MY LIFE WITH DEATH

MY LIFE WITH DEATH

Memoirs Of A Journeyman Medical Examiner

GARY D. CUMBERLAND, M.D.

Copyright © 2015 by Gary D. Cumberland, M.D.

Library of Congress Control Number:		2015912634
ISBN:	Hardcover	978-1-5035-9282-7
	Softcover	978-1-5035-9285-8
	eBook	978-1-5035-9281-0

All rights reserved. No part of this book may be reproduced or transmitted in any form or by any means, electronic or mechanical, including photocopying, recording, or by any information storage and retrieval system, without permission in writing from the copyright owner.

Any people depicted in stock imagery provided by Thinkstock are models, and such images are being used for illustrative purposes only.
Certain stock imagery © Thinkstock.

Print information available on the last page.

Rev. date: 08/10/2015

To order additional copies of this book, contact:
Xlibris
1-888-795-4274
www.Xlibris.com
Orders@Xlibris.com
718565

INDEX

Foreword xi

1. Why Be A Doctor To The Dead? 1
2. Forensic Pathology/Death Investigation Systems 20
3. Why Do An Autopsy? 26
4. It Ain't Necessarily So:
   What Forensic Pathologists Do And Can't Do 30
5. Who Am I? 48
6. Things Aren't Always As They Seem: Masquerade Deaths 70
7. You Always Hurt The One You Love:
   Homicide Among Friends And Lovers 110
8. The Meter Goes 'Round And 'Round: Death By Electricity ... 132
9. Suicide: Self-Inflicted Homicide 156
10. Drugs: Dying Sooner Through Modern Chemistry 174
11. Forensic Pathologist: Guardian Of Your Public Health 191
12. Death Of A Child: Types Of Pediatric Deaths 203
13. Death In The Summertime: Decomposed Bodies 230
14. My Friends? The Lawyers And Courts 242
15. Malpractice: The Suit That Never Fits Comfortably 253
16. The Worst-Case Scenario: Murder At Random 263
17. Two Wrongs Never Make A Right:
    The Murder Of Abortionists 279

Epilogue 287

Dedication:

To my parents Bonnie and Johnny Cumberland who made my career possible.

To my wife who helped me achieve it and put up with me along the way.

To my two children, Sarah Marie and John Robert, who made my life and career worth all the trouble and sacrifice.

A special thanks to my cousin, Pamela Skelton, for reviewing and correcting the grammar that I should have learned alongside of her in school (you always were smarter than me).

Special thanks also to my friend and colleague Frank Witter, M.D. who gave his sage advice from his vast medical expertise (you have yet to improve my golf game).

Finally, a very special thanks to my wife of nearly 40 years who not only edited the book but also encouraged me to finally get it done.

FOREWORD

One of the most interesting fields in medicine yet the least understood and appreciated is the field of forensic pathology. There are several reasons for underestimating my chosen field. In most jurisdictions of our country, the medical legal death investigation is handled by a lay coroner who is usually a funeral home director and has had no medical training that would qualify him for the job. In addition, it's almost a certainty that any new physician stepping out of his or her residency at a large multispecialty university-based hospital training program will have no exposure or contact with a forensic pathologist. This separation from the other academic training programs not only prevents the clinical physicians, those who do the hands-on patient care, from understanding the forensic pathologists' role but also limits the exposure of pathology colleagues who practice hospital-based anatomic and clinical pathology from having significant exposure to the subspecialty of forensic pathology.

Because hospital pathology has traditionally been a lucrative specialty in medicine, the pathology resident in training is usually bewitched by the call of the dollars and refuses to even consider taking the additional one or two years of training needed to be eligible for the reduced salary that government agencies are willing to pay.

Television programming has done the most to promote the profession of forensic pathology. *Quincy*, *NCIS*, and *CSI* times three have captured the attention of the public by showing death investigation at work, always with incredibly attractive people. I can remember sitting at a Super Bowl party when a commercial advertising one of the crime scene programs came on the air. Someone mentioned how handsome the male actors were and how drop-dead gorgeous all the female actresses were on the programs. One guy looked directly at me and commented how that's obviously not the case in real life. (I'm sure that he wasn't referring to me.)

I've made it a point to avoid watching these programs simply because the stories and findings, though technically possible or true, seldom happen that way in real life. What the shows tend to gloss over are the multiple cases per day required to keep up with the caseload or how long it takes, even with state-of-the-art technology, before a usable laboratory or DNA result is available.

Ironically, the job of a medical examiner can be routine to the point of being boring just like any other job. Despite these boring episodes, there are many reasons why I loved my work. These reasons include the straightforward case that suddenly takes a twist that causes me to think and rethink the findings to get a logical conclusion as to why an individual has died. It also includes the fun of knowing and working with the various law enforcement officers, attorneys, and crime laboratory personnel, the real crime scene investigators. This book has been written to present my career as a forensic pathologist and to include my training, years of practice, progressing to my retirement because of heart disease. Let me volunteer quickly that I am not, nor ever was, a giant in the field. Instead these are the cases that a journeyman forensic pathologist might face during a thirty-year career in a medical examiner's office.

Actual names are used only for police investigators, the Alabama Department of Forensic Sciences personnel, the Florida Department of Law Enforcement personnel, and my family. You are my friends, and I appreciate your willingness to teach me what little I know about your areas of expertise. Please take my using your name as the compliment that is intended.

Of course, any opinions expressed in this volume are mine alone and do not reflect the opinions of the employees or the various agencies of the States of Alabama and Florida. Also, note that the cases as presented are based on my recollections and thus may vary with those recorded in other sources. I have also taken the liberty of making changes in some cases to either protect an innocent participant or make an important point that, though not present in the case described, did occur in a similar case. This stretching of the truth allowed me to make an important point that might have otherwise been overlooked.

Finally, I would be guilty of gross negligence if I failed to express my personal gratitude to Dr. LeRoy Riddick, who taught me most of the forensic pathology that I know and has been a mentor, role model, and friend along the way. The state of Alabama, the Department of Forensic Sciences Division IV, and especially the county and city of Mobile, Alabama, owes much to this unsung hero who did so much to bring honesty, expertise, and credibility to the judicial system while taking the time to educate those of us who were fortunate enough to cross his path.

WHY BE A DOCTOR TO THE DEAD?

Early one spring morning, the phone began to ring. For the first two rings, my reaction was to pull the covers up over my head, trying to eliminate the noise. Finally, my wife, Beth, jabbed me with her elbow and demanded that I answer the telephone. I glanced at the clock and smiled to myself. The alarm was due to go off within a few short minutes; I had managed to sleep through the entire night without being awakened, a rare event for a Friday night on call. The voice on the other end of the line was a police operator from the city of Mobile requesting my presence at a death scene being investigated by the police. I wrote down the address and began to hurriedly get dressed. Though barely awake, my mind was already reviewing previous death scenes that I had attended. Because the address given to me by the police operator was in a nice upper-middle-class neighborhood, I already suspected that the case wouldn't be the usual Friday night homicide. As it turned out, I wasn't disappointed. I mumbled goodbye to a sleeping Beth as I headed out the door. I was immediately hit by the sight and smell of a spring morning in Mobile, with multicolored azaleas in bloom everywhere. It's the one time of the year that makes me glad to have left my Yankee origins for the South.

After a twenty-minute drive to the scene, I arrived to find several marked and unmarked police cars and an ambulance in front of the attractive ranch-style home. I walked through the front door and was greeted by the senior police investigator, Sgt. Boone. He quickly began to fill me in on the available background information. The deceased was a twenty-three-year-old single white female who lived at home with her parents. She was a student at the local university and was employed by a local accounting firm. Allegedly, the deceased had been home early the night before and complained about being a little more tired than usual. Because of this, she had elected to go to bed a bit early. The father had volunteered that the only noise that they heard coming from the room was a moaning-type noise that they passed off as a transient nightmare or the subject talking in her sleep. She was found dead shortly before the police called my home when she didn't awake for breakfast.

I walked into the deceased's bedroom to find her still in bed under the covers. The room itself was well kept, with no obvious medications or signs of struggle. A quick examination of the body revealed that she had probably been dead for several hours. She was cool to the touch and had rigor mortis (stiffening of the muscles after death) and livor mortis (settling of blood to the dependent surfaces of the body from gravity). There were no signs of trauma on the body. We quickly prepared the body for transport to our laboratory for an autopsy examination.

If I were to be honest with myself, I knew from the moment I walked into the room that this would be a complicated case. A police check into the deceased's background revealed that she was the type of young woman whom any family would be proud to claim as their own. She was not only attractive and well liked but also bright and hardworking. The only points of interest in terms of explaining her death were that she was under more stress than usual at her job because of the rapidly approaching tax deadline and was having the emotional ups and downs of an ongoing courtship so common at this age. All persons interviewed were emphatic in denying any drug use or alcohol abuse.

The family was completely devastated. Just imagine their morning. They awake on a beautiful Saturday morning and start their day only to discover that their daughter was lying dead in the adjacent bedroom. After the trauma of their discovery, the superimposed anxiety of having their home invaded by paramedics, police, and finally the medical examiner's personnel. In the midst of their shock and sorrow, they're expected to answer all sorts of probing and personal questions posed by these various agencies. I found myself empathizing with them, and because there was no obvious trauma, I immediately began to feel the pressure of explaining their daughter's death and having answers to their many questions. I was to be sorely disappointed.

Depending on the death investigation agency keeping the statistics, some 1 to 5 percent of death cases investigated fail to diagnose an anatomic cause of death. By this I mean that a complete autopsy to include a complete toxicology screen (to detect drugs and poisons in the body) as well as a complete microscopic examination of the organs (small pieces of each organ cut thinly and examined under the microscope) fail to reveal a disease process or injury that can explain why the person died at that particular moment. While most of these undetermined deaths are due to the inability to glean needed information from a body because of decomposition or postmortem destruction by animals or environmental exposure, a significant number of these undetermined deaths fall within this subset we call physiological deaths.

This is the same type of death seen in sudden infant death syndrome in that, instead of the death occurring on an organ or tissue level that can be viewed with the naked eye or microscope, the problem or process occurs at a molecular or biochemical level. Most investigators now feel that these types of deaths are related to a malfunction of the autonomic nervous system, that portion of our nervous system that's outside of conscious control and is responsible for controlling our breathing patterns and regulating our heart rates as well as our responses to dangerous situations. People who die this type of death are usually under external stress of some sort and die in their sleep. The autopsy shows only nonspecific findings that don't point to any one particular problem.

The autopsy examination that followed fell into this category. I finished the examination without an anatomic cause of death. The toxicology and microscopic examinations were equally unrewarding. Regardless of how thorough I have tried to be in this type of case, I still walk away feeling that there was something that I have missed. In cases such as this, I routinely consult other pathologists at the local medical school. They agreed with my negative findings and reassured me some people die suddenly without an anatomic cause of death.

As I attempted to explain the death to the family, I knew that I was leaving them with many unanswered questions. Was there something that they neglected to do that might have prevented the death? Should the younger sister worry about an inherited problem that she might be carrying? These were questions that in all honesty I couldn't answer. This is the type of case that makes me question why I chose forensic pathology as my medical specialty. These deaths haunt and affect the involved families for years to come. Yearly memorials in our local newspapers on the anniversary of the loved one's death are always a vivid reminder to me that, despite all of my training and experience, I've failed a family when they needed me most.

Initially, as I began my medical training at Southern Illinois University School of Medicine in Carbondale, IL, I was convinced that I wanted to be a family practice doctor. As the first male in my immediate family to go to college, much less medical school, my concept of medicine was my family's general practice physician in East St. Louis, IL, Dr. Richard Osland. I was aware that there were other specialties in medicine. My wife's father is a radiologist, but my mind at that time was oriented to family practice, that is, I wanted to be a caring, hands-on, primary care doctor.

This concept underwent a radical change at the end of my first year of medical school. Four pathology faculty from Springfield, IL, where the clinical portion of the medical school was located, came to Carbondale to give an introductory lecture on the field of pathology. This group was headed by Dr. Grant Johnson, a burly, balding, gruff-speaking pathologist who was the chairman of the department. About halfway through the lecture, after seeing autopsy slides and various laboratory procedures, I knew this was the area for me. That night I told Beth about my newfound field of interest. She was thrilled. As the daughter of a physician, she was familiar with pathology and knew that with few exceptions, it was an "8 to 5" type job. She had already informed me that she wasn't thrilled with the prospect of being the wife of a phantom husband in family practice medicine.

The sophomore medical school course in pathology only served to confirm my desire to go into pathology. The pathology faculty who knew of my desires were skeptical. It was common for sophomore students madly committed to the future practice of pathology to be swept away by the clinical medicine rotations in the following years to end up practicing internal medicine, pediatrics, or obstetrics. In addition, it wasn't unusual for sophomore students to pledge their undying love for pathology in the hope that it might in some small way positively influence their grade.

Such was not the case for me. Each ensuing clinical rotation seemed to strengthen my desire to be a pathologist. Basically, although I like the technical practices of medicine, seeing sick patients continually throughout the day wore on my patience. Autopsies were done on the obviously sick unto death, but you didn't have to talk to them or listen to the complaints for which modern medicine had no cure. So when the time came to interview for postgraduate training, I interviewed strictly for pathology programs.

Humorously, my decision to be a pathologist didn't go without some probing questions from my middle-class family who wondered what a pathologist did. My answers did little to clear the confusion. At my graduation from medical school, one uncle asked if I would graduate as a real medical doctor. Another, despite attempts to accept my decision, couldn't understand why I would want to work with dead people after all those years of training.

My father, who spent his whole career working as a machinist in a power plant, also had some reservations when he found out I was going into medicine. My father, you see, was a gifted craftsman. Every project he undertook looked like it came right off the cover of *Good Housekeeping* magazine. He could do finish carpentry, plumbing, and wire electrical systems; there was nothing my father was incapable of doing well. I, on the other hand, wasn't quite so manually gifted. When I replace the spark plug on the lawn mower, I always cross the threads, resulting in stripping of the threads out of the engine head. When I tighten the bolt, I always tighten it just a little too tight, to the point that the bolt on which I'm working on snaps. At one point during my high school years, my dad took me aside and gently explained to me that I would never be a craftsman. He said it wasn't because I couldn't understand what needed to be done or how to go about doing it, but instead, I just did not have the manual touch necessary to do the job correctly and know when to stop. I suspect that initially his fear was that I'd function this same way when I practiced medicine. He didn't have any problems assuming that I would be able to learn the material and pass the tests; his fear was that when I was out in practice, I would approach patients the same way I had approached projects at home.

To this day, my father has reservations when he learns that I'm about to start a home project. I remember talking to my father and explaining that I was going to install a ceiling fan in our bedroom. All of a sudden, the phone went silent. After a prolonged pause, my father quietly asked if it wouldn't be better to have an electrician come out and install the fan. I suspected that he had visions of the fan falling onto our bed in the middle of the night and Beth and I being chopped into pieces. By the way, the fan worked just fine after I installed it. The time I replaced the toilet in our home is an entirely different story.

When my father found out what a pathologist did for a living, he was pleased. He put his arm around me and said, "Son, I've never had any problem with your abilities in terms of thinking and knowledge base. My issue with you has always been the manual aspect of the job. Pathology is ideal for you. In pathology, you take the person apart, see why they died or what was wrong, and you don't have to put them back together again." He felt sure that I found my place in medicine.

Just so I can salvage at least a small modicum of my pride, I want the reader to know that I eventually developed great manual skills when it came to doing autopsies. Of course, there was that time when I sliced open my left arm on two consecutive days while sharpening my autopsy knife, but I choose not to count those.

I had initially hoped to stay and do my pathology residency at Southern Illinois University School of Medicine where I had been a medical student. All postgraduate students entering their first year as interns or residents in the United States medical school system are required to go through a national matching system to determine where they will do their postgraduate training. Senior medical students travel around the country and interview at various residency sites. In turn, the residency sites prioritize the students in terms of their desire to accept them into their program. The medical student lists his top 3 choices in order of preference, and the residency programs in turn submit their top choices of medical students to fill their residency spots in the order of their preference. Both sets of preferences are loaded into a computer program that matches the medical student with his highest choice of internship or residency that had chosen him or her as an acceptable candidate.

Because Southern Illinois University School of Medicine had limited their residency programs to one individual, I was automatically bumped down to my second choice, which was the University of South Alabama (USA) in Mobile, AL. Initially, both Beth and I were a bit disappointed that we were going to have to move to Mobile, Alabama, when an ice storm came through the area of Springfield, IL, resulting in downed power lines and freezing cold temperatures. We were without heat for several days. Suddenly, the thought of escaping from the Midwestern winters for a period of time to the balmy South didn't seem quite so bad.

The pathology residency at USA was similar to programs throughout the country and consisted of two years of anatomic pathology and two years of clinical pathology. Anatomic pathology is the study of tissues from the body to identify and document disease. Its main components are autopsy pathology (examination of the body as a whole), surgical pathology (examination of tissue fragments removed at surgery), and cytology (examination of individual cells, i.e., PAP tests for cervical cancer in females). Clinical pathology is laboratory medicine, that is, the diagnosis of disease by chemical tests on blood, urine, spinal fluid, etc. The clinical pathologist runs the hospital laboratory and aids the primary care physicians in making the correct diagnosis from laboratory results.

Right from the beginning, my interest centered on the anatomic portion of pathology over the clinical. As opposed to the clinical labs where most tests were run on machines that are continually becoming more automated, anatomic pathology was a hands-on experience that appealed to my basic need to do something manual. Also, unlike most pathology residents who objected to the smell and mess, I enjoyed doing autopsies. Each case was a mental exercise to explain why the patient had died. I was fortunately blessed with a strong stomach that only the foulest of odors seemed to bother me. In retrospect, I was a prime candidate for forensic pathology. As this is a contagious disease spread only from person to person, I lacked only one essential component, the communicating agent, that is, contact with a forensic pathologist. Little did I know as I began my first year of residency that contact was just months away.

The practice of forensic pathology wasn't completely new to me as I began my first year of residency. Dr. Grant Johnson, chairman of the Department of Pathology at Southern Illinois University, frequently performed forensic autopsies for the nonphysician coroners of the counties surrounding Springfield, IL. Twice, during my medical school training, he had given lectures to my class on the subject. I found the field interesting and had even toyed with the notion of doing some forensic training, but as in most aspects of life, if you don't have continual contact with an area, interest and enthusiasm wane. All this changed, however, in April of my first year of pathology residency. The Alabama Department of Forensic Sciences had decided to hire a forensic pathologist for their Mobile laboratory. Fortunately for me, they hired Dr. LeRoy Riddick.

I had first met Dr. Riddick the previous December when he had come to Mobile to interview for the job. He's one of those redheaded individuals who had turned prematurely gray for his forty-two years. Most people feel that with his curly white hair and bushy mustache, he bears a striking resemblance to photographs of Mark Twain, although Captain Kangaroo has also been suggested. Dr. Riddick's educational background is interesting, if not unique. Born in Memphis, TN, he did his undergraduate work at Princeton University, earning a degree in history. In addition, he has a master's degree in European history. After teaching some five years, he went to medical school in New Jersey and did his pathology training in New York City. Dr. Riddick then worked some five years in the Medical Examiner's Office in Washington, D.C., before accepting the call to Mobile.

To me, Dr. Riddick personifies the kind, absentminded professor. Burdened with a mind full of historical situations or books known only to an intellectual few, his conversations are punctuated with pregnant pauses during which I could watch the gears in his mind spinning all the while gesturing with his hands or scratching his prematurely gray hair. More than one person has begun to worry about themselves when they realized that they were beginning to understand some of Dr. Riddick's mumblings.

Dr. Riddick saw my interest in autopsy pathology and was always ready to share his forensic knowledge. I think he was relieved to find one pathologist in town who didn't get sick at the mention of autopsy pathology. As the time in my residency progressed, I found myself getting more and more involved in the day-to-day work of forensic pathology as time in my other pathology responsibilities permitted. I soon began to realize that I had found that essential ingredient necessary to become a forensic pathologist—a mentor who could teach and guide my learning experiences.

General pathology is the medical specialty dealing with the study and documentation of disease and injury. Forensic pathology is the study and documentation of disease and injury as it relates to the law and our court system. In the United States, there are more than six hundred board-certified forensic pathologists (pathologists who have done one or two years of full-time forensic pathology training and have subsequently passed an examination given by the American Board of Pathology). Only a small percentage performs the work of a forensic pathologist full-time. The remainder has elected to stay in the more lucrative private practices and do forensic pathology part-time, if at all.

Those forensic pathologists who practice their profession full-time are usually employed by some government agency. This explains why there's a significant salary differential between full-time forensic pathologists and those pathologists in private practice who do the work part-time. Because it's extremely difficult to rationalize a $100,000 plus annual salary to the citizens paying the bills, forensic pathologists working for a government agency when I began my practice usually earned less than this magic sum.

One of the neat aspects of medicine is that the training is one of the few remaining systems that adhere to the old teaching concept of master-mentor. This concept revolves around the idea that someone new to some aspect of medical training attaches themselves to someone who has achieved a high level of competence in that chosen field. The neophyte literally tries to learn as much from their mentor as possible through didactics and modeling the instructor's behaviors on the job.

This method of learning can be accomplished on many different levels, both from a distance where the mentor is monitored from afar and to the more ideal type where the novice is literally placed side by side with his mentor so that the observation aspect of the learning process can be reinforced concurrently by the didactics and allow the behavioral aspect to be emphasized and corrected on an ongoing basis. When thinking about it, this is not dissimilar to the type of learning that occurs during childhood where the child both observes and receives verbal instructions from the parents.

This learning method in medicine isn't usually adopted in its purest form until after medical school graduation and entry into what is called intern/residency training. This is the point in every physician's career where he or she has the title of physician but lacks the real world knowledge and skills necessary to effectively apply the head knowledge in a way that does good rather than harm. It's at this point that the mentor figure assumes his or her real value.

The whole basis of trying to gain acceptance in the best residency programs after medical school graduation is really the graduate's attempt to gain access to the best mentors. In fact, the reputation of the leading, most prestigious medical training centers is based on that facility's ability to attract and retain the best group of mentors over time. If the training center has the mentors, it then develops the reputation to attract the monies needed to build the best facilities and obtain the best equipment that attracts the best residents to compete for the opportunity to learn there. Over time, the reputation of the institution grows, and the Mayo Clinics and MD Andersons of the world are created.

In the world of forensic pathology, there are similar "big time" training centers like the Miami Medical Examiner's Office and the San Antonio Medical Examiner's Office, but because the field of forensic pathology is so small and relatively new, there's an inadequate number of good training centers available for those interested in the field to be able to learn their trade. This explains, at least in part, the vast variation in the level of expertise seen in medical examiner offices across the country. Hopefully, time will allow the specialty's training facilities to catch up with the other medical specialties,

My wife, Beth, has always claimed that I've made a career out of backing into my educational choices. I would rather think that my choices have instead chosen me. Looking at my history, this is not hard to believe. I started medical school thinking that I would become a family practice physician. I soon realized that I didn't enjoy working with sick people, so by default, I went into pathology. I had originally hoped to be able to stay in Springfield, IL, to do my pathology training, but to my surprise, I was transported from the cold, snowy Midwest to Mobile, AL, and the hot, humid South.

I had initially assumed that my career would consist of practicing hospital pathology somewhere in the Midwest; then I met Dr. Riddick and soon fell in love with forensic pathology. I was fortunate that Dr. Riddick had decided to assume the professional risk of moving to Alabama and taking on the trauma of establishing a medical examiner system in an area where coroners ruled supreme. I was especially fortunate that Dr. Riddick took a liking to me and was willing to accept me as a trainee. I suspect in some ways my wife, Beth, and I are both correct. I did back into my chosen profession, but providence also chose me by bringing Dr. Riddick into the area.

When Dr. Riddick first decided to take the plunge and move to Alabama, he wisely chose Mobile over the other locations that were available in Alabama. At the time, the Alabama Department of Forensic

Sciences, under the leadership of its director Carlos Rabrin, was in the process of establishing a system of regional medical examiners who would function as medical consultants to the elected lay coroners located in each county throughout the state. Dr. Riddick chose the Mobile location over the others available primarily because the University of South Alabama School of Medicine was located there.

Dr. Riddick realized that associating himself with the medical school would ease his entry into the local medical community and give himself some credibility as he tried to establish himself in the area. At the time of his arrival, I was in the second year of my four-year residency training in the Department of Pathology at USAMC. As soon as he realized that I had an interest in forensics, Dr. Riddick quickly took me under his wing. The end result was beneficial to both of us. I was soon spending all of my free time watching and learning from him in the autopsy room, and he in turn was using the relationship to prove to the pathology faculty that he was legitimate and could make valuable contributions to the pathology department with his willingness to teach students and residents.

Over time, I was spending more and more of my free weekends working with him in the autopsy suite. He in turn was allowing me more and more responsibility in the caseload till I was eventually doing forensic autopsies frequently under his supervision and oversight. Ironically, by the time that I had completed my four-year pathology residency and was eligible to take my national certifying examination in general pathology, I was actually just as ready to take the forensic pathology exams.

When it came time to deciding where I would do my forensic pathology fellowship by traveling to the various programs to be interviewed, I soon came to realize that the current level of my experience and training had already put me beyond where any one-year fellowship could take me professionally. When this information was coupled with the fact that the fellowship would require that I relocate my family for the year and in the process leave Dr. Riddick in the unenviable position of having to handle the caseload alone, the most reasonable solution was to stay put. To qualify for eligibility to take the forensic certifying exam, I was required to have either one year of full-time experience in a certified training program or two years of full-time experience at a location that the board deemed acceptable.

With Dr. Riddick's help, I was able to be hired by the state of Alabama to work under Dr. Riddick in the Mobile office of the Alabama Department of Forensic Sciences. This accomplished at least two good things. I didn't have to move my family across the country and away from the home we had previously purchased, and I got to continue to learn my trade under Dr. Riddick and work with the people in the forensic laboratory and the police agencies that I had worked with over the last couple of years. Hopefully, Dr. Riddick was relieved to have some help available so that he could at least take some long overdue time off.

Dr. Riddick was much more than a boss to me over the six years that we worked together. He became a true friend to me as I hope that I became to him. Like any situation where you must work closely with someone for hours on end, I'm sure that there were plenty of instances when I got on his nerves. Fortunately, we both had a relatively good sense of humor and could often laugh together about the absurdity of many of the stressful situations we encountered as we worked together. This was a valuable gift for both of us because the growth in the number of personnel in our state headquarters meant space was always in short supply. Until the state could come up with the funding necessary to build a bigger laboratory, Dr. Riddick and I were even required to share the same small office. Personal hygiene, as a necessity, became a high priority for both of us.

That is not to say that we didn't have our issues from time to time. As regional director of the Mobile laboratory, Dr. Riddick was responsible to the main headquarters for keeping our lab within our budget. I suspect that on the day in question, he just had some supple issue or cost overrun brought to his attention from headquarters because later that same day as I was doing paperwork and Dr. Riddick was busy autopsying the new cases that day, I was summoned to the autopsy suite.

Dr. Riddick had a habit of calling me back to the autopsy suite when he had an interesting finding to show me from the case he was currently dissecting. He would also call me back to the autopsy suite to correct one of my many missteps. He would stand beside the body continuing to conduct the autopsy with a scalpel in hand while he waxed eloquently over the correction in my behavior that he wanted, always punctuating his point by jabbing the scalpel he was holding into the air. The man knew how to keep a guy's attention.

The current issue involved overuse of the scalpel blades that we used to make all of the cuts that occurred during each autopsy. For the uninitiated, we used disposable scalpel blades attached to a reusable handle. Because the disposable blades were so sharp, they were also easily dulled. During the autopsy dissection, anything that touched the blade, even water, could render the blade dull and useless. Because the odds of hitting the blade against skeletal bone was a given, it often required five or six blades to complete an autopsy. If the individual being autopsied had had previous surgery where the surgeon had used metal clips to close the wounds, the number of blades needed to finish the exam went up exponentially.

Headquarters had called just that morning complaining about the number of scalpel blades we were using and their associated cost. As Dr. Riddick turned to start the internal portion of the autopsy exam, he picked up a scalpel, jabbed it in my direction, and stated that we were getting sloppy with our autopsy technique, and that was resulting in increased numbers of scalpel blades being utilized in the autopsy suite. Of course the implication was that it had to be my wastefulness causing the problem because in his own mind, he was totally innocent. He went on to state that from that point forward, we would only be allowed four scalpel blades per autopsy; no exceptions. If we needed more than the four, it would be our responsibility to buy our own blades to augment the shortfall. He emphasized his point by pointing to three additional scalpel blade handles, each sporting a gleaming new scalpel blade. There were no additional replacement blades anywhere in sight.

I had been working long enough with Dr. Riddick at this point to know that sometimes the best response is no response. Often if I would just stand there silently, Dr. Riddick would say what he thinks needs to be said in order to "vent his spleen." After he has had his say, the conversation usually moves along to more pleasant topics. Such was the case in this instance. As I stood there quietly watching the autopsy, he began to move on to less-controversial topics.

As Dr. Riddick continued on with the autopsy, he hit a piece of bone and dulled his blade. As he moved to replace the old blade with a new one, I said, "That's one." Unfortunately for Dr. Riddick, the case that he was autopsying had had multiple previous surgeries obviously done by a surgeon who had developed a serious love affair with the surgical supply representative who sold metal sutures because they were everywhere in the body. Dr. Riddick had no sooner picked up his second scalpel blade when he ran across another metal suture, dulling his blade. As he moved to set the dull blade aside to pick up the third scalpel, I said, "That's two."

At this point, I could see that I was beginning to irritate Dr. Riddick. He continued to work for some five minutes more before he hit another metal suture line. As he slapped the dull blade to the table and reached for the final sharp scalpel, I silently muttered, "That's three."

I could tell by Dr. Riddick's tense posture and the bright red discoloration of his face and neck that I had pushed this envelope about as far as I dare. I decided that a hasty exit at this point was the only way that I could guarantee my longevity. As I quickly scooted to the door, I heard Dr. Riddick let loose with a string of profanities, and I knew that he had just dulled blade number 4. With my body on the outside of the door, I stuck my head back into the autopsy suite and yelled, "That was number 4. Do you need to borrow some scalpel blades?" He never said another word to me about the number of scalpel blades that I used.

The other episode that I always remember about Dr. Riddick occurred shortly after we had moved into our new autopsy suite located on the campus of the University of South Alabama Medical Center. This new facility was a jewel. Designed personally by Dr. Riddick, it had a spacious floor plan that would allow four autopsy examinations to be conducted simultaneously, a separate smaller closed-off autopsy room perfectly sized for hospital autopsy cases, and a separate detached bad body autopsy room with its own separate ventilation system and body refrigeration unit.

Because the suite was shared with the pathology department associated with the medical school and medical center, Dr. Riddick had also designed in the plans a huge storage room to hold specimens and autopsy suite supplies. The walk-in cooler could hold a minimum of twenty bodies each on their own separate cart. The building that housed the autopsy suite proper was large enough to provide office and laboratory space for all the forensic disciplines that had previously been scattered about different locations.

It was easy to understand why Dr. Riddick took such pride in this new facility. In addition to being one of the finest full-service forensic science facilities in the southeast, it was also special to him because of the length of time he had tolerated doing autopsies in funeral homes and begging for permission to use the small autopsy rooms located at the local hospitals. Needless to say, the facility was his baby, and he took pride in making sure that it was clean and well maintained.

One day when we had been in the new facility long enough to feel comfortable there, Dr. Riddick was back in the autopsy suite doing cases. I, in turn, was doing the paperwork that drives every physician crazy. I got a phone call from the autopsy diener asking me to come back to the autopsy suite. Dr. Riddick had an issue he wanted to discuss. Because of my previous experiences with this particular scenario, I was a bit nervous. Was there some pearl of knowledge that Dr. Riddick was going to pass my way, or had I again fallen short of expectations in some aspect of my performance? Unfortunately, it was the latter.

As per his usual presentation, Dr. Riddick was just beginning to enter the abdominal cavity of a rather obese female when he saw me out of the corner of his eye and jabbed the scalpel into the air indicating that he wanted me to come closer. As I stood across the body from him, he began to complain that I wasn't making a good enough effort to keep the autopsy suite clean. He added that several times when he had used the suite after me he had noticed dried blood and tissue debris that hadn't been adequately cleaned up. He went on to impress upon me the responsibility I had to help keep the autopsy suite as clean and fresh as the day it was first used.

While Dr. Riddick continued the lecture, all the while jabbing his scalpel into the air to emphasize his points, I glanced over at Alberta, the head diener in the autopsy suite whose job it was to keep the autopsy suite supplied as well as cleaned. I gave her a "What's this all about?" look. She in turn gave me the "I have no idea where all of this is coming from" look. I continued to absorb the ongoing criticism while Dr. Riddick continued with the autopsy. Just at the point where his criticism of my lack of cleanliness hit its crescendo, Dr. Riddick lifted the woman's enlarged colon from the body cavity to place it on the dissecting table. Just as he hit midpoint of the turn, away from the autopsy table but not yet over the dissecting table, the colon filled to capacity with liquid stool burst, sending feces everywhere.

Dr. Riddick jumped, but not quickly enough to keep from being covered by liquid feces. Alberta screamed and jumped quickly enough to avoid any personal soiling of her scrubs. I jumped fast enough to avoid the flow but was soon squatting nearby doubled over with laughter. I just couldn't help myself. As I quickly moved to avoid the expanding mess and return to my office, I managed to voice my thanks to Dr. Riddick for setting such an excellent example for me regarding autopsy suite cleanliness. I could hear his profanity all the way down the hall to my office.

So having given you my educational background and residency/fellowship experience, am I a real doctor? There are all kinds of doctors in the world. The doctorate is considered the highest academic degree in just about every academic field of endeavor. You can therefore be a doctor of biochemistry, a doctor of economics, or even a doctor of basket weaving under water at midnight. Many of my attorney friends are quick to tell me that they're also doctors; their degrees are Juris Doctor.

By tradition in the United States, if people use the title of doctor in front of your name, you are usually a medical doctor, doctor of osteopathy, dentistry, or podiatry. Your doctorate is in some field of medical care. Although all the other earned doctorates carry an equal or even a higher level of academic achievement, the socially accepted common usage of the title doctor is usually reserved for those in some health treating field. In most other situations, the use of the title of doctor is restricted to instances when the individuals are functioning in their area of expertise. When I was in the premedical and basic sciences portion of my training, it would have been considered an insult not to use the doctor title to those PhDs who were teaching me basic sciences.

So who are these PhDs and what do their degrees mean and how were they earned? In my humble opinion, because the PhD is the highest academic degree that an individual can earn, it deserves the greatest respect. The title of PhD is actually an abbreviation for the full title of doctor of philosophy. So that the reader doesn't get any more confused than I've already made this issue, let me volunteer that the term "philosophy" as used here is not exactly defined the same way that the word "philosophy" is commonly used today. When your child comes home from college and states that he or she is pursuing a degree in philosophy, the discerning parents immediately begins wringing their hands, wondering how their child expects to be able to earn a livelihood with a degree in philosophy.

If this were my child, I would feel exactly the same emotions because, as used today, the study of philosophy involves the study of general and fundamental problems connected with reality, existence, knowledge, values, reason, and mind. These are nice things to ponder on a winter day in front of a blazing fire but fall short of the practical tools needed to earn a living in the current world in which we live. The word "philosophy" literally means love of wisdom, again an admirable pursuit, but it probably won't pay the bills. Back in the "old" day when the degree of doctor of philosophy was founded, the use of the word "philosophy" meant just that, the love of wisdom. It signified that the recipient had jumped the academic hurdles necessary to be considered an expert in his field. The degree in the academic world is as high as anyone can get. That is not to say that that all PhDs are created equal. There are PhDs, and there are PhDs. By this I mean that the respect that a PhD receives is, in my opinion, practically dependent on the field of study for which it was awarded. A doctorate awarded in education is not nearly as rigorous as the one awarded in astrophysics. Both individuals are doctors, and both individuals have their niche in society. I wouldn't want everyone who pursues a PhD to get their degree in astrophysics because all the venues of study make a contribution to society, but the reader should realize that not all PhDs are created equal.

I also need to admit that not all medicine-related doctorates are equal in terms of their academic difficulty. The doctorate degrees in podiatry, optometry, chiropractor, and dentistry are not as demanding as the medical doctor or doctor of osteopathy degrees in terms of their intensity and academic difficulty. I might also admit at this point that although the medical doctor and osteopathy doctorates are difficult and demanding, they can be easier to obtain and a lot less demanding than some of the PhD degrees earned in the hard sciences like physics, chemistry, and astronomy (rocket science can be hard).

Finally, I need to explain the difference between being a medical doctor and being an osteopath; there is not much difference in today's world, but that was not the case in the early to mid-1900s. When the medical doctor degree as we now know it was evolving, there were few standards in terms of the actual training required to be allowed to practice as a medical physician. In the 1900s, there was a push to develop formal medical schools to educate and qualify individuals to practice medicine with state requirements necessary to obtain a license to practice as a physician. These early medical schools concentrated on anatomy, diagnosis, surgery, and what little pharmacology was known at the time.

The schools of osteopathy started formalizing and developing standards necessary to be considered qualified to practice osteopathy at the same time as medical schools. Instead of concentrating their courses of study on the use of drugs and medicines to help relieve pain and aid the body to heal itself, they also focused on spinal manipulation as a means of treating and curing their patients. Initially, the osteopaths were closely related in their treatment modalities to those currently utilized by chiropractors. Until the 1950s, osteopaths often limited their practices to manipulation procedures. Over time, however, the training and education given to future osteopaths became more and more similar to the training that medical doctors received in their medical schools such that today there is essentially no difference between the practices of medicine and the practices of osteopathy. Although medical doctors claim a bit of superiority over osteopaths, they are every bit as qualified to practice medicine as the medical doctors; we just don't want to admit it.

One other point that I need to interject at this point is when an individual is granted a degree as a medical doctor or doctor of osteopathy, he/she is often only halfway in terms of formal training. Most states require at least one additional year of training under the auspices of an approved internship program, usually at a medical school–sponsored hospital overseen by competent teaching physicians who direct their continuing education. In addition, most physicians go on to do an additional two to six years of specialized training in similar training facilities before they actually go out into the world to practice independently. I spent an additional six years in training as a resident and fellow before I worked independently as a forensic pathologist.

So why did I take you on this academic journey? To explain to you where the forensic pathologist or medical examiner falls into the sundry doctors that you encounter in our American society. The bottom line is that I'm a medical doctor who has taken additional years of training to be qualified to practice forensic pathology. Because I've taken all of the same medical training in medical school as, say, a cardiologist, I'm qualified as a physician. Yes, I'm qualified to write prescriptions, but I don't because I don't see patients. This makes me a physician, but not a clinician, someone who sees and treats patients. I take great pride in claiming that I am indeed a doctor. I am without a doubt a physician, but I'm not a clinician. If you're totally confused by all this, don't worry because it has more bearing on my pride than it does on your ability to understand what is in this book. Hopefully, it will also give you a bit of peace the next time you have to surrender yourself to the care of your private physician.

FORENSIC PATHOLOGY/
DEATH INVESTIGATION SYSTEMS

As previously stated, most forensic pathologists work in a government agency responsible for determining the cause and manner of death of those individuals who die within a defined area within a state or county. The medical-legal death investigation systems used by these various government agencies in this country fall into two main types, the coroner system and the medical examiner system. The American version of the coroner system is the older of the two systems and, with a few modifications, was brought over by the early American colonists from England in the early 1600s. The term "coroner" is probably a corruption of the title "crowner." In the twelfth century, the crowner was appointed by the judicial system to investigate deaths and arrest suspects. Since lands and possessions were often surrendered to the crown in such cases, the ruling royalty obviously had a vested interest in who was appointed coroner or crowner and how loyally he served the crown. In addition, the coroner had basically equal but separate legal authority from the sheriff of the region; thus, the two offices could keep a check on each other's authority and activities. This also explains the current tradition in American common law where only the coroner of a county can arrest or serve subpoena on the sheriff.

When I first entered the field, the position of coroner was used in some twenty-eight states. In most jurisdictions, the coroner's authority is restricted to those persons dying outside of hospital facilities, usually from some type of trauma. Unfortunately, except in a few select jurisdictions, the qualifications for coroner require only that the person be eligible to stand for election, that is, be eighteen years of age with no previous criminal record. As a result, in most jurisdictions of Alabama, one of the states with which I am familiar, most coroners are funeral home directors. They obviously have a financial interest in death and have, in all fairness, accepted the job in most areas because of the lack of interest by other parties, particularly the medical profession.

In the remaining twenty-three states and in the larger metropolitan areas of thirty-nine states, the office of coroner has been replaced by a medical examiner system. The first major step in the establishment of a medical examiner system occurred in New York City in 1915. The coroner was replaced by a physician who was given the authority to investigate deaths resulting from criminal violence, suicides, and sudden, unexpected deaths in apparently healthy individuals or those who die in any suspicious or unusual manner. This new law made two significant advances in the sphere of death investigation. First, it gave the medical examiner the authority to autopsy as he deemed necessary to determine the cause of death. Second, the position was established through the civil service system so that the office was no longer political, requiring the office holder to stand for election. This, in my opinion, allowed the medical examiner more freedom to do his job without as much political pressure, particularly around election time. The first statewide medical examiner's office was established in Maryland in 1939. Since obviously there are not enough forensic pathologists to cover every jurisdiction in a state system, the central office is usually directed by a forensic pathologist with the individual jurisdictions manned by a physician or a trained lay investigator who is responsible to the director.

It's probably obvious to all that I'm partial to the medical examiner system. In the interest of honesty, however, it should be stated that any system is only as good as the people who run it. It makes no difference if the medical examiner's office is held by a physician with multiple letters behind his name if he's unwilling to develop an interest in the job and work to continue to learn and improve his investigations. I know coroners whom I would put up against any physician medical examiner in a statewide system. In my opinion, the main advantages of a medical examiner system are (1) separation from the political arena and (2) standardization of nomenclature in death certification by having physicians examining bodies and signing the death certificates.

In Alabama, the system of death investigation is a compromise between the two previously described systems. This, in turn, has all the advantages and disadvantages of both systems. In the classic coroner system, the coroner investigates each death and makes a decision as to whether an autopsy is indicated. He then usually calls in a pathologist to perform the subsequent autopsy if he feels it is indicated. This pathologist is usually a hospital-based pathologist with little or no formal training in forensic pathology. He issues a written report on the autopsy findings to the coroner, who in turn completes the death certificate on the case.

Because of a historical reluctance by Alabama pathologists to perform autopsies on obvious criminal cases that will end up going to court, the Alabama Department of Toxicology and Criminal Investigation stepped in to fill the void. Initially, these autopsies were performed by nonphysician crime laboratory personnel with some formal training in pathology.

As time went on, however, the autopsy duties were eventually passed down to crime laboratory personnel whose only qualifications for the job were those acquired through on-the-job training. To be fair to the criminalists doing these autopsies, it should be mentioned that their abilities to acquire and document evidence taken from the body were often far superior to the abilities of hospital-based pathologists, who, without forensic training, tend to be poor at maintaining a chain of evidence so necessary for subsequent testimony in court. On the other hand, however, death investigation was being placed in the hands of a nonphysician, someone who hadn't been trained in the natural disease processes so often a significant finding in cases of sudden, unexpected death. After all, the cause of death is a medical diagnosis.

In the mid-1970s, the Alabama Department of Forensic Sciences attempted to remedy this problem by hiring forensic pathologists to do all the autopsy consultations sent to the department. It was during this era that Dr. Riddick came to Mobile. Thus, all autopsies done for medical legal purposes in Alabama are currently performed by board-certified forensic pathologists. Lay coroners in the counties of Alabama, instead of having to locate a local pathologist to do their autopsies, have access to forensic pathology experts who can do the various cases and testify in court, all paid for by state revenues. The major drawback to this system is that the initial decision as to the depth of investigation and the need for an autopsy still rests with the lay coroner or, in most jurisdictions, someone with no formal training in medicine or death investigation.

There are exceptions to this generalization within some jurisdictions of Alabama. Jefferson County, where Birmingham is located, opted to replace its coroner with a medical examiner manned by a forensic pathologist in 1975. Mobile County maintains the office of coroner but has appointed Dr. Riddick as its coroner within the framework of the Mobile Laboratory of the Alabama Department of Forensic Sciences. Thus, our office functions as the coroner's office of Mobile County as well as serves as consultants to the lay coroners of some eight surrounding counties. The citizens of Mobile County are in effect served by a medical examiner system. I want to emphasize, however, that these counties where there is a medical examiner system still exist within the framework of the outdated coroner's laws of Alabama.

The state of Florida has a medical examiner system, which partially explains my willingness to accept a position in Pensacola. The system in Florida was generally an improvement over the coroner system in Alabama, but like any bureaucratic organization, it was far from perfect. The main deficiency revolved on how the state was divided into medical examiner districts. Because of the volume of cases, large counties, such as Miami in Dade County, have a medical examiner's office that serves only that one county. Unfortunately, to financially support a medical examiner's office, the less populated areas of the state had to combine their caseload. On first blush, this makes all the sense in the world until it's time to develop the operating budget necessary to run the office. In that case, the medical examiner had to write and defend a separate budget for each county that comes under his/her jurisdiction. This can vary from two up to six separate counties depending on the population of that area of the state. Because smaller counties have a smaller cash flow than their larger sister counties, a larger percentage of their budget is going to support an office that they're required to support by state law.

If that isn't bad enough, the smaller counties each have their own sheriff's office and municipal police forces who are equally laboring under restricted budgets that keep them from getting the training that they need and the specialized equipment needed for good death investigation.

The main advantage of the Florida system is that each medical examiner's district must be run by a board-certified forensic pathologist who is empowered by statute law as to which cases fall under the office's jurisdiction as well as an oversight commission composed of law enforcement, funeral home, pastoral, and medical examiner personnel with the authority to oversee and enforce statewide policies regarding the functioning of each medical examiner. In addition, rather than being an elected official, each district medical examiner is appointed by the governor based on his or her qualifications. This helps keep the medical examiner out of the political arena.

Regardless of the title given to the death investigation agency in a community, its real ability to serve a given constituency is best determined by the laws that define its investigative powers. In my opinion, the minimum requirements should include adequate qualifications for the medical examiner/coroner, a definition of the types of cases to be referred to the office for investigation, a legal penalty for failing to report the said cases, and adequate funding to support the operation.

For a relatively rural state such as Alabama, the ideal system, again in my opinion, would include medical examiners certifying all medical-legal death cases in the larger metropolitan areas. Those more rural jurisdictions without a sufficient volume of cases to support a forensic pathologist should be manned by trained medical investigators who are directly responsible to the forensic pathologist in the metropolitan areas for the decision-making aspects of handling death cases. This would allow even the most rural county access to quality death investigation and take a medical decision out of the hands of untrained lay coroners.

I suspect that a system similar to this won't be forthcoming in my lifetime. The reasons for this are many. Probably most important is the fact that dead people don't vote, or at least are not supposed to vote, and thus are no one's constituency. Legislatures would much rather spend limited tax dollars on projects that are much more visible to the citizens doing the voting.

In addition, most of us spend a considerable amount of psychic energy denying our own mortality and thus would prefer not to think about death in general, much less in a personal way. Interestingly, coroners, at least in Alabama, wield a considerable amount of political clout. As many of these individuals are funeral home directors and thus have a vested interest in death, they're reluctant to relinquish an office that either fattens their purses or can be used as a stepping stone in local politics. Finally, those groups that you would expect to push for a more modern system, law enforcement agencies and the criminal justice system, at least in Alabama, are quite content with what they have available to them now. Although they may have to occasionally pat the ego of a local coroner, they're having all death cases of a criminal or potentially criminal nature examined by a forensic pathologist. Thus, the investigations and the prosecutions of their high-profile cases are usually as good as they would be under a well-defined medical examiner system. They have no reason to overcome the political inertia of the antiquated coroner system.

As a result of all the above, one can rest assured that the citizens of Alabama will continue to function in a system of death investigation, probably until I retire or die, that will remain relatively unchanged since Alabama came into the union in 1819.

WHY DO AN AUTOPSY?

There's no doubt that the decision as to whether an autopsy should be conducted comes at a bad time for the family and loved ones left behind. They've just lost someone precious to them, and along comes a nurse or physician asking if the body of their loved one can be subjected to additional trauma.

In natural death cases that occur in a hospital setting with a physician willing and able to sign the death certificate, the legal next of kin has the authority to either agree to an autopsy or deny permission for an autopsy.

In medical legal cases, the medical examiner or coroner has the statute authority to perform an autopsy on anyone who dies as the result of some type of trauma, dies due to undetermined natural causes, or dies due to a potential infectious agent or disease. In most jurisdictions, the medical legal cases are itemized specifically in statute law and are well defined.

The statute law is established with the understanding that the public's or state's need to document or determine the cause of death outweighs the individual family rights. Ironically, in many situations of a traumatic death in homicides, the person who is the legal next of kin and would thus under natural causes have the right to decide whether an autopsy is permitted might be the person responsible for causing the loved one's death.

Regardless of what type of death has occurred, there are several good reasons why a complete autopsy by a well-trained pathologist should be done. Below I've listed just five reasons to conduct an autopsy. I suspect that many individuals in the field could come up with many more.

The first reason is to make the certification of the death as accurate as possible. To be honest, when I'm watching television and see a news report talking about the leading causes of death in either our local community or within the nation, I chuckle to myself.

The reason I chuckle is that I know how inaccurate the cause of death is documented in this country. Death certificates are being filled out by coroners who have absolutely no medical training or background. In addition, many death certificates are being filled out by physicians who, though quite competent to care for their patients while they are living, have had absolutely no training or guidance in terms of how to sign a death certificate.

As the medical examiner in Mobile County, it was often quite comical to see the items listed as the cause of death by physicians who should have known better but did not. The classic example is the physician who lists cardiopulmonary arrest on the death certificate as the only cause of death. Cardiopulmonary arrest simply means that the heart and lungs have ceased to function. He gives no indication as to the cause of death, that anatomic abnormality which resulted in both the heart and lungs ceasing to work.

As with most things in life, you only need to follow the money. After the death certificate is signed by the physician, coroner, or public health official as to the cause of death, that certificate, along with thousands of others, are eventually combined and analyzed first on a state level and finally a national level. Statistics derived from these certificates are then used to determine the leading causes of death in the community and in the nation. That data is then used to determine the areas into which federal tax dollars are diverted for medical research. Law enforcement, public health, safety issues, and various federal grant monies are also allocated based on this data.

Finally, insurance companies devise their insurance rates for various types of policies from the data. Thus, the more accurately the deaths are certified across the country, the more wisely our already-stretched tax dollar and our budget dollar can be disbursed.

The second reason to do autopsies is to be able to give law enforcement officers accurate information as to the cause and manner of death. One of the cardinal rules in forensic pathology is that there is often a difference between appearance and reality.

While the death scene of a young white female may appear to be a straightforward case of suicide on superficial inspection, a closer inspection of the background, scene, and autopsy findings may in fact reveal a well-disguised homicide. We call these masquerade deaths.

Probably, the most common examples of this involve fire deaths where initially the scene suggests someone falling asleep in bed while smoking when in fact the case involves a homicidal stabbing with the scene set on fire to cover up the death. Of course the reverse is equally true and probably more sobering. What on first pass may appear to be an obvious case of homicide may actually be a suicide disguised for reasons of revenge or shame.

Obviously, it's only by the careful examination of all types of cases that justice can truly be done. In my opinion, this includes a careful autopsy examination in at least all violent or suspicious deaths.

The third reason for an autopsy examination is to help determine insurance settlements. As we all know only too well, life insurance has become big business, with all of us paying a large percentage of our income to maintain policies that protect our families.

Because we all pay so much for our individual policies, we all would like to see the beneficiaries of the policies receive all the money they deserve. Insurance in our society has become a necessary evil, and I'm sure most of us groan a bit each month as we write out the checks. Because of this as well as our common desire to see the underdog win out against the big corporate giants, it's natural for us to be sympathetic to the recipients, especially if they have just lost a loved one; yet on the other hand, we all must pay premiums based at least in part on what insurance companies must pay on death claims. Obviously, if we're all to get what we truly deserve in the way of death benefits from insurance policies and at the same time pay as little as possible in premiums while we're alive, the cause and manner of death must be documented as honestly and accurately as possible.

The fourth reason to autopsy is for our society as a whole. In my opinion, it's extremely important for society to know why it is dying. Besides the economic reasons already stated, autopsy pathology is needed to help advance medical science, and the autopsy has been in a large part responsible for our current level of medical sophistication.

The autopsy as a tool to document injury and disease can also provide valuable data that can be used to make our automobiles, our industrial plants, and our environment safer by correlating disease with environmental pollutants and injuries with design flaws. It is by doing the autopsies and correlating the data that these trends can be correlated and changes initiated to make our daily lives safer.

The fifth reason is much more personable. The autopsy can be used to explain death to the family who has just lost a loved one.

As Dr. Riddick is so fond of saying, the play *Hamlet* by Shakespeare revolved on the main character, Hamlet, trying to understand and put the death of his father into perspective.

The autopsy can usually determine anatomically why a person died and can often allay anxiety and guilt associated with the death. It can often assure the family that they had done everything possible to save the loved one or provide evidence to the family that the disease was too severe or advanced to have made any further interventions on their part futile. Sometimes we're even able to assure the family that the death was either most probably painless or at least the pain wasn't prolonged.

In addition, a documentation of the diseases noted in the deceased might give family members a clue as to possible medical problems they might have inherited and might have to face at some future time. Only by understanding death as well as we possibly can are we able to put its emotional trauma behind us and work to take up our own lives again. We all have known someone haunted by a loved one's death years after his or her exodus.

Finally, the public needs to realize how few autopsies are performed in our modern society. In the not-too-distant past, each hospital had to perform autopsies on a percentage of their in-house fatalities to pass state and federal certifications. This rule has been dropped for economic reasons—no insurance company will pay for the pathologist to do a routine natural death autopsy.

Many will claim with the diagnostic tools that we have available today, an autopsy should be unnecessary. Unfortunately, although almost miraculous in their ability to see smaller and smaller lesions, when the physician really wants to know the cause and mechanism of death, there's nothing at this point in time that replaces a complete autopsy.

I find it ironic that despite the historical fact that many if not most of the significant medical breakthroughs have occurred or have been documented by the autopsy examination, our society has allowed this valuable tool to become underutilized. The autopsy has done much to improve the longevity and quality of our lives. Hopefully, it will remain a valuable tool in the medical researcher's arsenal.

IT AIN'T NECESSARILY SO: WHAT FORENSIC PATHOLOGISTS DO AND CAN'T DO

Before you read any further, it's important that we define some terms used continuously in forensic pathology. The solid understanding of these definitions will help assure that you, as the reader, understand some important points later in the book. The three terms that we need to define are the "cause of death," the "mechanism of death," and the "manner of death." In all medical examiner cases, these are the three diagnoses that we try to make. They are, therefore, foundational to the interpretation of all death cases.

The first term that we need to define is the "cause of death." Simply stated, the cause of death is that disease process or injury that sets in motion a series of pathophysiological processes that are eventually incompatible with life. Don't you just love the way that particular definition just rolls off your tongue? Since this definition and the next are related to each other, I think it would be better if I define the second and third terms before I attempt to explain what they mean in practice.

The second term is the "mechanism of death." The mechanism of death is the pathophysiological processes or events initiated by the cause of death from the above definition that result in a person's death, usually within minutes.

Finally, the manner of death is a medical legal classification of the circumstances of death. The circumstances of all deaths fall within one of the following subtypes: homicide (one person responsible for the death of another person), suicide (one person taking his own life with intent), accidental death (a death resulting from a chance happening or act of God), natural death (a death resulting from some natural disease process, e.g., cancer, heart disease, etc.), and undetermined (the manner of death cannot be determined with certainty after a good investigation into the circumstances of the death to include a complete autopsy examination with complete toxicology analysis of the body fluids).

Now that we have the boring medical definitions out of the way, let me try to clarify and simplify what I want to communicate by giving you examples. Suppose that I'm walking from my office to my parked car when a witness sees my wife pull a gun and shoot me once in the chest.(I had forgotten my wedding anniversary again, and this time, my usually levelheaded wife snapped). The paramedics are called, and I'm rushed to the hospital where I'm immediately taken to surgery and treated for a gunshot wound to the heart. I survived the surgery, but because of prolonged shock, that is, not enough blood circulating to keep oxygen going to my brain, I'm in an irreversible coma.

My life is maintained for some seven days by a respirator and other sundry machines in the intensive care unit. Finally, because of a lack of brain activity, I'm declared legally dead, and my kidneys are harvested because I'm an organ donor. At the end of the harvesting procedure, all machines are turned off, and all my living functions cease. I'm now dead by any definition.

In this case, the mechanism of my death was shock resulting from cerebral hypoxia (too little blood and oxygen to the brain) resulting in irreversible coma and brain death. The cause of death, the disease or injury that started all of my pathophysiological problems, is the gunshot wound to the chest. The manner of death, because my death came at the hands of another person, is homicide.

The observant reader has probably noticed several interesting points in all of this. One point to ponder is that in most circumstances, the cause of death is due to a physical or anatomic abnormality, and the mechanisms of death deals with an abnormal functioning of the body components due to the abnormal anatomic change. Without this structural or anatomic change, the pathophysiology would not occur. That's why some forensic pathologists talk about the proximate cause of death, that first trauma or injury that allows the pathophysiology to kick in and ultimately result in death.

The other point of interest is the realization that the same injuries on a body can be due to different manners of death depending on the circumstances under which the injury was received. For instance, a contact gunshot wound to the side of the head is usually associated with a suicide in which the person places the barrel of the gun directly on the skin before discharging the weapon. This same injury, however, could have also been inflicted by another person in an execution-type shooting and thus be a homicide where one person is responsible for the death of another.

Please note that I said homicide and not murder. "Homicide" is the medical term we use to describe one person responsible for the death of another person. This term has no legal or judicial connotations. Thus, it's possible to commit a homicide but have no legal consequences; for instance, killing in self-defense would still be classified as a homicide even though the criminal justice system decides that no laws were violated.

Another wrinkle in the classification of the manner of death involves suicides. To be correctly classified as a suicide, the person must take his/her own life with intent. If you can't prove intent, the death is classified as an accident, essentially saying that the person accidentally took his/her own life. In many ways, accurately culling out which deaths are true suicides can require more work and be more time intensive than many homicides. Reasons for this might include the overlay of religious, insurance, and family guilt issues. We'll talk about this more in a later chapter.

I realize all of this on first blush appears pretty straightforward. Surprisingly, there are many physicians who confuse the cause and the mechanism of death. There are probably several reasons for this confusion. The most likely reason is simply the lack of education. At no time during my training prior to my forensic fellowship did I ever learn about these definitions and how they relate to an accurate signing of a death certificate.

When this fact is coupled with the fact that the mechanisms of death are those processes that physicians are trained to combat, they work to reverse the shock by replacing blood volume or giving medicines to cause the heart to contract stronger or to control an irregular heart rate.

After working for hours or days to reverse these pathophysiological processes, it's not surprising that they are often more fixated on the pathophysiology that they're unable to reverse than the cause of death;

that disease or injury that started all the bad pathophysiology in the first place.

Finally, whether we want to acknowledge it or not, death is considered a failure by most physicians. Death is the entity that we've spent years training to overcome even though we all realize that 100 percent of our patients will eventually die. We're indoctrinated to believe that life is precious and that our job is to defend our patients from anything that shortens or compromises that precious gift. Anything less is considered unacceptable. As this all comes full circle, you begin to see the reasons behind the need for an accurately signed death certificate.

Let's use one more example to drive home the points which I hope that you now are coming to accept and understand. Suppose that as I was leaving my office one evening during a Midwestern ice storm. I slip and fall on the ice-covered pavement, fracturing my skull, and am rushed to the local emergency room only to be pronounced dead on arrival. The subsequent autopsy shows fractures of the skull with appropriate contusions (bruises) and bleeding into the brain.

Most people would agree that this situation is best classified as an accident or a chance happening, but what if I was walking down the sidewalk and a mugger jumped from the bushes, and after a brief struggle, I was thrown to the sidewalk, resulting in skull fractures and death? Because my problems began at the hands of another individual, the manner of death should be classified as a homicide.

Assume that I had just had some severe financial reversals, my wife had left me for a taller and more handsome man, my job was being eliminated for budgetary reasons, and my body is found on the sidewalk with the same fractures. Reliable witnesses stated that they had seen me leap from a fifth-story window. The manner of my death would be suicide, that is, I probably took my own life with intent.

Finally, if my body was found with the same skull fractures, but this time on dry pavement, with no other injuries to suggest an assault, no background medical history of depression or medical problems to suggest suicide, no witnesses to my death, and after an extensive investigation, no evidence of foul play or logical explanations for my death, the manner of death would be best classified as undetermined, that is, the true circumstances surrounding my death are unknown.

As you can readily see, the determination of the manner of death rests to a large extent on the investigation of the circumstances surrounding the death. Although findings at the autopsy table can be strongly suggestive of a particular manner of death, without good scene and background information, the examiner may be fooled. For example, if the body shows up in the morgue with a contact gunshot wound to the right temple, that is, the barrel of the gun in contact with the scalp or skin at the time of discharge of a weapon, in the majority of the cases that would be a suicide, but if the police investigation informs me that the deceased was a well-known drug dealer and had been seen previously that evening arguing with some unidentified men over money, death may be due to an execution-style gunshot wound to the head and thus be a homicide.

Equally obvious is the needed legwork to obtain the information to correctly classify the death. The death certificate is many times filled out by a physician who has a busy clinical practice, but who has neither the time to investigate nor the hired professional investigators who can sort out the information to correctly classify the death. In my opinion, the best way to obtain the necessary details and see that justice is done is by employing a professional, trained investigative staff working full-time to aid police agency's investigation as well as obtain the information necessary to correlate autopsy findings with the background investigations.

Another aspect of death investigation that's often misunderstood is the actual autopsy examination. Many times after I've talked to family members regarding the results of an autopsy examination on a family member or loved one, it's obvious that they really don't understand what the autopsy entails. In many instances, this is probably a real blessing because the procedure when thought about outside its medical trappings can have gory overtones. First, let me qualify what follows by saying that the autopsy is a medical surgical examination and, as such, is done for specific reasons which are not taken lightly by those involved. Think of the autopsy as a scientific, medical exploration and refrain from visualizing the procedure in terms of someone you know about who has undergone the procedure.

As with all procedures that take place in a hospital when a patient dies, family members must give consent for the autopsy examination. The examination is usually requested by the physician taking care of the patient and is used primarily by clinical physicians to determine how well their therapy was working or to discover if there was some disease process that was missed and potentially could be corrected in future patients.

In these instances, the actual cause of death is usually already known, and the autopsy examinations requested are used to elucidate the underlying mechanisms of death. The main thrust of these autopsies is to make clinical-pathologic correlations, that is, taking available clinical information including X-ray examinations and laboratory tests on blood and trying to explain any abnormal results by the autopsy findings. Again, as the cause of death is usually already known, these correlations are usually related to various mechanisms of death.

In a medical-legal or forensic autopsy, however, the primary goal in most cases is to determine or document the cause of death, that is, to determine what disease or injury was primarily responsible for the death. In addition, unlike the hospital autopsy where the family must get permission before an autopsy can be performed, forensic autopsies are done for the good of the community and are thus previously authorized by law with or without the blessings of the next of kin.

Obviously, there's some overlap in cases. If an individual is shot during an altercation and rushed to the hospital where he or she remained alive for several weeks before death, the case would still be considered a medical legal case. Someone has to document the injuries so that testimony as to the cause of death can be presented in court. This said, however, the actual procedures of these two types of autopsies are the same with some modifications.

Autopsy examination itself is divided into two parts: the external examination and the internal examination. The external portion of the examination is a careful inspection of all clothing, body surfaces, and body orifices to document disease and injury. This is not unlike the physical examination performed on patients by their private physicians when they go for a checkup. In a forensic autopsy, this is an extremely important portion of the examination. The surfaces of the body are those areas where contact is made with the environment and thus contain important clues as to the cause of death and contain valuable pieces of trace evidence that could help understand what happened.

Thus, in all forensic cases, all items of clothing presented with the body, all signs of therapeutic intervention, and all injuries on the skin surfaces themselves are carefully documented with diagrams, photographs, and written descriptions. In the hospital autopsy, the more important information is usually located internally so that on most of these cases, the external portions of the examination don't go into the level of detail seen in the forensic autopsy.

After the external portion of the examination is complete, the internal portion of the examination is begun. This involves the opening of the body cavities and the systematic examination of all internal organs for disease and injury. In addition, all evidence located within the body is collected and documented. The usual approach into the body cavities is by a Y-shaped incision. With the surgical blade, an incision is made extending from the front portion of both shoulders to the lower portion of the front chest in the midline in a "V" shape. The "Y" is formed by extending the incision from the apex of the "V" down the midline of the abdomen to the pubis.

Once this initial incision is made, the skin and muscle of the chest and abdomen are dissected toward the sides so that in the chest area, the ribs are exposed, and the organs of the abdominal cavity are exposed inferiorly. With a saw or sharp knife, the ribs and intercostal muscles (the muscles located between the ribs) are cut along each of the sides of the rib cage.

This allows the front chest wall to be dissected freely, exposing the organs within the chest. At this point, the sac covering the heart is open, and blood is retrieved from the heart and peripheral large blood vessels for toxicology examinations (examinations for drugs, alcohol, or poisons).

This is done routinely in all forensic autopsies. Urine, if any is present, is collected at this time directly from the urinary bladder located in the pelvis. The circumstances of the case will dictate whether specimens are drawn for bacteriologic studies from the various body compartments.

Once the specimens are collected, the organs are removed from the body cavities in a systematic fashion. In a complete autopsy—all forensic autopsy should be complete autopsies—all of these organs are then individually examined, weighed, and usually photographed if significant disease or injury is present. In the process of this examination, small portions of each organ are removed and placed in a fixative before being embedded in paraffin, sliced thinly, and stained for examination under a microscope, again to help document disease and injury.

Finally, the cranial cavity is opened. This is accomplished by an incision into the scalp extending from behind one ear, across the back part of the top of the head to just behind the opposite ear. Once this incision is made, the scalp is reflected to the front and back from the incision to expose the underlying bony skull. With an oscillating saw, the top of the skull is cut and removed, exposing the underlying brain. This organ is then removed, weighed, and examined like the other organs.

Most laboratories, after completing the autopsy examination, put all the organs back into the body cavities where the funeral director can prepare them for burial. All the skin incisions made are then sewn shut, and the body is washed and prepared for release to the funeral home. Please note that all incisions made on the body are located so that when fully clothed, the body can be displayed in an open casket funeral. The incision made on the head is placed far enough back that it's well below the pillow top in the casket.

Finally, let me reaffirm that the autopsy is a medical procedure and is thus done, at least in our laboratory, with considerable respect for the deceased. Let me reemphasize the important role that the autopsy has played in advancing the quality and quantity of life through its contribution to medical knowledge. Although at first thought repulsive to all of us, the autopsy continues to be a useful medical tool.

There's a sign hanging in the autopsy suite of Southern Illinois University medical school that states it more eloquently than I. "This is the place where death can rejoice to be of service to the living."

Television and novels, in addition to glamorizing the forensic pathologist, have also given us problems in terms of what the public and even law enforcement and attorneys think that we should be able to determine from the examination of the body. Quite often, at the scene of a homicide after my quick examination of the body, I get the distinct impression that the homicide detective expects me to look him square in the eyes and state, "The assailant in this case is obviously a middle-aged oriental male trained in the martial arts who walks with a limp caused by poliomyelitis. He held a small-caliber murder weapon in his left hand and was lying on his right side when the weapon was discharged. The death occurred at 8:42 yesterday morning. Neither the victim nor the assailant had breakfast."

Although I'm being facetious, there's considerable pressure placed on the pathologist to deliver information that's impossible to glean from the body alone. As previously stated, in most instances, an autopsy examination in and of itself can't differentiate between contact gunshot wounds resulting from a suicide versus an execution-type slaying, nor can we know for certain the relative positions of the assailant and victims at the time the weapons discharge.

What we can say is that the bullet tract in the deceased courses in a particular direction, that is, front to back, right to left, and head to toe. The relative positions of the two participants are any combination that could potentially make this tract through the body possible to include the absurd possibility that one of the parties was standing on their head. To say with a reasonable degree of certainty where the victim and assailant were in relationship to each other, bullet trajectory must have an additional point of reference, that is, a hole or mark where the bullet lodged or ricocheted somewhere in the scene of death. Another unanswerable question involves the amount of purposeful activity the victim could have performed following the fatal wound to the body. Again, with a few exceptions, there's no way to know for certain. There are multiple factors involved that potentially change the possibilities. These include the physical condition of the deceased, such as disabilities from natural diseases, vital organs disrupted by the wound or wounds inflicted, emotional state of the deceased at the time of entry, etc. Although there are some wounds that render the recipient unable to function instantaneously, for example, wounds transacting the spinal cord or massively destroying the brain, I've learned from experience and from cases described in the forensic literature that just about any amount of activity after a fatal wound is possible and has been reported.

Possibly the greatest fallacy regarding what the pathologist can and cannot determine involves the time of death. My wife has seen me jump up and yell at the television (I try to restrain myself more in movie theatres) when the medical examiner narrows the time of death to a matter of minutes. This is rarely possible even under the best of circumstances.

Instead, the best that we're able to do is give a broad time frame measured in hours during which the death could have occurred. Even then, many expert forensic pathologists feel that examiners are treading on thin ice when they commit themselves to any estimate of the time since death. Indeed, the forensic pathologist who develops a means of accurately determining the time of death can rest assured that he'll be permanently enshrined in the annals of the profession.

The means used by most forensic pathologists to at least give a rough estimate of the postmortem interval are the same parameters that have been used for decades. These include rigor mortis (stiffening of the muscles of the body after death), livor mortis (the settling of blood to the dependent portions of the body after death), and algor mortis (the cooling of the body after death).

As a general rule, rigor mortis begins some three to four hours after death and reaches its peak after about twelve hours. It then slowly dissipates over the next twenty-four hours. Rigor can often be first observed in the smaller muscle masses such as the muscles of the face. As time progresses, the rigor spreads to the larger muscle masses of the trunk, arms, and legs.

Environmental conditions affect the development of rigor, with the whole process taking longer in a cold environment as compared to a warm location. Once rigor in a muscle is broken, it'll not return. Since muscle contraction is a chemical reaction between muscle molecules, energy is required to make the reaction occur. Once the body is dead, the muscle uses up the stored energy and causes the muscle contraction. Since there are no longer any available energy molecules, once the muscle in rigor is forcibly lengthened or allowed to sit over time, the muscle molecules are no longer able to react and contract the muscle.

Livor mortis is simply the settling of blood in the body by gravity after the heart has ceased pumping it around. It tends to start developing within minutes and tends to peak somewhere between six and twelve hours. It gives Caucasians a deep bluish hue at dependent areas of the body. It becomes what we call fixed lividity at five to six hours after death. Lividity occurs because the blood after death is initially liquid. Immediately after death, the lividity will move by gravity as the position of the body is moved. As it begins to congeal, it becomes trapped in the capillaries where it is found and won't change regardless of how the body is repositioned.

This can be useful in a homicide investigation when the pattern of lividity noted on the body doesn't conform to the position of the body where it was found. The bottom line is that the body had been moved or repositioned after the lividity had become fixed.

Algor mortis, or the cooling of the body after death, tends not to be as useful an investigative tool because there are too many variables that must be included in any result. What has the temperature of the environment been where the body was discovered? How much insulation of the body has occurred because of clothing or blankets? Was the temperature of the deceased normal at 98.6 degrees at the time of death, or was some disease process involved that would result in an initial temperature higher or lower than the generally assumed normal temperature? Despite these complications, it's routine to take a body temperature when first examining the body at the scene. This is usually accomplished by sticking a thermometer directly into the liver after making a small incision into the overlying skin. Multiple formulas have been published that extrapolate back to the time of death based on the rate of body cooling varying with the body mass.

Again, while often useful, the variables involved in each of these methods make any generalization as to their usefulness in the individual case difficult. For example, a body found outside a shelter in freezing temperatures couldn't be expected to go through the rigor mortis and algor mortis at the same rate as a body found inside the warm building. Thus, any statement based on these parameters must be qualified by the environmental surroundings and issued with caution.

Interestingly, examination of the stomach contents and their correlation with the last documented meal is probably one of the better methods for placing the time of death within a three- to five-hour framework, the usual length of time necessary to empty a normally functioning stomach. Even this can be variable, however, if the time between the meal and death was characterized by a stressful emotional state or there's a superimposed gastrointestinal disease.

Other methods used to obtain a relative time of death include the measurement of various chemicals shown to increase in the body fluids after death. All methods for making this difficult determination have been met with variable success.

One technique that I found useful for estimating the postmortem interval is the analysis of vitreous potassium. In this technique, the clear fluid from the main chamber of the eyeball is removed by a syringe and analyzed for its potassium content. In the living body, there's an increased concentration of potassium inside the cell as compared to the fluids that bathe the cells and exists as the liquid portion of blood.

This increased potassium inside the cell is maintained by an energy-requiring pump mechanism and is necessary to keep the cell alive. After the cell dies, this increased intracellular potassium concentration slowly leaks out of the cell into the surrounding fluids. Under controlled situations, one would therefore expect to see increasing potassium concentrations in the extracellular fluids over time, and if that leak was slow and constant, the potassium concentration could be used to estimate time since death.

Although great in theory, the problem was finding a fluid both compartmentalized from the other body fluids and relatively resistant to trauma. Blood wasn't useful because after death, blood begins to clot, releasing large amounts of potassium erratically as red cells rupture. The blood is also susceptible to bacterial contamination from the gastrointestinal tract. Cerebral spinal fluid, the fluid surrounding the brain, was also tried but there was an erratic increase in the potassium levels, probably due to the large number of cells lining the fluid tissue interfaces.

Finally, the vitreous or eyeball fluid was considered. It had several advantages. First, it was relatively sequestered as a fluid in that it doesn't turn over rapidly nor have contact with the blood other than by small arteries and veins that feed the area at the posteriorly located optic nerve. Second, because of the eyeball's location in the bony socket in the skull, it's protected from trauma. Thus, even in cases of severe trauma, vitreous fluid can usually be obtained for analysis. Because there is a relatively small number of living cells lining the vitreous cavity in relation to the fluid volume, there tends to be a slow steady diffusion of potassium into the vitreous fluid over time.

In point of fact, of all the fluid compartments of the body examined for this potassium flow, vitreous fluid, although far from perfect, proved to be the best for estimating the postmortem interval.

Even with all these positive attributes, problems still exist. For instance, no one knows what the normal living potassium concentration of the vitreous fluid is. Since potassium is commonly measured in the serum portion of the blood, this is the normal level assumed for vitreous fluid, but since eyes are only removed surgically for severe conditions, and since most people are reluctant to allow anyone to stick a needle into their healthy eyes, even for science, we don't know for sure what the normal level of vitreous potassium is in a healthy living individual.

Another problem is that we don't know what effect environmental conditions have on the rapidity of potassium leakage into the vitreous fluid. Is potassium leakage the same in a cold environment as compared to a body found in heated apartment? We simply don't know for sure. Finally, the rate of potassium leakage has been shown to be erratic past a certain postmortem interval, usually about twenty-four hours.

In important cases, I feel that I've obtained useful information from the vitreous potassium levels. I would be hesitant to use the vitreous chemistry results as the only evidence used to convict a suspect. Instead, I found that its real value was its use as an investigative tool. Let me explain. Anyone who watches television detective shows knows that the lie detector or polygraph can't be used as evidence of guilt in the courtroom, yet this same device is used routinely to sort out suspects so that efforts can be concentrated on individuals who demonstrate through their polygraph results that they're lying about their involvement in the death case.

The vitreous fluid analysis falls within this same category. Although it's not reliable enough for courtroom testimony, it can still help the medical examiner determine the relative time since death, making it useful to use as a gauge to confirm or eliminate a time of death estimate obtained from the other methods. (One modification described in the literature that I found useful is obtaining vitreous fluid from one eye at the scene, then draw vitreous from the other eye after a measured twelve hours. This gives two separate points that can be plotted on a graph of time versus the potassium concentration. My experience has been that this method gives a reasonable estimate of the approximate time of death.)

Although not perfect, ease of obtaining the fluid from the eyes, plus the availability of equipment to run the tests at just about any hospital, makes the analysis of vitreous fluids worthwhile.

A case where the time of death had some investigative importance involved the strangulation of a young white female in her apartment. When the victim failed to show for work after the weekend off, her boss became worried and, after not getting an answer at her apartment, called the police that same afternoon to investigate. The police broke into the apartment and found the subject strangled in her empty bathtub.

Immediate information from a maintenance man working in the area indicated that the woman had been out walking her dog earlier that same morning. If this was correct, the assailants couldn't have gone far. Based on examination of the body at the scene, I felt the subject had been dead for at least twenty-four hours, much longer than the maintenance man had reported. The degree of postmortem change in the internal organs noted at autopsy only confirmed my impression.

As a result of my opinion, the range of search was broadened, and the assailant was captured in Texas the next day. Once in custody, the suspect pled guilty. I was relieved when his timetable in his confession confirmed mine.

Interestingly, as the postmortem interval increases, most investigative parties involved in the case willingly accept broader and broader time frames. If the body is found decomposing outdoors, the time of death can be most accurately estimated by analysis of insects present on the body by a forensic entomologist (a scientist who studies the life cycle of insects). We've had several cases where their input has proved invaluable.

Probably the most aggressive way to get a handle on the time of death in that interval where temperature, rigor, and lividity are no longer of use is to present your case to the body farm at the University of Tennessee. Associated with that university in its anthropology department is a farm unlike any other in the country. They don't grow crops or raise livestock. Instead they grow decomposing bodies. I joke, but in fact, that's not far from the truth.

Scattered about the farm in areas selected for their varying exposure to the elements are a multitude of bodies being studied for their rate of decomposition. The farm takes human bodies donated to medical science and places them in environments that approximate actual cases that police agencies submit, cases where knowing an accurate time of death is critical to solving the case.

If your case is accepted for investigation, the body farm takes all pertinent information as to the location of the body, environmental and seasonal parameters, and sex and size of the victim, then goes to great lengths to duplicate the entire scene with a donated cadaver that closely matches the deceased, and then the decomposition process is followed until the degree of decomposition matches the photos and crime scene information from the actual unsolved case. When the decomposition matches up to that identified victim, the police then have a working frame of time to use in eliminating or including potential suspects for their investigation.

Although the idea of allowing Aunt Susie to lie in a field and decompose over time can be shocking to the uninitiated, you must remember that all these bodies have been donated to the University of Tennessee body farm for just this purpose. In addition to giving evidence on an individual case that might be unsolved, the decomposition is carefully followed and documented in all cases over time so that an incredible amount of information about decomposition under varying conditions can be applied to other cases that didn't make the cut to have their own cadaver for study.

My personal experience with the body farm is limited to scientific journal articles. One time I did have the opportunity to see the value of the farm on a death case with which I was peripherally involved, the death of a young coed from the University of South Alabama. The body was found on the weekend that I was preparing to leave to take my board examination to be certified in anatomic and clinical pathology. While Dr. Riddick was working the case, I was sitting in a room trying to cram as much information as possible into my already-challenged brain in the hope that I would pass the four-day examination to take place in San Diego that next week.

The case involved a freshman coed attending the University of South Alabama (USA). On a Thursday afternoon in February, Kathryn, a pretty coed, had plans to go shopping with girlfriends. She was attending USA with her high school boyfriend and a female friend from her hometown. The shopping trip included the hometown female friend, Jamie, and another friend named Trish. According to Jamie, she and Kathryn were getting ready to leave for town when Kathryn realized that she had left something back in her dorm room. She left to retrieve the unknown item and was never seen alive again.

Kathryn was reported as missing to the Mobile Police that evening, but by policy, they refused to launch an investigation until twenty-four hours had elapsed. The police thus began their investigation in earnest on Friday afternoon when Kathryn failed to return.

On Saturday morning of that second day, the student body of USA organized a campus wide search, and the body of Kathryn was located in a wooded area on campus at about ten on that same morning.

When discovered, Kathryn was lying on her back on the ground with two gunshot wounds to the head. The scene and subsequent autopsy examinations failed to show evidence of sexual assault, and

Dr. Riddick, who had assumed the case, saw no significant changes of decomposition during either the external or internal exams.

In addition, the victim's clothes were intact, and the body showed no defensive-type wound on any of the body surfaces. Had Kathryn not had the gunshot wounds to her head, she could just as easily been sleeping where she had been found.

Based on Dr. Riddick's scene examination as well as the complete autopsy examination, he estimated that the death had occurred some eight to twenty-four hours prior to the discovery of the body. If this was the case, Kathryn had to have been alive for some twenty-four hours before sustaining the gunshot wounds that took her life. Trying to fill in those missing twenty-four hours became an investigative priority for the police.

All of Kathryn's friends had solid alibis for the eight to twenty-four missing hours. The fact that Kathryn had no defensive wounds on her body suggested that she had been with someone that she knew and trusted. Interviews with everyone who might have had contact with Kathryn produced no viable clues.

The investigation went through the usual convulsions of an unsolved homicide with added stress inflicted by the media and university. No city or university wants to live with the fear of a homicidal killer on the loose. The university didn't want the fear of a recurrence or the prospect that the killer might be a student at their school.

I was involved in one case soon after Kathryn's body was found that was initially suspected as being related to her killing. One of the USA campus police was found dead in his home not far from the university campus. The cause of death was determined to be due to a suicidal overdose of sleeping medication. The finding that caused police to perk up regarding the coed killing was that the security guard had obtained copies of the autopsy report and was making his own case file, including photos of the deceased and all of the newspaper articles related to the death.

Although it would have been nice to have the security guard committing suicide over a guilty conscience because he had killed the coed, it was subsequently discovered that the guard had an alibi for the interval of time under question. He was working on campus for that time interval and hadn't been out of his partner's sight. A more thorough background check on the guard revealed that he was a police "want to be" and had been previously turned down multiple times by local police agencies because he'd been unable to pass the mental/social exams required by the police agencies. I suspected he had hoped that his solving the big murder case would open doors to the local police agencies. That was not the case.

The case went cold for two decades until a reporter for a local television station did a multipart report on the unsolved case. It wasn't long after these stories aired that the Mobile Police received a call from the Pascagoula, MS, police stating that they had been telephoned by an Alcoholics Anonymous counselor who had a patient who had confessed to killing a woman in Mobile in her distant past. The woman's first name was Jamie, and she had recently moved to Jackson, MS, to live in a halfway house.

As they investigated the report further, the police discovered that a letter written by Jamie in which she had allegedly confessed to the murder was being stored in a file located at the home of Jamie's stepfather. He gave them the original letter, and the police were able to get fingerprint matches from the letter's paper that matched Jamie.

It had begun to look like a slam-dunk case until it was presented to the district attorney to get an indictment for Jamie's arrest. In reviewing the file, the assistant district attorney noted the estimated time of death given by Dr. Riddick (eight to twenty-four hours prior to discovery of the body) and an investigator's typed report claiming that Jamie had been spending that night with a family of old friends who now lived in Mobile. They stated that she had been with the family for the entire evening and had even stayed in their home during the night in question. Jamie had a solid alibi, making it impossible to tag her as the killer.

The police investigators contacted Dr. Riddick, asking how firm he felt about the time of death in the case. Dr. Riddick indicated how variable the findings could be in determining the time of death for any particular case and was willing to concede that his estimate was subject to error. The district attorney was still unmoved and wanted more evidence to use in court should the time of death issue be raised. That's where the body farm comes into the story.

It's not every day that any death investigator gets the chance to solve a twenty-year-old case. The body farm agreed to take the case and within weeks had female corpses lying out in their woods in an environment that duplicated the original crime scene as closely as possible. The body was examined daily for signs of decomposition, insect infestation, and animal infestation. At the end of the twenty-four-hour and forty-eight-hour time intervals, there were no significant changes to the body as compared to those seen in the original autopsy findings.

Jamie was taken to trial, and after a full day of deliberation, the jury found Jamie guilty of first-degree murder. Though it took twenty years, justice was finally served. It also proved to me how estimating the time of death in individual cases can be difficult even in the hands of an expert with the vast experience of my mentor.

In summary, there are definite limitations as to what information can be generated from the examination of the body, even by an experienced forensic pathologist. Learning your limitations is probably the hardest lesson of all. Interestingly, the acknowledged authorities in this area of endeavor are the investigators who choose their words most carefully. Perhaps that's why they're the acknowledged experts.

WHO AM I?

Obviously before a death certificate can be issued in a death case, the body must first be identified. Sometimes this involves no more than comparing the deceased's likeness to photographic identification present with the body or the positive identification of the deceased by relatives present at the time of death. Sometimes in cases of skeletonized remains found in the woods, however, I feel fortunate to be able to identify the body, much less able to determine the cause and manner of death.

Probably equally obvious, the procedures used to identify the deceased vary with the condition of the body and location where the body is found. For instance, if a decomposing body is found in a locked apartment known to be rented by an elderly male who lives alone and who has a long medical history of heart disease, a tentative identification can usually be made by mail and personal effects found in the apartment. This can be further corroborated by interviews with people living around the deceased who can confirm that indeed, the subject lives in the said apartment and hasn't been seen for some time. Positive identification can then be made via dental records or fingerprint comparisons.

If the body is found in the woods with no tentative identification, the process of identifying the deceased becomes more difficult. Most people don't realize that fingerprint comparisons are the only means available to identify a body if we have no idea who that person is. A match by DNA testing is now possible, but the library of known DNA results is still in its infancy. Fingerprints, as most people know, are unique to each individual. To date, no two individuals have been found to have the same fingerprint patterns.

One point that I didn't know before starting in this line of work was that the fingerprint pattern on each finger of a given person can be different, and that knowing this sequence of patterns can help make the positive identification. In retrospect, this makes sense and explains why the police take prints on all fingers making sure that each finger is identified as to its digit number and hand. The Federal Bureau of Investigation probably has the world's largest library of known fingerprints. They've comprised their libraries from local law enforcement agencies as well as the records of everyone entering military service.

One interesting corollary to this is that we're entering an era where the fingerprint records of the FBI won't be as valuable in identifying unidentified remains. As the number of generations pass with our nation maintaining an all-volunteer system of recruiting, larger numbers of these exempt individuals will have no fingerprints on file.

Another complication with the use of fingerprints as a means for identifying unknown bodies is that, other than the FBI, there's usually no local central depository for the fingerprint records of a community. Instead, each law enforcement agency maintains its own files, usually in varying degrees of organization.

In addition, most police agencies don't fingerprint all arrests routinely, usually because of manpower constraints in procuring the prints as well as maintaining the fingerprint libraries. Hopefully, the era of computerization will help alleviate this problem and give individual law enforcement agencies access to each other's files for purposes of conviction as well as identification of unknown bodies. An example of this involved a 35-year-old white male found lying beside the road as a victim of a pedestrian–motor vehicle crash in Mobile County.

Because there was no identification found on the body, we took and submitted fingerprints to the surrounding law enforcement agencies with no matches obtained. While the prints were sent to the FBI for comparisons, Brian Delmas, our fingerprint examiner, sent copies of the prints to the major police agencies in the southern states.

Long before the results had returned from the FBI in Washington, we were able to make a positive identification via a known set of prints on file with a police agency in Tennessee. This process, however, still took several weeks to complete and could potentially cause a deceased's family considerable grief during the waiting period. This has become a nonissue since my retirement by a federal depository of fingerprint information available to local agencies via Internet-linked computers.

The bottom line to this discussion is that if fingerprints are available from the deceased, they remain the best means for obtaining a positive identification.

If the body is sufficiently decomposed or skeletonized so that fingerprints are no longer available, the identification of the remains becomes a process of elimination. The first step in this procedure is to develop a general description of the deceased.

Working with an anthropologist, a scientist who studies archeological bones from past civilizations, we attempt to determine the sex, race, age, and height of the deceased. The sex is usually best determined by the configuration of the pelvis. If unavailable, a less-reliable determination of the sex can be obtained from the skull. The race can be categorized by the configuration of the skull into Caucasian, Negroid, or Oriental/American Indian. The age is approximated by determining the closure of the various growth plates in the bones. Interestingly, these epiphyseal or growth plates in the bones responsible for the increase in bone length with age, close or fuse at different ages in the same individual.

Thus, by determining which plates are open and which have already closed, an approximate age at the time of death can be obtained. Finally, an approximate height can be obtained by measuring the length of the long bones, bones from the arms and legs, and comparing the measurements to standard tables gathered by the anthropologists. Once the approximate age, sex, race, and height are obtained, these figures are compared against missing person records on file at local police agencies. All suspects fitting the description within a broad range are selected for further study.

In addition to determining the above, examination of the remains also includes the search for unique characteristics, such as features on the skeleton which are unique to that individual alone and thus of potential help in establishing a positive identification. The unique features used as points of identity between the missing person and the unidentified remains include, in order of usefulness and uniqueness, dental fillings, dental extractions and dental repair work, bony changes from previous trauma, and congenital (from birth) abnormalities of the bones. Thus, dental records including dental X-rays and all medical records including X-rays from all suspects must be collected and compared to either the remains themselves or preferably to X-rays taken of the skeletonized remains. As you might imagine, this is quite often no simple investigative undertaking. An incredible number of man hours usually go into snooping out all this information. From experience, we've found that this type of case is best left to one investigator. This cuts down on the duplication of the legwork and allows for all potential suspects to be systematically eliminated.

Statistically, dental fillings and dental X-rays are the most fruitful avenues of investigation. The three-dimensional metal filling put into a tooth cavity usually renders a unique configuration when converted to a two-dimensional X-ray of the tooth.

In addition, the dental X-ray allows investigators to identify which tooth the filling is in. Thus, particularly in those cases where multiple teeth have fillings for comparison, dental fillings come close to fingerprints in terms of uniquely identifying the individual.

Unfortunately, many dentists don't routinely take X-rays of the teeth with fillings. In their defense, in many instances, it's neither cost-effective nor worth the risk to expose the patient to unnecessary radiation. From a forensic pathologist's point of view, however, there's nothing more discouraging than to have a body with a mouthful of fillings and no dental X-rays for comparison.

An example of the use of dental X-rays to establish a positive identification occurred when a set of skeletal remains was found in an illegal dump site on the east side of the Mobile River. The body was almost totally skeletonized, with only fragments of leathery dermal tissue along the left side of the face and posteriorly along the back side of the body. The remains were infested with beetles and larger insects that were beyond the maggot stage.

Examination of the body back at the lab revealed a female pelvic configuration (there are few things more embarrassing than identifying remains as female based only on clothing to find out later that the remains were those of a male transvestite). The skull appeared Caucasian, the height was estimated at five feet four inches to five feet six inches, and the age was estimated between thirty-five and forty years. This information was circulated to the local police agencies for comparison with their missing person files. Local possibilities included only one person.

The family of the suspected missing person was contacted to find out the suspect's dentist. The dentist, in turn, had good written records of the patient as well as multiple X-ray studies. These records and X-ray studies were compared to the deceased, and a positive identification was made within twenty-four hours of the discovery of the body. The deceased's boyfriend was interviewed by the police, charged and subsequently proved responsible for her death.

The point to be noted here is that although our office was unable to ascertain the exact cause and manner of the deceased's death because of postmortem decomposition, a positive identification of the remains was necessary before law enforcement agencies could prove that a crime had been committed.

Obviously, if fingerprints and dental patterns are not available for identification, things become more difficult. Occasionally, however, lady luck smiles on you with some long-standing bony change of skeletal trauma or disease that allows investigators to comfortably identify the remains. This type of case was presented to our office one autumn from Baldwin County, AL. A highway crew was cutting weeds on the median of the interstate highway that separates Mobile and Baldwin counties. In an area of the median that widens into thick woods, a partially buried skeleton was discovered.

Examination of the skeleton back in the laboratory revealed characteristics that I thought represented an elderly black male. Even at first glance, I saw changes in the bones of the lower legs that offered hope for a positive identification. The right leg of the skeleton was markedly smaller in diameter and length as compared to the left leg. This was indicative of a long-standing disease involving the muscles of the right leg, most probably a disease like poliomyelitis. This would waste the muscles of that leg and thus result in weakening of the associated bones from disuse.

The identification was subsequently solved by going through the partially buried, dry-rotted clothes. A plastic Florida driver's license was recovered with the photograph of an elderly black male leaning on a homemade crutch. A telephone call to the police agency of the community identified on the license confirmed that some five years previous, this elderly gentleman wandered off from his home in Florida in his pickup truck. He was known to get easily lost during his wanderings and had been listed as missing by family members the next day when he failed to return.

Interestingly, records of the police agency near his location of discovery had recorded towing a broken-down pickup truck from this very location some five years previous. Upon contacting the family about the deserted vehicle, the son had come to the area looking for his father but failed to find him after a several days search. Because the man was well into his seventies with a history of heart disease, he had likely become disoriented during his drive and, upon running out of gas, walked into the median to either sleep or start for help. I felt sure that he died from natural causes at the site where he was found.

The point should be made that in some skeletal remains cases the identity of the remains is never ascertained. This is more likely the case in areas where there's a high volume of drifters passing through. Unfortunately, the jurisdictions that I've worked in Mobile and Pensacola have characteristics that fall into this category. Located at the intersection of 1-65 and 1-10 along the Gulf Coast, we tend to have a large number of people passing through the area either heading toward the Florida panhandle or toward the New Orleans area to the west.

Many of these drifters carry no identification, and their subsequent identification can be quite difficult. One avenue of help in identifying individuals from other regions of the country is a national computer identification program called the National Crime Information Center. By completing several pages of identification criteria to include dental patterns, tattoos, and scars found on the body as well as hair, eye color, and approximate age and height determinations, the computer compares the known characteristics from the unidentified body to a similarly completed missing-person-type form completed by the police agency reporting the individual as missing. All possible matches based on statistical criteria are supplied to both agencies, and via telephone and mailing correspondence, possibilities are eliminated or investigated further. If the match appears to be a strong possibility, copies of dental X-rays and medical records are exchanged. It's not unusual to get a positive identification by this method.

One such case investigated by Dr. Riddick involved a white male estimated to be in his early twenties who was found badly decomposed lying in a drainage ditch in a nearby county. All avenues of local identification were exhausted while the forms were being prepared by the department to enter the deceased into the computer program. The follow-through on several subsequent potential matches turned up fruitless. Just as we were beginning to think that the body was never going to be identified, our office received a call from a police agency in the northeast.

Allegedly, the suspected match was a sailor stationed in Pensacola, FL, some sixty miles from where the body was found. As the chances for a match appeared good, arrangements were made to send the dental records to our lab for comparison. The dental records were a perfect match and thus allowed us to positively identify the remains as the missing son from New England.

In some cases, it's the radiologist who's called upon to help make a positive identification. Radiology is the medical specialty dealing with the study and interpretation of X-rays as well as those new-fangled imaging techniques, nuclear magnetic resonance and ultrasonography. Obviously, after years of studying X-rays, these physicians are experts in their interpretation. Some radiologists have taken a special interest in using X-ray comparisons to make a positive identification.

Although every human bone has the same general architecture, every person has individual characteristics that make his/her bones unique. There may be changes as obvious as a thickening of the bone at a fracture site to things as subtle as the location of holes in the bone where blood vessels penetrate to feed the inner bone marrow tissues.

Thus, by comparing known X-ray films taken while the subject was alive to X-ray films taken of the skeletonized remains, a forensic radiologist is usually able to find sufficient points of identity or nonidentity to determine if the skeleton belonged to the person shown on the premortem X-rays. For this process to work, you must first have some suspicion as to the identity of the deceased. The investigator must also have access to premortem X-rays of the suspected subject and matching skeletal remains to X-ray for comparisons.

Fortunately, especially in the more elderly segments of the population, most people have at least had a chest X-ray somewhere in their past. Unfortunately, it's not always easy to get access to the X-ray films themselves. In many instances the X-rays were taken during military service and it often takes an act of God to get the records released.

In other instances, the X-ray department who are custodians of the films may have already destroyed the X-rays as a matter of policy. X-ray films, because of their size and bulk, are difficult to store indefinitely. Thus, most radiology departments have policies in place requiring X-rays over a certain age be routinely destroyed. Although some hospitals put the X-rays on microfiche for permanent storage, the cost is often prohibitive for most hospitals. For the forensic pathologist hoping to use the X-rays for identification purposes, there aren't many things more depressing than finding that the X-rays have already been destroyed.

In the younger age groups, it's not uncommon to find that X-rays have never been taken. If dental records are also nonexistent, it's quite possible that a positive scientific identification can't be made on the skeletal remains.

For X-ray identification, the most fruitful areas of the body for obtaining a positive comparison are X-rays of the head and pelvis. Both areas have the potential for yielding sufficient individual differences because of their complexity. This in turn allows the three-dimensional orientations of the bones to render a unique two-dimensional X-ray photograph.

In the skull, the shape of the frontal sinuses, those air-filled spaces in the bone of the forehead, often is unique enough to allow a positive identification on its own. X-rays of the pelvis, in addition to giving the sex of the skeleton, also have enough uniqueness to allow a positive identification. Other areas of potential use to the forensic radiologist are X-rays of areas of previous skeletal trauma, chest X-rays, and spinal X-rays.

Most radiologists, like physicians in general, are reluctant to get involved in any endeavor that might result in a courtroom appearance. Thus, although there are usually radiologists associated with most hospitals, it can sometimes be difficult to find one who's interested in the forensic applications of X-ray studies. In Mobile, we were fortunate to have Dr. B. G. Brogdon in the radiology department of the University of South Alabama.

In addition to being an acknowledged expert in clinical radiology, Dr. Brogdon has also published and presented seminars extensively in forensic radiology. He has proved himself invaluable on many occasions.

One such case involved the skeletal remains of a young black female found in the woods near a rural community in Washington County, AL. Preliminary examination of the bone and clothing at the scene indicated that the remains were consistent with a nineteen-year-old resident of the community who had been missing for some ten months. Although fractures of the skull indicated blunt force injury to the head as the cause of death, I quickly realized that obtaining a scientific identification would be difficult.

One reason for the difficulty was that not all of the bones of the skeleton were present. Various scavenger animals had taken portions of the skeleton to parts unknown. The skeletal fragments remaining also showed evidence of gnawing artifacts. More disturbing, however, was the complete absence of dental fillings or evidence of dental extractions. Our subject had probably never been to a dentist or at least not had any dental repair that could be used as points of identification.

Huey A. Mack Jr., the forensic investigator on the case, began checking the medical history of the deceased in his usual thorough manner. He was able to ascertain that the woman suspected of being the skeletal remains had delivered a baby at the local hospital about one year before. When her medical records were checked, a report of a pelvic X-ray was noted. The X-ray, initially ordered to determine if the bony birth canal would be large enough to pass the baby's head, was still on file in the hospital X-ray department.

Although pleased that we had an X-ray to use for comparison, it was too early to start celebrating. The scavengers from the woods had taken or destroyed most of the pelvis. Of the seven bones comprising the pelvis, we only had the three bones that formed the right side of the pelvis: the right ilium, right ischium, and right pubis bones. The left side and posterior portion of the pelvis were nowhere to be found. Determined to do the best we could with the bones we had, we began taking X-rays. This was no easy matter.

To make the detailed comparisons of bony structure necessary for a radiologic identification, the recovered bony fragments must have the identical orientation to the X-ray beam that the original had. Thus, by trial and error, using modeling clay as a base to hold the bones upright, we began the process of trying to adjust the strength of the X-ray so that the amount of X-ray penetration and thus degree of X-ray film exposure would also match the original.

With the invaluable help of the technicians from the radiology department and multiple exposed X-ray plates, we eventually duplicated the original pelvic X-ray in both orientation and exposure. Dr. Brogdon, supervising this tedious process, was quickly able to find six points of unique identity between the pelvic X-ray and the X-ray of the skeletal fragment. His expertise in the process gave us a positive scientific identification in a case otherwise destined to go unsolved.

Needless to say, skeletonized and decomposing bodies can be among the most interesting and satisfying cases faced by the forensic pathologist. They can also be among the most frustrating and humbling. Regardless of a person's station in life or his/her personality, there's always at least one person somewhere who loves him or her. Thus, every case remaining unidentified deprives that loved one's opportunity to know the fate of their relative and the opportunity to go through a normal grieving process so necessary to put the loss behind them.

Finally, mention should be made to the one category of case that makes even the best-equipped and staffed medical examiner's office cringe—mass disasters. Any time multiple individuals die in the same incident, potential families of the victims and the media become actively involved. Mass disasters can be the result of a natural disturbance in nature as a tornado or hurricane, but in this age of rapid transportation, the cause is usually due to the crash of a train or airplane with multiple passengers on board.

When a crash such as this occurs, the cause of death in the passengers is usually obvious. The real problem involves the positive identification of the passengers who have died in the crash. In airplane crashes, identification is normally complicated by the explosion and burning of the airplane on impact. Thus, instead of working on severely traumatized and burned bodies that are relatively intact, as from a house fire, investigators are instead forced to attempt identification on severely traumatized, possibly charred fragments of bodies.

Fortunately, on larger airplanes, all seats are assigned, and the airline maintains a list of the passengers and personnel on board the plane. Although I've never been personally involved in the investigation of the crash of a large plane with multiple passengers, medical examiners involved with such cases have vouched for the cooperation of the airlines in making passenger lists available as well as working actively with the families of the deceased to obtain pertinent medical and dental records to aid in the identifications.

If ever there was a category of a case where teamwork is necessary, this is it. It's usual to recruit the aid of dentists, anthropologists, and outside forensic pathologists. Duties for teams of professionals at the scene of the crash include securing the scene to prevent vandalism and theft of valuables and the systematic collection and documentation of all pieces of evidence, from human fragments to possessions found at the crash site.

Finally, all fragments are taken to a central depository where dentists, anthropologists, and pathologists work together to try to reconstruct the human jigsaw puzzle necessary to establish a positive identification on the victims. Of course, all of this is done under the pressure of the families waiting for positive identification on their loved ones and the news media wanting instant answers regarding victims and cause of the death.

Regardless of how thorough or experienced the group of workers is in this type of investigation, there's always a certain percentage of the bodies that remain unidentified by scientific criteria. In addition to the trauma that renders identification difficult, there's inevitably a small percentage of passengers aboard who either have used a ticket listed in another name or are traveling under an assumed name for personal reasons. Obviously, all parties concerned in the crash are anxious for positive identification on all victims for reasons of death certification, so life insurance policies can be filed, and families can bury their loved ones and begin to rebuild their lives.

The closest that I've personally come to this type of case involved the crash of a twin-engine airplane in a rural county north of Mobile County. We received the call early one spring evening that the plane had crashed into a wooded area after experiencing engine trouble on a flight from Florida to St. Louis, MO. After being assured that none of the bodies would be moved or the scene disturbed, we headed north.

Upon arriving at the scene, we first did a quick overview and began to document the scene with photographs. Although there was no evidence that the severely charred fuselage was still potentially flammable, it was obvious that police and fire crews standing by were anxious to begin to get the bodies out of the wreckage. It's one of those curious quirks of human nature that everyone's immediate reaction, mine included, is to begin tearing the plane apart to get all the bodies out. Instead, after documenting the scene with sketches and photographs, we systematically began removing the bodies, making certain that photographs were taken at each step and that all associated valuables were kept with the bodies.

In the meantime, the Flight Safety Board and the Federal Aviation Agency were on their way to investigate the crash. Concomitantly, a search for a list of all passengers on board the plane was begun at the airport of the flight's origin. Special care was used in attempting to identify the pilot and copilot of the plane.

Removing the bodies from the plane was complicated by the fact that the plane had flipped over and was lying upside down at the crash site. Identification of the passengers and pilot was more difficult because there was extensive charring of the bodies from the fire after the crash.

Despite these handicaps, we were able to positively identify the bodies removed from the plane, eight in all, within some forty-eight hours of the crash. This was accomplished by dental record comparisons, personal effects, and medical record comparisons. Complete toxicological studies were carried out on all of the victims in addition to complete autopsies. It was interesting that none of the victims died as the result of blunt force injuries sustained in the crash. Instead, all of the victims died as the result of smoke inhalation and carbon monoxide poisoning sustained as the plane caught fire on impact.

The subsequent analysis of our work in documentation both at the scene and at the autopsy table has to date withstood the scrutiny of the federal agencies involved as well as attorneys representing various interests. Although I realize that the magnitude of this case comes nowhere near that encountered in mass disasters involving large passenger airplanes, this case hopefully gave our office a framework on which to build should a larger disaster come our way. Hopefully, this will never happen.

Another technical breakthrough in forensic investigations that has occurred during my career is DNA analysis. If I had to pick one improvement in technology that has changed forensic investigation more than any other, it would have to be DNA analysis. There have been impressive advancements in toxicology with gas chromatography/mass spectrometry (GC mass spec), where small molecules of an unknown substance can be analyzed and compared to a library of hundreds of thousands of substances and matched to the exclusion of all others, and there has been marked advancements in comparison of fingerprints and the ability to develop latent prints on various surfaces throughout a crime scene, but nothing compares to DNA analysis.

So how does DNA fit into the forensic picture? To understand this, we have to go back and look at the anatomy of the individual cell.

If you remember your high school biology, you recall that the cell is an individual living unit and that your body is composed of trillions of individual cells. Each of these cells is composed of a cell membrane, protoplasm, and nucleus. Within the nucleus are forty-six individual chromosomes organized in twenty-three pairs. One half of these chromosomes come from your mother, and the other half come from your father. This explains why you can have your father's blue eyes and your mother's blonde hair. The vast majority of human cells contain this complement of forty-six chromosomes. The only exceptions include red blood cells, which lose their nucleus early on in their maturation process, and the sex chromosomes from the sperm and egg produced by your parents, each of which have one half of a normal cell chromosome complement (twenty-three each). These forty-six chromosomes contain a complete set of instructions that help maintain and make you into a living human being. These chromosomes in turn are composed of a molecule known as deoxyribonucleic acid (DNA).

DNA has been called the most extraordinary molecule in the world. That's ironic because it's relatively inert and exists only to act as a template to make proteins and more DNA. If stretched out into its total strand length, every cell nucleus contains about six feet of DNA. Since our bodies are composed of an estimated ten thousand trillion cells (finally a number larger than our national debt) and each of these cells contains the equivalent of six feet of DNA compacted into the small nucleus, you come to realize how much DNA our bodies actually contains as we walk around every day.

It's obvious that the human body is good at making DNA. That's a good thing because without it, we wouldn't be alive; yet despite its necessary role in the function of the cells that make us humans, DNA is an incredibly inert molecule. It doesn't react or decompose readily when exposed to environmental extremes. In fact, it's so inert that it maintains itself under conditions and in situations where most molecules would decompose. That's why DNA is so valuable at crime scenes. It maintains its structure even under drying situations and, in the case of the movie *Jurassic Park*, in the bellies of mosquitoes that have been petrified in amber.

This in turn makes the recovery of blood and tissue substances at a crime scene important because the DNA from the sample obtained at the scene can be compared to known samples of living individuals to prove or disprove that they were at least at the crime scene depositing their cellular samples.

This unique physical characteristic of DNA's inertness is based on its composition and structure. It's so brilliantly simple that for years, scientists failed to appreciate its role in the survival and replication of every cell on the planet. The DNA molecule is composed of four basic molecules called nucleotides. This means that in essence, the whole book of instructions necessary to make us each into the unique human individuals that we are, are coded in an alphabet composed of just four letters. These four nucleotides are arranged in a structure known as the famous or infamous double helix. The best way to picture a double helix structure is to imagine a spiral staircase, much like the type seen in the Washington Monument or the Statue of Liberty.

In this model, each step of the stairway is formed by two nucleotides held in place by phosphate molecules that form the stairway railings. The four nucleotides—adenine, cytosine, guanine, and thymine—connect to each other such that a cytosine is always attached to guanine, and an adenine is always attached to a thymine. This monogamous relationship occurs because the three-dimensional shape of the four molecules will only allow the bonding between molecules necessary to match up and lock into the double helix shape, not unlike how the pieces of a jigsaw puzzle fit together in only one way based on their shape.

Since DNA is the alphabet that each cell uses to duplicate itself each time it divides to form another cell, it's important that each cell division produces an exact duplicate of itself so that it can perform the same function as the cell from which it divided. Thus, liver cells divide to make liver cells that do all the same functions as the cell from which it divided. To do this, the nucleotide sequence on each step of the double helix must be exactly the same in terms of their order and nucleotide type.

The beauty of this system is that if the DNA molecule is split apart at the two nucleotides, the middle of each step in the double helix, and then pulled apart, the two strands will always be the mirror image of each other. If each separated strand is then used as a template on which you attach additional nucleotides, you end up with two DNA molecules with the exact same nucleotide sequence because only a cytosine can attach to a guanine and only a adenine attach to a thymine. Once the DNA information is exactly duplicated, one copy stays in its cell of origin, while the other copy goes into a new cell produced by cell division. Both cells have a complete copy of the DNA needed to function properly.

In addition to DNA completely reproducing itself and thus passing on the genetic code from one individual to another during procreation, the other function of DNA is to code for proteins. Proteins, which are composed of amino acids, are responsible for the structure and metabolic activities of all cells. The sequence of nucleotides in a DNA molecule gives the information necessary to take individual amino acids and place them into the proper sequence so that a three-dimensional protein, which actively does its programmed job correctly, is produced.

The public probably thinks that with all that we know about the DNA molecules that we would understand its code and function completely. Ironically, however, some 90 percent of our DNA consist of stretches of nucleotides that for years we thought coded for no particular proteins and produced no particular benefit to the cell or organism. We now are beginning to realize that these areas of DNA code that were previously thought of as useless "junk DNA" actually have a complicated regulatory function in protein production. This comes as no big surprise to many of us nonscientists who couldn't understand why God would put so much useless filler into such a simple ingenious code.

The aspect of all this biochemistry of interest to forensic scientists is that each DNA molecule is unique to the human or organism that it codes for. In fact, there's never been a human being since God created Adam and Eve who has had exactly the same DNA sequence that you have sitting here, reading this book, nor will anyone coming along after you ever duplicate your DNA exactly. I need to quickly add the disclaimer here that the only known exception to this fact is the DNA sequence of identical twins. They will both have the exact same DNA nucleotide sequence because both twins come from the same fertilized egg that splits into two individuals shortly after conception.

Although my DNA is 99.9 percent the same as yours and every other human being past, present, and future, that 0.1 percent difference and the variability within that 0.1 percent make each of us unique within the human population. It's also this 0.1 percent difference between individuals that makes DNA such a valuable tool in forensic investigations.

By using the correct nucleotide probe combinations that are specific for those areas of DNA which are unique between individuals, it's possible to identify a DNA sample from a crime scene as belonging to a given individual to the exclusion of anyone living or who has ever lived on the earth. Knowing that makes it easy to understand why DNA has become such an important tool in crime scene and rape investigations.

With the exception of fingerprints, forensic scientists have never had a tool that could uniquely link one individual to the scene of the crime. In addition, police agencies are in the process of collecting this DNA information from criminals who have been convicted of previous crimes and developing a database much like what has been done for fingerprints so that unknown samples can be compared to the known database to uniquely identify or exclude a suspect from the crime being investigated. The use of DNA to prove the involvement of one individual in cases of serial murders is an immediate example, and everyone has heard how DNA has been used to prove the innocence of a jailed convict who was released based on DNA evidence.

The origin of the idea of using DNA profiling as a forensic tool is credited to an English scientist named Alec Jeffreys. Since everyone knew that DNA varied from person to person, there should be a way to use that information to include or exclude suspects who either matched or failed to match a DNA sample retrieved from either the victim or the crime scene.

The beauty of Jeffreys's idea, however, was that instead of having to analyze the entire nucleotide sequence from both the unknown and suspects, he instead developed DNA probes composed of a sequence of four to six mirror image nucleotides from the variable regions of human DNA. He then uncoiled the DNA molecules of the sample being examined and exposed the uncoiled DNA to the probes that he had developed. The DNA probes would either attach to the uncoiled DNA from the sample or remain unattached depending on whether there was a perfect mirror image nucleotide match between the probe and the unknown sample.

The unattached DNA fragments are then eliminated, and the results will show either a positive result for the probe when it perfectly matches the nucleotide sequence on the sample and attaches or a negative result to the probe if no attachment occurs.

Based on the rate of occurrence of the mirror image nucleotides that match the sequence of the nucleotides in the probes within the population of humans, scientists can statistically determine whether two samples of DNA came from the same individual. The positive or negative results from these various probes can also be classified and stored in a computer database, much like fingerprints. This is the database police and federal agencies are building when obtaining DNA samples from convicted criminals. Once an unknown sample has been processed, it can often be used to quickly confirm whether a previously convicted suspect is a repeat offender.

Just like most things in life, however, the methodology used in the DNA profiling wasn't perfect; for one thing, the method required a relatively large sample to get results. That works fine when profiling suspects and can get plenty of DNA with a cotton swab rubbed against the inside of the subject's cheek, but in many instances, the DNA sample recovered from a crime scene that should be from the suspect in the crime isn't large enough to get a definitive profile. There aren't many things more frustrating than having a suspect in custody whom police strongly suspect committed the crime only to have the DNA results return as insufficient specimen for analysis.

An additional problem seen in many of the early DNA cases involved contamination of the specimen by the victim's blood or vaginal cells in rape cases where the large amount of victim DNA obscured the small amount of suspect DNA present. Thanks to the curiosity of several basic scientists, however, another technique called polymerase chain reaction (PCR) was discovered.

The PCR technique starts with a DNA sample. In our example, we'll assume that we're starting with a one double helix strand of DNA. In the first stage of PCR, the DNA strand is heated to near boiling, causing the DNA double strand to separate into its two mirror image single strands. The temperature is then lowered, and a short sequence of DNA called primers are allowed to attach to complementary sites on the separated mirror image DNA single strands from the sample. These DNA primers function to bracket the target sequence on the sample DNA to be copied.

The temperature is then again raised, and an enzyme called polymerase is added. The polymerase enzyme is a protein with one function: to take loose nucleotides and attach them systematically to single-stranded DNA to make a double helix. Since the only sequence that will attach has to be the mirror image of the single-stranded DNA that the primer has attached to, the resulting new single-stranded DNA has to be the mirror image copy of the original sample. As the process is repeated over and over, the targeted sequence of DNA determined by the DNA primers used accumulates such that millions of copies of the original DNA sequence determined by the primers accumulate in about two hours if the automated process is continuously allowed to progress. That's a lot of DNA to work with when the reader considers that he began with only one fragment of double-stranded DNA.

Anthropologists now routinely use amplified DNA to trace the migration of different human population groups around the world throughout our short history here on earth. PCR is also being used to rapidly identify strains and types of bacteria from hospital patients so that treating physicians can more rapidly prescribe an appropriate antibiotic to treat infections.

This is just the tip of the iceberg in terms of PCR applications. The technique was deemed so important that Dr. Mullis was awarded a Nobel Prize for its development. Thus, a powerful tool used in many different fields of science is now available to researchers. I suspect that eventually there will be a systemized depository containing all known DNA samples obtained during an individual's military enlistment as well as those obtained because of criminal activity. Although I personally don't expect DNA analysis to completely replace the need for fingerprint libraries, the two techniques together give the forensic investigator a set of powerful tools that can be put to good use.

Sometimes a low profile is the best profile, especially when talking about the profile that the medical examiner's office has with both the print and electronic journalists.

Any time your job requires dealing with the media, it's always wise to remember that individual reporters can make the office look either good or bad to the public, even if the circumstances are exactly the same. I always tried to remind myself that reporters out there have a job to do with all the issues that most jobs have, but with the added burden of time constraints because of the need to get the information or video into the main office before their predetermined deadlines.

Let me add that there are some reporters who are just jerks. They're the people who would be jerks regardless of what job they were doing. They seem to be hardwired to be that way. Add the fact that many of the reporters have a chip on their shoulders thinking that their duty in life is to assume that everyone is hiding something and they're anxious to do whatever it takes to dig the information out and collect their Pulitzer, letting the dead bodies they cause fall where they may. As I type this, I'm forced to realize that if I substituted the practice of medicine in place of reporting, I would be describing most of the physicians whom I work with.

Having said this, I've always dealt with individual reporters by assuming that they're reasonable people just trying to do their job. When investigating death cases, there's often information that's sensitive either to family members left behind or to the police who use the particulars of a case to screen witnesses. Although technically the medical examiner's release to the media should be limited to the cause and manner of death, I've always tried to give them the most information possible without compromising the investigation.

I soon learned whom I could and couldn't trust just by how they handled my requests to keep the information given "off the record." If the information is in the paper the next day, that reporter is only given the bare minimum information from that point forward, but by far and large, I felt as though I enjoyed a good relationship with the media in that we both knew each other's boundaries and tried not to cross them. Everyone who interacts with the media on a daily basis hopes that they never have to deal with a reporter who goes out of his way to magnify the ME's mistakes and isn't beyond telling half-truths and even lying to make himself look good to his readers.

As I started out saying earlier, many times a low profile is the best profile. This is usually easier said than done, particularly when an ME first starts his/her career. I would be less than candid if I didn't admit that there's something special in seeing yourself on television or pictured in the newspaper that first time. People come to know who you are out in public, and your friends are usually gloating, having seen you in the media. I'll never forget how proud of myself I was the first time I was interviewed for a national television program. I could hardly wait for the comments to come up in just about every personal interaction that I had for the next two weeks. I suspect that to a certain extent, this is an understandable reaction when it first occurs, but if it continues for any length of time, you're asking for trouble. The Bible is correct in stating that pride comes before the fall.

Fortunately, the situation that I'm about to relate occurred later in my career when I had developed a sixth sense about whether or not I should put myself out in the media forefront. I received a call from the crime scene team from the Florida Department of Law Enforcement (basically the state of Florida's version of the FBI). Jan Johnson, the senior crime scene analyst, asked if I could come out to the campus of the University of West Florida located just north of Pensacola and examine a bone that had been recovered at the excavation site for a new dormitory.

The call arrived midafternoon on a Friday in early spring when the leaves were just coming out and flowers were beginning to bloom. It was one of those gorgeous days that occur in Pensacola before the heat and humidity of summer chases everyone indoors. After driving onto campus, I immediately saw where I was wanted by the collection of spectators and the three mobile television news vans located at the site.

I had to park about a block away because of the spectator traffic, but after a brief stroll, I met up with Jan Johnson standing near where they were currently digging the foundation for the new dorm.

Jan had called out her whole team to help with the excavation. The reason for the concern in finding the bone was that a young female who had disappeared some years previously was known to attend the university and that the sheriff was excited to possibly have more clues in a case that had gone cold and unsolved.

When I asked Jan where the recovered bone was located so I could take a look, she stated that it was currently being examined by two PhD professors in anthropology, but they should be finished shortly. I could see the two professors huddling over the bone and whispering to each other. They soon walked over to where I was standing, and after some brief introductions, they were anxious to tell me what they thought.

The bone recovered was obviously human. It was an intact right femur and, on inspection by the professors, was thought to be that of a young adult female who stood about five feet four inches. I looked briefly at the bone, placed it beside my own leg (I'm five foot four inches tall, don't laugh), and could tell that it was compatible with the suggested height. I thanked the professors for the consultation, turned to Jan, and asked how she planned to proceed with the excavation. She explained her idea and stated that she would deliver the femur to me after it had been registered in their computer system and promised to call me if anything else of import was discovered.

As I was leaving to walk back to my car, I could see the two professors talking to the television reporter as they taped the interview. One of the reporters who knew me asked if I wanted to add any comment to their analysis. I stated that they had done a good job and that I had nothing to add. I slowly walked to the car, having a nagging thought in my mind that I couldn't bring to the conscious, reasoning part of my brain. I drove home still trying to put together what was bothering me.

That evening, all three television news programs went on and on about the bone, the possible link to the unsolved murder with my two professor friends on camera waxing eloquent about the findings, what it showed to their trained eyes, and how it could end up helping the investigating police. I chuckled to myself because it was obvious that both professors were enjoying the limelight immensely. As I watched them perform, I was glad to let them have their moment in the spotlight. Later on, I was even happier.

Jan Johnson and her team spent the whole weekend doing their usual thorough crime scene excavation. This required hours and hours in the hot sun in addition to the backbreaking work of digging for more bones. They failed to find any additional human bones to go along with the intact femur already found. This was peculiar because if the body had been disarticulated, with different parts buried separately, where was the rest of the body?

On the following Monday, the femur recovered was submitted to the FDLE forensic laboratory, and an attempt was made to extract DNA from the bone marrow. The sheriff's office had already obtained DNA samples from the suspected victim's home by collecting hair from her personal hairbrush and materials from her toothbrush.

The DNA analyst was baffled by the bone from the beginning. To obtain the bone marrow sample for analysis, he had to saw into the inner portion of the bone where the bone marrow normally resides. Despite multiple attempts to get into the marrow, he kept hitting solid material.

He finally decided to take a sample of the cortex or outer dense part of the bone to analyze it. He noted that the sample wasn't bone at all but instead melted at relatively low temperatures. The femur was made of a dense plastic material. What we had suspected to be a human femur was instead a plastic anatomic model of a human femur.

In retrospect, this actually made perfect sense. It would seem that someone had snuck an anatomic model out of the anatomy laboratory to do a little extra study, probably before a big examination. Instead of trying to sneak the model back into the lab from which it came, he/she instead elected to get rid of it by throwing it out into the woods of the yet-undeveloped part of the campus. It had been there long enough to be buried in a shallow grave, waiting for the construction team to find it when they came to build the new dorm on that site.

As you might imagine, the television and newspapers had a field day with the error. One newspaper ran the title to the story as "Laboratory Model Bone Fools Two Tenured Professors from the University of West Florida Department of Anthropology." No one mentioned me or the medical examiner's office, not even in passing.

Let me come to the defense of the anthropology professors by stating that the detail, texture, and weight of the anatomy models produced are so realistic that if put side by side with a real skeleton, it's nearly impossible to tell the difference. This level of detail has been developed because it has become politically incorrect to use real human skeletons.

At one time, skeletons obtained from unclaimed bodies collected in third-world countries could be bought by medical supply companies specializing in medical models for academic training. These bodies were defleshed and dried out before they were rearticulated and sold to reputable sources. That's no longer the case. I realized what was happening and paid an outrageous sum of money to buy one of the real skeletons before they were no longer available. I shouldn't have bothered. The plastic replica models are every bit as good as the real thing.

The main lesson to be learned from this story is that there really are times when the best profile is a low profile.

THINGS AREN'T ALWAYS AS THEY SEEM: MASQUERADE DEATHS

It's not unusual at a party, meeting, or some other social gathering for people, once they have found out my line of work, to ask about my favorite or best case. What they hope to hear is a case where like *Quincy* or NCIS on TV, my testimony or findings had been crucial to "breaking the case."

I would be less than honest if I didn't admit that in the vast majority of cases, my findings don't in and of themselves "break the case." Homicide cases are made or lost based on old-fashion investigation. It's still the homicide detective with time-honed experience who makes the case. My testimony, in addition to letting the judge and jury know that indeed an individual has died at the hands of another person, is used predominantly by the homicide detective as a yardstick against which to measure the stories of witnesses in the case. For example, suppose that one witness states that the attacker was only about two feet away from the victim when the fatal shot was fired, while an equally convincing witness states that the assailant was more than ten feet away at the time of the incident.

By looking at the gunshot wound on the body of the deceased, I can tell the police that the distance between the gun and the victim is more compatible with ten feet rather than two feet. This enables the homicide detective to put the testimony of both witnesses in perspective in terms of other statements they might volunteer.

Occasionally, however, I do have cases that, when finished, allow me to go home feeling that I've earned my pay. The vast majority of these cases fall into an easily recognized group. They're cases in which the initial investigation makes the death appear like a homicide, with my subsequent autopsy examination proving to everyone's satisfaction that the death was actually due to a natural disease process or that the deceased took his own life.

One case clearly stands out in my mind regarding this point. The reason for this is obvious; an innocent person doesn't go to jail, and the family of the deceased has closure concerning the death of a loved one. I hadn't been with my Mobile job long when I received a call from the local police to come to a homicide scene in a federally subsidized housing project.

The scene was a small cottage home rented by a little eighty-year-old man not weighing more than one hundred pounds. The scene of death was in the back bedroom of the house, allegedly the bedroom of our diminutive friend. Upon entering the room, the police found an attractive white female who appeared to be in her early thirties lying on her back, clad only in T-shirt and panties. By the time I had arrived, the police officers had the suspect in the living room, undergoing interrogation. The story given by the old man was that he had been widowed for some years and was living alone in the house.

About a week before this evening, the attractive woman had come through the front door and informed the suspect that she had no place to live and had decided to move in with him for a while.

Obviously catching our friend off guard, he had freely given his permission. In point of fact, this elderly gentleman was probably lonely, and I'm sure that the thought of having such an attractive visitor to keep him company didn't hurt his feelings.

Well, as the week progressed, the old man realized that the arrangement wasn't all that it had initially seemed. The young female kept late hours, coming and going as she pleased, when she pleased. Because of her late hours, the suspect was unable to keep his doors locked. Since the neighborhood wasn't all that safe, he had begun to keep a .38-caliber revolver in the headboard of his bed.

Allegedly, on the day of her death, the deceased had been out all day; where, the elderly gentleman didn't know. At 9:00 p.m., she came storming into the house, rattling things in the living room and bathroom. She marched into our suspect's bedroom to find him lying buck naked on his double bed. I'll vouch for the fact that it was an extremely hot, muggy night and that the house had no air-conditioning.

Once our lady had entered the room, she stripped to her T-shirt and panties, hopped into the bed, and started to make passes at our suspect. Possibly flustered by the advances, our suspect alleged that he began to fight her off.

While he was struggling to get out of the bed, our attractive female was rummaging through the sliding compartments of the headboard. By the time our elderly friend had escaped to the living room, he heard a shot. He returned to the bedroom to find his roommate dead. At this point, the sequence of events becomes a bit blurry. He did, however, have enough sense of mind to call out the window to some neighbors to get the police and an ambulance.

I arrived and walked into the bedroom to find the deceased lying on her back with her arms at her side. Her jeans were on the floor next to the bed, while her purse and a partially consumed bottle of liquor were sitting on the vanity next to the bed. Lying at the right side of the subject near her right knee was a .38-caliber revolver. A few blood-smeared footprints led from the bedroom to the bathroom immediately adjacent to the scene of death. A quick examination of the body did little to alleviate my anxieties.

The woman died as the result of a contact gunshot wound to the head, that is, the barrel of the gun was placed directly on the scalp when the bullet was fired. Although this went well with a suicide, the wound to the head was on the left side of the head while the gun was found by the right knee. Although a person can do some purposeful activity following a gunshot wound to the head, a contact wound with the full force of the bullet and explosion of the powder to push the bullet out of the barrel both impacting on the brain usually results in a marked concussion-type effect that renders the person unconscious immediately.

In addition, the blood-stained footprints couldn't be explained. They obviously weren't from the deceased for the abovementioned reasons, and the elderly suspect claimed he wasn't in the room at the time of the shot and denied remembering having been close enough to the body to have smeared the relatively localized stains and pools of blood from the body on his feet.

As I watched the police lead our suspect off to jail through a flood of TV news camera lights, I was left with many unanswered questions. The police were maintaining that our elderly suspect had attempted to entice the young female into having sexual relations with him. When she refused to comply, he had taken his revolver out to further encourage her compliance; then, either in a fit of rage or by an inadvertent discharge of the weapon while holding the gun to her head, he killed her.

From the examination of the scene, I couldn't refute that scenario. The bloody footprints presumed to be from the suspect and the location of the deceased on the right side of the bed where the suspect would have ready access to the left side of her head all tended to agree with the police version of the death. Besides, who would believe that a young woman as attractive as the victim would march unannounced into the home of an unknown elderly gentleman and set up housekeeping? Well, maybe I'm a soft touch, but I believed that the guy was innocent. The old man was pathetic looking. He convinced me that he would have to get his nerve up to kill a fly. Besides, the story was just unbelievable enough to be true.

The subsequent autopsy examination initially did little to allay my fears. Examination of the head revealed that there was indeed a contact gunshot wound present. Unfortunately, the bullet had entered on the left side of her head. As I examined the other external surfaces of the body, however, the tide began to turn. Oriented horizontally across the anterior aspect of her left wrist was a well-healed, faint scar. The deceased was one of those people who scar faintly, but based on the thin linear nature of the scar, I could be sure it was caused by a relatively sharp object. It wasn't a tear-type scar.

In addition, most people are aware that a scar in this relatively protected portion of the arm indicates a previous suicide attempt. People who attempt suicide once are likely to try it again. The real turning point in the examination of the body came, however, when I reflected the scalp over the skull.

When a bullet perforates the skull, it creates a beveling pattern just like the beveling one sees when a bullet or BB goes through a pane of glass. At the entrance site on the skull, the hole is smaller on the outer table of bone than on the inner table of bone. This entrance wound was unusual. In addition to the nice, smooth circular entrance hole, there was a similar round hole immediately above it, also connecting the internal and external surfaces of the skull. This gave the defect a figure "8" configuration.

After seeing this, I immediately reflected the scalp back to find a faint scar hidden within the hair. This probably, as much as anything else, shows the importance of doing a complete autopsy on everyone who needs to be autopsied. Even a careful inspection of all external body surfaces can miss some lesions. By correlating both the external and internal examinations, most of these missed areas can be found. In this case, the combination of both the defect in the skull and the faint surgical scar pointed to previous surgery on the head and brain—a craniotomy.

Since this type of surgery is usually related to trauma, I called the medical records at the hospital where we do our autopsies; it happens to be the major trauma hospital in our area. The information that I received from medical records was more than I had even anticipated.

Our attractive roomie had had a craniotomy some four years previous to remove a blood clot from the surface of the brain, a subdural hematoma. She had sustained a head injury in an automobile crash in which she had not only injured herself but also, as the driver of the vehicle, lost her husband and infant child.

Interestingly, since that injury, she had been referred to a psychiatrist for ongoing problems with headaches and depression. Other hospitalizations included two previous suicide attempts. One was an attempt by incising her wrists, as noted at autopsy, and another for an attempted drug overdose. Additional evidence gleaned from the chart indicated a moderate mental retardation and a hysterical type of personality.

Obviously, this fit well with our findings at the scene. Hysterical types are known to throw themselves at strangers in manipulative situations. It explained her moving in with our elderly gentleman without knowing him previously. In addition, people who attempt suicide once are likely to do it again. Another interesting point is that it isn't unusual for people committing suicide to direct their destructive act at the organ or portion of their body causing them physical pain or anguish; for example, a woman with severe menstrual pain may shoot herself in the pelvis, while an elderly male with angina-type heart pain might shoot himself in the chest. In our case, because the deceased had ongoing headaches and depression, it wouldn't be unexpected that she would shoot herself in the head and, interestingly, at the site of her previous craniotomy.

I was relieved the next day when the police returned, questioning whether the death was really a homicide. Allegedly, the old man had stuck to his story despite prolonged interrogation. The only point that he would concede involved whether or not he had reentered the room after the shooting had taken place, thus explaining the bloody footprint.

Additionally, a background check on the deceased's whereabouts before coming home revealed that she had had a rather severe argument with her current boyfriend and had announced to everyone that she was going home to commit suicide. Allegedly, she threatened this quite often. In my opinion, she carried through with her threat. Only because of a good investigation to include the scene of death and a thorough autopsy examination of the body did an innocent man walk away free, although I'm sure a bit "shell-shocked."

Sometimes the results of a masquerade-type death can be much more sobering. It was early one Friday evening when I received a call from one of my investigators that there was an elderly white male found dead in his apartment in the downtown region. The investigator stated that the police felt that all the findings at the scene indicated a natural death. I was busy at home trying to repair the damages to my lawn inflicted by my part-gopher dog. I was hurriedly trying to get some grass seed scattered before an impending rain. As the investigator calling was our most experienced agent and as the scene was only a few minutes away from his home, he volunteered to run down and investigate the death. He stated that he would call me if he felt it was necessary. This suited me just fine.

Later that night, I called the investigator to discover that the apartment did indeed look in order and that the seventy-year-old subject had a long history of heart disease and was expected to die at any time. The only problem with the case was that the deceased had probably been dead a couple of days and was beginning to decompose. I went to sleep that night thinking that everything had been handled appropriately.

The next morning, I arrived in the lab to find three autopsy cases in addition to our elderly gentleman. The family had been contacted and volunteered that they didn't feel that an autopsy was necessary. With three autopsies ahead of me that morning, I was easy to convince. I agreed that our examination would be limited, that is, I would limit our examination to the external portions of the body to rule out trauma, but I wouldn't examine the internal organs.

As I'm sure that you already have an idea of what the final outcome in this case will be, let me at least partially defend myself. In cases of elderly people with long medical histories who die at home, it's not unusual for us to do an external examination and send them on to the funeral home. This accomplishes several things. First, it allows us to look at the body to rule out physical trauma as a cause of death. It also gives us an opportunity to draw blood for toxicology studies to rule out an alcohol or other drug overdose as the cause of death. This information in turn allows us to comfortably sign the death certificate on these individuals after investigating their past medical history and talking to their personal physician.

In fact, I suspect that I would be strung up by the citizens of Mobile County if I autopsied all the little old Aunt Susies who died at home. With this said, it's not at all unusual for us to do an "external only" type exam on this subpopulation of cases. This case, however, wasn't a straightforward case. I had chosen to ignore something that made all the difference in the world.

I would be less than honest if I didn't admit that I hurriedly did my external examination on this case. As reported, he was decomposing and was at that stage of decomposition where there's a large amount of purge (decomposition fluid coming from the mouth and nose) as well as early skin slippage. In my opinion, when I know that I'm going to do a full examination on a decomposing body, I resign myself to the smell and the mess. On external exams, I go to greater lengths to avoid getting messy, and thus, the examination is often more superficial than it should be.

The examination itself revealed nothing that bothered me. There was a lot of skin slippage around the neck, but this isn't unusual in bodies in this stage of decomposition. I finished my exam, content that our subject had died as the result of natural causes, most probably due to heart disease.

I was in the middle of my second of three autopsies later that morning when we received a call from the daughter of our decomposing subject. She stated that in going into her father's apartment, she had noticed several items of furniture missing, including a relatively new portable television. Based on this, she felt uneasy about her father's death and wanted a complete autopsy performed. Needless to say, this didn't make my day, but as it's the policy of our office to perform autopsies on natural disease cases if the family requests them, I agreed to the complete exam.

As I did the neck dissection portion of the internal exam on the above subject, I began to get sick to my stomach, not because the body was decomposing, but because there was a large amount of hemorrhage in the muscles of the neck. This was too much blood to be explained by decomposition. Further dissection confirmed my worst fears. There was a fracture of the larynx (voice box) as well as the hyoid bone (a horseshoe-shaped bone that sits at the base of the tongue and is frequently fractured during strangulations). In retrospect, the skin slippage on the front of the neck failed to hide the curvilinear abrasions (scrapes) caused by the assailant's fingernails.

This elderly fellow had been strangled. Believe me when I say that I went to great lengths to make the rest of my examination as thorough as possible. Probably the only people as upset as I was by the results of the autopsy were the homicide section of the police and the subject's family. The homicide detectives were left with a cold, contaminated death scene to work. The family was left with the knowledge that their loved one died at the hands of another individual. As far as I know, this homicide remains unsolved.

Needless to say, this case taught me several things, some of which I already knew, at least from an intellectual point of view. First, all decomposed bodies should have a complete autopsy. Decomposition can hide subtle injuries on the surface of the body that indicate fatal trauma internally. Second, elderly individuals with long medical histories and enough natural disease to explain their death can still be the victims of a homicide.

To this day, I get a cold chill when I think about this case. I wonder how many cases of elderly people released to the funeral home directly from their residence without the benefit of a physician viewing their bodies are actually the victims of homicide. Although not common, I'm sure that their relative inability to fight off an attack makes them victims more often than we think. Partially because of this case, I try to go to all scenes when I am called. Although I too might have thought that the case was a natural death at the scene, I would like to think that I wouldn't have approached the case with a preconceived impression and would have pushed more strongly for a complete autopsy from the beginning.

Incidentally, the rain I was trying to beat with my grass seed that Friday evening was a good one. In fact, it rained so hard that all of my seed was washed away with the loose soil I had used to fill the holes that my dog had dug. Sometimes you just can't win.

Sometimes things happen on this job that would depress anyone. In the early evening of a day in April, I received a call from Brian Delmas, our chief investigator, stating that we had a homicide scene in a small town in the northeast section of Mobile County. After a thirty-minute drive up a winding two-lane road at dusk, no small danger in itself when Delmas was at the wheel, we arrived in town. The home we were looking for was a nice middle-class ranch-style home in the middle of town. City police officers meeting us at the scene informed us that the wife of our middle-aged victim had been in New Orleans seeing a physician. She had left town some five days previous with the children and had planned to visit some relatives on the way back home from her appointment.

We were escorted to a back bedroom used as a combination guest room/storage room. There, slumping on the floor with his back against the bed, was our subject. It was immediate at first glance and first smell that he had been dead for several days. Allegedly, his brother hadn't heard from him for a few days and, after getting no response on telephone, decided to drop by to check on him. He claimed that the back door was unlocked, not unusual in the more rural areas of Alabama, and that he had done nothing to disturb the scene.

The scene around the body was interesting. There were several rifles set along one wall of the room. Immediately below the victim were newspapers spread out and several opened gun cleaning kits, one immediately at his feet and another sitting on a desk nearby. All rifles were neatly standing butt down against the wall, glistening from having recently been cleaned with gun oil. By the time that we had arrived, the city police had decided that instead of a homicide, they were investigating an accidental shooting. He had obviously shot himself while cleaning the last of the rifles in the room.

Brian and I were skeptical. Based on the degree of decomposition, we both estimated we were dealing with three or four days. We checked the mailbox and confirmed that he hadn't brought in the mail for four days. I became even more skeptical about an accidental death when I examined the body. There was one gunshot wound to the chest, but instead of finding an intermediate-type wound with a tattooing around the wound caused by burning powder, the wound appeared to be a contact wound, that is, the barrel of the gun placed directly against the skin of the chest. The exit wound was on the back side of his chest just below his left armpit. The missile had then traveled upward and perforated the wall behind the deceased just below the junction of the wall and ceiling. This indicated that the missile tract through the body and through the room had traveled sharply upward, admittedly consistent with the theory of an accidental shooting. This type of case confirms the reason for good background information. The information doesn't always change one's mind in and of itself, but it usually can make the investigator feel better about his/her conclusions. The deceased was a forty-five-year-old white male who had made his career as a roughneck on the oil rigs in the Gulf of Mexico. Allegedly, some two years previous, he had hurt his back on the job, requiring that he lay off from work for some nine months.

To get the compensation that he felt he deserved from the injury, he had sued the oil company owning the particular rig on which he had worked. He was compensated with enough money to pay his hospital bills and support his family while unemployed. Unfortunately, when he was healthy enough to return to work, he was unable to get a job on any of the rigs. All companies were reluctant to hire him because of his back injury. As a result, he had been unemployed since the injury.

While talking to his immediate family members, it became obvious that he was running out of money. Although he had received a good salary on the rigs, he, like most of us, was unable to save much money. Allegedly, as time went on, he became more and more depressed over his inability to work. His only real assets remaining were his life insurance policies; obviously, these were of no use to his family with him alive. When his wife suggested that he go with her and the children to New Orleans, he declined, stating that he wanted to stay home in case a job offer call came in. In my opinion, there were no job offers.

Without mentioning anything to the immediate family, I told the city police that my immediate impression was that we were looking at a suicide. I had learned through experience not to say too much to the family and police at the scene until all the information was in and I had completed the autopsy. No matter where a body is found, it's difficult to duplicate the good lighting and facilities that we have at the laboratory.

Obviously, if I could tell everything about a case at the scene, there would be no need to do an autopsy and certainly no need to make the tax payers pay for the expensive facility we have available to us.

The autopsy in this case only confirmed my impression of the gunshot wound at the scene. It was indeed a contact wound, indicating that the end of the barrel had been placed in contact with the skin of the chest. The angle of the trajectory of the missile through the body and the room made the possibility of a homicidal killing unlikely. In my opinion, based on the autopsy findings and the background information, the deceased had committed suicide, probably to collect the life insurance for his family.

The reason that Brian and I were both skeptical upon entering the room and seeing the gun cleaning apparatus was that this setting is classically used by people to cover up their own suicides or by family members to make the death appear as an accident. Although I had never seen a case personally, I've read about them in many of the forensic textbooks and forensic literature. With that knowledge, Brian and I both approached the investigation with suspicion.

After finishing the case, I called the police chief and informed him of my opinion and how I planned to sign the death certificate. He informed me that the wife had returned to town and was on her way in to talk to me about the case. I've been accused on more than one occasion by friends and fellow physicians of going into forensic pathology so that I wouldn't have to talk to people. I would be less than honest if I didn't admit that this was at least partially true. I was in for a rude awakening once I started working cases.

I suspect that other than the time that I spend actually doing the autopsies and paperwork, the majority of the rest of my time is spent talking to relatives explaining the cause of death, lawyers representing the families in death cases, or insurance companies trying to get insurance claims settled. It's a part of the job but nonetheless can be uncomfortable.

Obviously, I wasn't looking forward to telling the wife that her husband had committed suicide. When she arrived, she was an attractive, petite woman who was obviously grieving. Brian and I both sat down with her and carefully explained our reasons for feeling that her husband's death was a suicide. It's not unusual for family members to disagree with our opinion. Sometimes their anger at having lost a loved one is looking for a place to go, and we're obviously fair game, but instead of denying, she continued to sob into her handkerchief. Upon gaining a bit of control, she informed us that all life insurance policies had suicide exclusion clauses. They wouldn't pay off in cases of suicide. She and her children would get nothing. At this point, I had to fight back tears of my own. It was my opinion that was denying her and her family what little financial support they had left. We talked about her husband for a few more minutes, and then she left to return to her home and her children.

I felt terrible. If ever there was a case where I would be tempted to change my opinion, this would have been it because only a hard person wouldn't want to help this family. Unfortunately, I had to be truthful. Although I obviously wasn't with her husband at the time of his death and would never know for sure what had happened or what was going through his mind, it's still my job to take the patterns present on the body and at the scene, put them into the perspective of the background information, and arrive at a cause of death and manner of death. I have to rationalize that the harm that this opinion generated for this family would be offset by the good that a consistent search for the facts would produce over the years.

One lesson that most physicians learn relatively early in their careers is to never plan social engagements when they're on call to potentially go to work. It's like the kiss of death. I can go several months on call, say, on Friday nights, and never experience my first beep. But if Beth and I plan to have friends over to the house or go to a local movie, I can bet that I'll be called out at least once.

Such was the case one Friday night when we had three other couples over for a meal of fried oysters recently purchased from a local fisherman. Fresh seafood is one distinct advantage of living in the South. Although I knew that I was on call, things at work had been so quiet that both Beth and I agreed that the party was worth the risk. Sure as rain, as I was busy deep-frying oysters that were being consumed faster than they could be cooked, the phone rang.

The Mobile Police were investigating a shooting that had occurred near the hospital where our office was located. They requested a pathologist to go to the scene to help out. Needless to say, Beth wasn't overly thrilled. Neither was I. I knew full well that the chance of there being any oysters left by the time I returned was slim at best.

I arrived at the scene to find a large middle-aged black male lying facedown in his driveway immediately behind his car. Lying next to him was a recently purchased bag of groceries. On the back left rear fender of the car was a .38-caliber revolver that had obviously seen better days. The grips of the gun were covered with white adhesive tape, and the cylinder was loose within the frame. A brief examination of the deceased revealed an indeterminate range gunshot wound to the neck (the barrel of the gun was far enough away from the skin that no powder or smoke was deposited around the wound).

Neighbors in the surrounding houses reported that the deceased had been observed pulling into his driveway. Although not seen immediately after that, reliable witnesses stated that shortly after seeing the victim pull his car into his driveway, they heard a loud noise, either a car backfiring or a gun going off. They strongly maintained that there was only one shot or noise. Some ten minutes later, someone went outside to find the subject lying as described.

The real question at the scene was whether or not we were dealing with a homicide. If so, the shooting had the appearance of a drive by killing or the work of a crazy assassin. Because the wound was indeterminate in range, the body was of little help, other than ruling out intimate contact between the victim and the gun.

In addition, the gunshot wound was a through-and-through-type wound, so there was no bullet to match to the weapon found at the scene. Finally, although the chamber of the gun beneath the hammer contained an empty cartridge, so did the two chambers immediately adjacent to the most recently fired chamber. As I left the scene that night, I still didn't know whether the death was a result of a homicide or an accidental discharge of a defective weapon.

Before I go any further, I need to explain a point about my philosophy concerning handguns. I'm not an easy sell when it comes to accepting a person's death as due to an accidental discharge of a weapon, particularly a handgun. The reason is that handguns are only produced for one reason, to be used against other humans.

In addition, for an accidental shooting to occur, many sequential events must occur; for example, the weapon must be loaded, the weapon must be pointed at another individual, all safety devices must be disarmed, and the trigger must be pulled. In my opinion, for all of these to occur without intent is outside the realm of probability without an extremely good explanation.

As a result, the number of cases that I've classified as being due to the accidental discharge of a handgun can be counted on one hand. My impression is that this is a widely accepted consensus among certifying forensic pathologists. The autopsy examination the next morning only confirmed my findings of the previous night. The answer to the problem wasn't solved until the weapon was examined by the departmental firearms expert, Mr. Dale Carter. As in cases of electrical deaths where the autopsy of the electrical appliance can be as revealing as or more revealing than the autopsy examination of the body, examination of the weapon in this case solved the mystery.

As previously stated, the weapon was in poor repair, even to the eyes of a person who knows as little about guns as I do. Dale's subsequent examination revealed that the gun was susceptible to accidentally discharging when dropped, struck, or jolted. Dale explained that the safety mechanism that normally separates the hammer of the gun from the firing pin was defective and allowed any jolt to the hammer to be transmitted to the cartridge of the bullet. In his opinion, the gun was susceptible to an accidental discharge with minimal manipulation.

Background information on the case collected by the police confirmed Dale's conclusion. Allegedly, the deceased had no known enemies at work or play. The revolver in question was indeed his weapon and was used on a part-time security job. The grocery receipt found in the bag near the body indicated that the groceries were purchased some twenty minutes before the call was placed to the police reporting the death. No suspicious or unusual strangers had been reported in the neighborhood.

What had probably happened is as follows: After pulling up into his driveway, the deceased stopped the car and reached beneath the front seat to collect his revolver from its usual hiding place. Then, walking around to the trunk of the car, he opened the trunk lid to remove the recently purchased bag of groceries. Possibly, in the process of trying to hold on to the groceries with one arm, he slammed the trunk lid closed with the arm and hand holding the weapon. The jar produced by the slamming trunk lid was sufficient to cause the weapon to discharge, striking the deceased in the neck.

This case proves the value of the team approach to death investigation. By working closely with a competent firearms examiner who knows weapons inside out, I was able to comfortably certify the death as an accident. The police, in turn, could halt their investigations on the case to work in more fertile areas needing investigation. Thus, it represents one of my few cases of death due to the accidental discharge of a handgun. Incidentally, by the time I returned home to the party, fried oysters were merely a pleasant memory in the minds and stomachs of our guests.

Although not at all common, every once in a while, I was called by law enforcement to examine injuries on a patient hospitalized and suspected of being a victim or perpetrator of some violent event. This, to be quite honest, is usually a bit awkward for me. Although I spent a considerable amount of time during my medical training working with patients in a hospital, because of the time interval since those years, I always feel a bit like a fish out of water. The clinicians I knew who saw me while on the clinical floor of the hospital always did a double take. What was I doing there, looking for potential cases?

Thus, I was a bit reticent when I received a call from the local sheriff's office asking me to meet them at the intensive care unit of a local hospital to help them sort out a mystery. When I arrived at the intensive care unit, the history that I was given was totally different from what I was expecting. In most instances, the police want me to examine and interpret various wounds on the victim to help guide them in their investigation. The classic example is interpreting a gunshot wound on a victim who's been assaulted.

I should interject here that clinical physicians are poorly trained in gunshot wound interpretation. But to come to their defense, that's not their primary focus. They're there to save the life, not interpret gunshot wounds for the police or the judicial system. In fact, the whole specialty of forensic pathology was developed just to have the expertise available to correctly interpret wounds in criminal cases. The problem is that most physicians don't realize how incompetent they are at wound interpretation. Instead, they state an opinion, and because they're a physician, everyone thinks they know what they're talking about. It can lead to some tragic mistakes which in turn can ruin lives. I know of one case in the upper Midwest where an emergency room physician misidentified entry and exit wounds to the chest of a shooting victim.

He stated that the entry wound was on the back of the deceased while the exit wound was located anteriorly. The mistake made a truthful statement by the defendant look like a lie; "He was coming at me so I shot him in the chest to protect myself." Yeah, sure. He ended up spending several years in prison before it could all be sorted out; a life ruined because a clinician in an emergency room wouldn't admit that he just didn't know.

In this case, the story was bizarre not because of the injuries, but because of how the injuries came about. The alleged victim and ICU patient in this case was an eighty-year-old white female found unconscious at the base of a flight of stairs in an industrial park that had previously been a navy air base. The area had been developed during the World War II era when there was a need for training massive numbers of pilots for future combat overseas. Like many of these facilities, after the war, it was no longer needed for training purposes and was given to the local county. They in turn rented various parts of the facility to private companies for manufacturing sites.

Because the base also had provided housing and teaching halls for the pilots in training, this part of the base had at one point been leased as a temporary campus for the University of West Florida, a state university founded in the early 1970s. The University of West Florida had long ago moved to a new campus some five miles to the north. This part of the industrial site had since remained vacant over the ensuing twenty years.

The initial suspicion of the sheriff's office was that our patient had been abducted and left in the industrial park after a robbery. Fears of foul play escalated further when the paramedics who had been called to the scene described our victim as severely bruised on the head, arms, and legs; had a suspected left hip fracture; and was partially disrobed, with her slacks and underwear pulled down around her ankles. There was no obvious physical evidence of sexual assault when she was examined at the hospital, but a sexual assault couldn't be completely excluded. A CT scan of the victim's head showed changes of cerebral contusion (bruising of the surface of the brain) as well as evidence of intracerebral hemorrhage (bleeding into the brain, commonly called a stroke).

The victim's car was located not far from where she was found, and there was no trace evidence of significance discovered outside or inside the vehicle. The building where the victim was found was a vacant dormitory. The two-story building was constructed so that each dorm room exited onto a front patio or balcony. Access to the upper-story dorm rooms was made possible by sets of exterior concrete stairs extending from the balcony of the upper floor to the ground at the front of each building. Our elderly subject had been found at the base of one of the concrete staircases.

The sheriff's office was baffled. They didn't know if they were dealing with a criminal assault and attempted rape or an accidental fall down some concrete steps. Should they call out the troops for a countywide search? Who would they be looking for? The only evidence they had that a crime had been committed was the victim herself. The family was beside themselves and wanted answers. The local news media was also involved, increasing the pressure on all parties concerned. When I finally arrived at the hospital, everyone was looking to me to give them the answers as to what happened.

To get a good investigative outcome in most cases, the key is to ask the correct questions and not allow preconceived opinions to influence how information is interpreted. I had the advantage of being able to listen to everything without being previously influenced by the family, paramedics, and sheriff's investigators. My follow-up questions were what was our victim's physical and mental state prior to her injuries and why would she have picked the vacated dormitory facilities as a place to go.

In medical examiner cases, the general public thinks that all answers in the death investigation come from the autopsy examination when in fact, the autopsy examination in most cases only confirms what the investigative evidence from the scene and background medical history have indicated all along. Indeed, as in our previous infant case above, without reliable background information, you're guaranteed to come up with the wrong answer almost as often as the correct answer. That's why the time-consuming, labor-intensive background investigation with all information gleaned and sorted is so important in death investigation cases.

This case was a prime example of that fact. Our victim's past medical history was almost as pertinent for its negativity as much as for its positive findings. Our patient still lived alone and was quite self-sufficient, taking care of all her own financial and physical needs. She had her own car and was described as a slow, yet careful driver who limited her driving to daylight errands and social visits. Her family claimed that she was still mentally sharp and, although starting to slow down a bit, was able to hold her own intellectually as well as physically.

The only known connection between our victim and the vacated dormitory facilities in the industrial park was our lady's daughter. When the University of West Florida first opened its doors to students, the daughter was in one of the founding classes. Although not the actual dormitory building where she had lived, the location where her mother was found wasn't far from where the daughter had lived during her freshman year. Interestingly, the daughter had a second-floor dormitory room.

Finally, since our victim was a patient at a hospital, I was able to review all her laboratory and radiology studies. The CT of the head showed evidence of an intracranial bleed as well as contusions of the cerebral cortex. The intracerebral hemorrhage, stroke, was in a location where it wouldn't be trauma related. Instead, our elderly lady had suffered a significant stroke in addition to the bruising on the surface of her brain which was consistent with trauma (cerebral contusions).

The question remained as to whether we should be actively looking for a potential suspect. Everyone looked at me to make the call one way or the other. I knew from experience that the longer the police waited to find a suspect in an assault case, the less likely they were to find the perpetrator. I also knew that if the findings in this lady were due to accidental causes, anyone arrested would be arrested for a crime he or she didn't commit.

I elected to call off the search for a suspect at that time. This decision didn't sit well with the family who wanted justice for their unconscious loved one. Even the sheriff's detectives on the case gave me a questioning look. This was my thought process at the time. I felt confident that I could explain everything that had happened, and what we were seeing was a combination of natural disease with superimposed accidental injuries. I strongly suspected that our elderly female victim began having bleeding issues in her brain. This natural disease process can come on catastrophically or can come on slowly over hours with increasing symptoms.

In her case, the hemorrhaging probably began slowly, making her more and more disoriented. She became delusional and ended up driving to see her daughter, thinking that she could find her daughter at her old dormitory complex at the industrial park. While walking around the vacated complex, she fell down the flight of concrete steps of the dormitory building where she was found. All this is well and good, but how did her underwear and pants get pulled down around her ankles? The forensic literature reported a study in which stroke victims having hemorrhaged into the closed skull perceived a need to urinate or defecate because of the pressure being put on the sensory areas of the brain that normally controlled those sensations.

This might explain why her clothes were found around her ankles and why she had fallen down the steps. From a trauma point of view, the pattern of injuries that I saw on her head, arms, and legs were much more consistent with a fall than having been inflicted at the hands of an assailant.

Our elderly lady never did recover from her injuries. She experienced a steady downward course to death without ever regaining consciousness. Since she was a questionable case with a traumatic overlay, she became a medical examiner's case. When I conducted the autopsy, the findings both externally and internally agreed with my original interpretation. I was relieved because I didn't want to be the one responsible for allowing someone assaulting elderly females to go free. When all of the paperwork was completed in the case, I sat down with the family to discuss the findings. Although initially they were a bit angry with my findings, I think I was finally able to convince them that their loved one hadn't died at the hands of another. I, in turn, was thankful that I had been there to keep an innocent suspect from having to go through a trial and possible prison sentence for a crime that he or she hadn't committed.

Webster defines *asphyxia* as a lack of oxygen or an excess of carbon dioxide in the body that results in unconsciousness and death, usually caused by interruption of breathing or inadequate oxygen supply. Asphyxial deaths represent a significant number of cases coming into the medical examiner's office. They can be associated with homicides, suicides, accidental, natural, and undetermined modes of death. If anyone stops to think about it, everyone stops breathing when they die, so when we talk about asphyxia, we're really talking about a mechanism of death, not a cause of death. Something or someone must cause the asphyxia to occur.

Remember, the mechanism of death is the pathophysiological processes that come about as a consequence of the cause of death. Some disease or injury must occur causing a change in the body that allows the mechanism of death to occur, something causing an interruption of breathing or an inadequate oxygen supply to cause the asphyxia to occur. This disease or injury is the cause of death and should be noted as such on the death certificate.

The most common cause is asphyxia due to drowning where water being inhaled into the bronchial passages and lungs proper blocks the air from getting into the lungs to exchange oxygen and carbon dioxide. The second most common cause of asphyxia is probably due to smoke inhalation where the smoke replaces the oxygen in normal air with carbon monoxide that blocks its ability to attach to hemoglobin in the red blood cells. The added irritation of the smoke to the bronchial passages also inhibits that process by causing constriction of the air passages, just like an asthma attack.

Sometimes the manner or mode of death in asphyxia cases can be controversial. The actual cause of death is usually pretty obvious, but the manner of death can be mislabeled. This mislabeling can cause the surviving family unnecessary grief and, in some instances, negatively impact life insurance policy benefits.

Death by hanging is a common way to take one's own life. Many of these suicides take place in jails where the thought of facing either the upcoming jail time or the embarrassment of having to face family can often convince a person that suicide is a reasonable way to exit his/her circumstances. In many jurisdictions, individuals deemed to be at risk for a suicide attempt always have any clothing item that might be used to hang themselves taken away before they're placed in a holding cell, which is usually monitored continuously by video cameras. Despite how thorough the police try to prevent suicides, if the inmate is determined to take his or her own life, it's amazing how resourceful the prisoner can be to get the job done.

I had one case where a young black male was arrested in a small white community for shoplifting and drug use. Because the young man begged the police not to call his grandmother to report his whereabouts, the police worried that the young man, who had no previous criminal record, might be tempted to take his own life. Let me remind you that this case takes place in the Deep South and involves a young black male and a police force composed of all white males.

Because of the parties involved, the police took great pains to take his belt, shoelaces, or any item that could even remotely be used to hang himself. This incident occurred before the advent of video cameras, so the young man was placed on a suicide watch where the police officers visually checked on him every fifteen minutes.

In the middle of the night, the prisoner pretended to be asleep as he waited for the guard to make his rounds. Once the guard had checked on him, he hurriedly wrote a note of apology on the wall of his cell with toothpaste, then used his nylon socks to make enough noose that he was able to suspend himself from the ceiling bars. Fifteen minutes later, the rounding guard found the victim, and despite multiple attempts at resuscitation, he was pronounced dead by the paramedics.

Just to show you how naïve I can be, I did the scene examination, finished the autopsy, and signed the case out as a suicide just as I would have handled any other. Send in the next case. From my simplistic viewpoint, we had a young man who got involved with illegal drugs and was caught stealing to help support his habit. While awaiting his court date, he was distraught to the point that he hanged himself while in the prison. The only issue that I could see was that the jail probably needed to review their protocol for handling suicide risks. I couldn't see any other problems, certainly nothing to indicate foul play on the part of the police.

A few days later, I had my first-ever visit by the Federal Bureau of Investigation. The agent who visited me was in charge of the local civil rights desk. It was his job to investigate and determine if any civil rights had been violated in the arrest and police handling of the case. I explained that it was a straightforward case of suicide by hanging and that I saw no evidence that the young man had been mistreated physically during his time in jail. The FBI special agent paused and looked at me as though I had just fallen off the turnip truck. He then went on to explain that anytime a young black male hangs himself in the jail of a predominately white community, it's never a straightforward case.

He then systematically went over the entire case, asking me questions when appropriate and educating me on the other sundry aspects of the case. It was just like the agent had said; there are no straightforward cases that involve civil rights issues. After going over the autopsy findings in detail, the special agent noted that he could see only one significant error in the way that I had handled the case. I should have had an acknowledged leader from the black community, a respected black physician, to witness the autopsy. Had I done that, it would have been easier to convince the black community that my findings were accurate and unbiased.

To be honest, regardless of anyone's findings in this death, the black community was going to demonstrate their displeasure. As most people realize, the pastors in the black community have a considerable sway over their peers. The television stations were soon showing press conferences where the black pastors were calling for an economic boycott of the town where the death occurred. In an attempt to try to at least moderate the public reaction, the FBI convened a meeting between the black pastors, local police, the FBI, and me.

I entered the meeting feeling assured that I would be able to explain my finding and in the process convince the black pastors that the young man committed suicide and had not been subjected to any physical harm by the jailers. The reason for this confidence was that I had grown up in East St. Louis, IL, a community which was predominantly black. I was stupid enough to think that this fact gave this short white boy credibility with his audience. It didn't.

The meeting took place in the conference room of one of the local black churches. In addition to the FBI, local police, and yours truly, there were eight black pastors representing most of the black churches in the community. As we sat down to start, one of the pastors stated that we should begin the session with an opening prayer. As a person who takes his religious convictions seriously, I assumed that a prayer would help get the discussion off to a civil start. I was wrong. The pastor finished his prolonged prayer with amen, and all the pastors went immediately into attack mode.

The volume in the room increased severalfold, and I immediately realized I was in over my head. When my turn came to go over my findings, I started by introducing myself and where I grew up. They couldn't have cared less. As far as they were concerned, I was just another white representative of the law enforcement community who was spouting the establishment line. As I tried to explain the lack of physical injuries that would indicate police abuse, the presence of the toothpaste suicide note on the wall of the jail that matched the victim's handwriting, and the point that it's extremely difficult to commit a homicide by hanging without causing other injuries on the body, I realized none of these mattered because the truth didn't fit into their political agenda. While all of this was going on, the FBI agent would occasionally look at me with an I-told-you-so smile.

I left the meeting frustrated because I realized that regardless of how thorough a job I had done and regardless of how many pieces of evidence point to my interpretation of the case as being the correct interpretation, it didn't matter because the pastors didn't believe me because I was one of them, the white law enforcement community. My FBI friend put his arm around my shoulder as we walked out to our cars and told me that my failure to enlist the help of that black physician had destroyed my credibility. He told me not to take it personally. Their reaction was based on the historical record in the South and the political agenda of the black community.

The result was a several-month boycott of all the businesses in the predominantly white community by all of the blacks in the county. Many of the mom-and-pop stores went out of business in the town because of the lack of business, and eventually, the downtown area became a ghost town. Had the findings in the case supported the claims of police abuse by the black community, I would have been there doing all I could to see justice done. Unfortunately, sometimes facts just don't matter.

Part of the fun of being a medical examiner is that from day to day, it's impossible to predict what's going to happen next. On one particular day, I was quietly going about my business in the medical examiner's office, trying to catch up the never-ending backlog of paperwork being demanded by my secretary, Rose Hall.

Let me digress a bit here and sing the praises of excellent secretaries or administrative assistants everywhere without whom nothing would ever be completed. Rose was a gifted administrator who had the ability to handle several important issues at the same time and keep all parties happy while doing it. She had an incredible phone personality, able to soothe an irate attorney or, in a few well-placed phrases, a family member. She was equally gifted at being able to commiserate and empathize with someone who has recently lost a loved one. Other than my wife, Beth, I've never met a woman who could handle me so competently, keep me out of trouble concerning scheduling issues, and keep me moving on current projects.

First thing in the morning, she would hand me a list of cases that needed to be completed that day and would give me subtle reminders when I was falling behind. At the end of the day, she would approach me about those items not completed and, without a hint of disappointment or anger, call the party awaiting the result, explaining that it was going to take another day. She was so good and so essential to my professional life that if told that I had to give up either Rose or my wife, I would at least hesitate before responding. I hope my wife doesn't read this.

The phone had rung, and the caller was one of the detectives from the sheriff's office who needed our presence at a death scene, in this case the county sanitary refuse facility (dump). They had the body of a young white male who had been found by the site personnel when they had arrived at work that morning. When we arrived at the site office some thirty minutes later, we were taken past the security gates (why security gates at a dump?) and into the sanitary landfill area proper.

We were soon led to a distant section of the landfill where a cluster of police cars and a fire truck sat while a group of uniformed police stood about scratching their heads. When we arrived, the police huddle broke up, and they led us across mounds of trash to where the body of a white male, who looked to be in his thirties, lay partially covered with trash. He was completely clothed but had the ragged, dirt-encrusted look of one of the homeless men seen at various street corners in Pensacola begging for money.

A quick check of the body confirmed he was indeed dead and had been dead for at least twenty-four hours. This was determined by an early loss of the rigor mortis that occurs after death as well as by getting a core body temperature by incising the skin in the upper right quadrant of the abdomen and jabbing a thermometer into the liver to get the reading.

A quick look at the external surfaces of the body failed to show evidence of major trauma; there were no stab wounds or bullet wounds noted. The only evidence of any possible trauma were a few friction abrasions (rug burns) on the arms and side of the face. The police wanted to know if they had a homicide case on their hands as well as how in the world did the dead body get into the limited-access dumpsite. The people from the landfill, which was privately owned, were worried that they were going to be held liable in some upcoming civil lawsuit. I felt certain that I knew how our victim had died and how he came about being in the landfill. He got in by hitching a ride.

Although there was a security fence present about the facility, anyone who really wanted in to the place could have found areas in the surrounding ten-foot chain-link fence where they could have either crawled under or over the barrier. Although the landfill has items that in the right hands have some value, pieces of copper, scrap metals, and assorted discarded appliances, but without a vehicle to carry the stolen loot out of the landfill, it wouldn't be cost effective to try to walk off with anything there.

Another thing that I noticed about the location of the body was that it was found near relatively fresh trash rather than in areas that had obviously been exposed to the sun and rain over any significant period of time. In fact, a copy of the previous day's local newspaper was lying near the body. In other words, the time since the victim's death matched the time frame of the trash pile where he was found.

Although I had a pretty good idea of the sequence of events leading to this death, I've learned through bitter experience that it's best to wait until all data is in before trying to make a brilliant diagnosis. An investigator can often end up looking more like the village idiot than Sherlock Holmes. I kept my theory to myself until after the autopsy following Mark Twain's theory that it's better to be quiet and be thought an idiot rather than to open your mouth and remove all doubt.

The findings at the autopsy were consistent with a death due to asphyxia. There was a congestion of all the tissues and organs of the body, pulmonary edema (fluid backed up into the lungs), and petechial hemorrhages (small pinpoint hemorrhages) located on the conjunctivae of the eyes and surface of the heart and scattered over the skin surfaces. These are all classic signs of asphyxia. The toxicology studies showed only a small amount of alcohol in the blood. He wasn't intoxicated. There was an interesting finding in the stomach. In the lumen of the stomach I found multiple fragments of recently chewed and swallowed pickles, the type of slices usually put on hamburgers sold at the fast-food restaurants. These findings confirmed the theory that I had generated at the scene. Our victim had indeed hitchhiked into the land site in the trash compartment of a garbage truck. That ride was also what caused his death.

I suspect that our victim was doing some dumpster diving, looking for food that had been thrown away by one of the fast-food restaurants. While he was sitting in the dumpster, eating his pickles and minding his own business, the garbage truck drove up to empty the dumpster. Before the victim could get the driver's attention, he and the dumpster were lifted and dumped into the garbage truck. As you're probably aware, those big trucks that cruise around picking up trash have a large hydraulic plate that is used from time to time to compress the trash down in the storage compartment so that the truck can pick up larger amounts of refuse and avoid extra trips back to the landfill to dump their contents. The driver compressed his load of trash not knowing that in the process, he was asphyxiating our homeless man. All of the trucks from this landfill worked the commercial businesses in the city and had a front-loading mechanism that lifts the entire trash dumpster over the front of the truck to empty it. The driver never saw the contents of the dumpster or heard any calls for help because of the noise generated by the hydraulic systems.

In our case, external compression on the abdomen and chest caused the asphyxia. To breathe in oxygen and exhale carbon dioxide, the body uses muscles to increase the volume of the chest cavity. This is a passive flow of air into the lungs dependent on the increased volume of the chest cavity, causing a negative pressure inside the chest. These muscles include both the diaphragmatic muscle as well as chest muscles external to the chest cavity. If a person is trapped in an environment tight enough that he or she is unable to expand his/her chest and abdomen, it's impossible for the individual to draw the air into his/her lungs to get oxygen. Adults tend to use both their chest muscles and diaphragm.

A quick trip to the beach where the men are parading around shirtless will demonstrate the use of the chest muscles for breathing. The reason for this is that most men are trying as much as possible to hold their stomachs so they look to be in better shape. This process takes the diaphragm out of the breathing process and allows men to expand their chests by using only their chest muscles. They think this impresses women.

Children and infants, on the other hand, haven't matured physically to the point that they can make use of their chest muscles alone. Instead, watch an infant breathing while asleep in his or her crib, their abdomens pooch out with each inspiration. This is because the diaphragm is descending into the abdominal cavity to increase the chest volume and exchange air.

This means that anything that prevents the diaphragm from descending into the abdominal cavity to pooch out the abdomen will interfere with the child's ability to breathe. This can cause asphyxia in children when they play on the swing set. If the seat of the swing is the belt type, don't allow your children to swing when they're lying across the seat on their abdomens and suspending their weight on the seat. All of their body weight is being supported by their abdomens as they swing back and forth. This weight compresses their abdomens and keeps the diaphragm from being able to descend properly. This in turn limits the chest volume and air exchange, potentially leading to unconsciousness and death. Cases of asphyxia by this mechanism have been reported in forensic literature. It's a risk seldom talked about in parenting literature.

One thing that the medical examiner's office has taught me is that everyone has issues in their lives. Most of us also spend a considerable amount of energy trying to keep them hidden, with varying results. One afternoon in the middle of the workweek, I was called out to a scene in an upper-middle-class neighborhood to help the local police investigate an apparent suicide. The victim was a forty-eight-year-old white male who owned the house and lived there with his wife of twenty plus years and their teenage son. He was found hanging in the master bathroom of the home and was discovered by his wife who had just returned home from grocery shopping. She claimed that this was her husband's usual afternoon off each week and that he had been his normal, cheerful self when she left for the store. She further volunteered that they weren't having financial problems or any marital issues that would explain her husband's suicide. From her previous experience as a nurse, she realized immediately that her husband was dead and did nothing to modify the scene of the death. Her emotions were appropriate for the circumstances.

When I went into the master bath to examine the body, the husband was still suspended by a rope from a hook mounted above the closet door.

Let me interject here that there's really nothing worse than finding the body of someone you care about suspended from their neck. These suspension-type hangings should in no way be confused with judicial-type hangings. In judicial hangings that are done properly, the knot of the noose is placed on the side of the neck, and the executioner has calculated the amount of slack needed in the rope to snap the neck of the victim when the floor of the platform drops away. That snap of the neck transects the upper spinal cord and, if done correctly, results in an instantaneous or near-instantaneous death.

Suspension-type hangings kill by means of a slow strangulation of the victim. The weight of the body puts more and more pressure on the structures of the neck, first causing a blockage of the veins, draining the head and neck, then the arteries trying to get blood to the head and neck, and finally obstruction of the airway so the person can no longer get air into the lungs. Since the veins are the easier to close off, there's a short period of time when blood is still being pumped into the head and brain but is unable to escape the head because the veins are blocked. The end result is an intense purple-blue discoloration of the head and face. The increased swelling that accompanies this process distorts the facial features, and the pressure of the noose on the neck causes the tongue to protrude from the mouth with that same blue-purple discoloration. Once the heart begins to fail, all of the blood begins to pool in the legs and feet, causing rupture and pinpoint bleeding into the skin of the legs and feet in addition to a marked swelling of the suspended lower extremities. The end result is a grotesque sight, which, in many instances, bears little resemblance to the loved one in their natural state.

In this case, the deceased was fully dressed, but I did notice that the fly to his pants was open, his belt was only loosely hitched, and he wasn't wearing underwear. The ligature around his neck wasn't the usual type. The deceased had used a one-and-a-half-inch bathrobe belt made of cloth, probably from the wife's clothing based on the pink color of the material. In addition, it was tied to a wall-mounted hook in such a way that, although secured to the hook, the end of the noose around the deceased's neck could be quickly released by a jerk on the loose end. This case didn't fit the findings of the routine suicidal hanging.

I asked to speak to the wife, and after she had related the same story that she had previously shared with the police, I politely asked, "Were there any pornographic materials found near your husband's body that you decided to put away before the police arrived?" Her face turned a bright red, and at first, I thought she was going to hit me. She quickly regained control of herself and admitted that there were some filthy materials lying on the bathroom floor in front of her husband that she didn't want anyone to see. When she showed me the materials, I could understand her feelings. The materials weren't the routine photos of men and women in compromising positions but were materials that involved gay bondage scenarios with the associated photographs. I felt sorry for the wife, but it also helped me appropriately interpret the case. This was a case of autoerotic asphyxia.

Back in the 1980s when this case occurred, autoerotic asphyxia was practically unknown in the general population. This was just as well because it's an extremely dangerous practice. Autoerotic asphyxia was how David Carradine, the actor in the television series *Kung Fu*, died while in Bangkok, Thailand.

The theory behind the act is that hypoxia or lack of oxygen when a person is experiencing a sexual orgasm causes the sensations of the orgasm to increase greatly in terms of its duration and intensity. Various methods have been used to cause the hypoxia from the inhalation of amyl nitrate at the point of orgasm to having the sexual partner squeeze your neck. The suspension type of autoerotic asphyxia is particularly dangerous because it's usually practiced alone; therefore, no one is available to help if complications occur.

In the suspensions, the participant usually tries to tie the ligature in such a way that a quick jerk will release the tightness. Sometimes that fail-safe doesn't work either because the ligature won't release or because the person has become hypoxic to the point of unconsciousness and is unable to release the ligature. I suspect this is what happened in this case.

From the medical examiner's point of view, classifying the case as an autoerotic asphyxia changes the manner or mode of death from suicide to accidental. In the autoerotic deaths like this, it's not the intention of the individual to take his/her own life. Death occurs because they accidentally asphyxiated himself/herself while pursuing a sexual high.

As in most medical examiner's cases, there was a subplot. This particular case of autoerotic asphyxia was no different. The father who asphyxiated himself was aggressively suing a surgeon in town who, during an inguinal hernia operation on his son, had accidentally cut one of his vas deferens. This prevents sperm produced in the associated testicle from participating in the ejaculation that takes place during male orgasm. Men have a vas deferens associated with each testicle, so the odds that the surgical mistake will make the boy sterile are remote.

It should be noted that a cut vas deferens doesn't affect the associated testicle's ability to produce the male hormone testosterone.

I suspect that the father's fear in all the legal proceedings revolved around the masculinity of his son and the effect the surgical error would have on his manliness. It was almost as if the father was afraid that his son might end up with the same sexual perversions that he had to live with or maybe not. I am not a psychiatrist by any stretch of the imagination.

One type of asphyxial death that again was relatively unknown in the early 1980s but has since become much more commonly identified, especially among the food service industry, is the type of asphyxia that I diagnose as asphyxia due to aspiration of a foreign object. The media calls it a café coronary. It tends to occur most commonly in overweight males who don't adequately chew their food before attempting to swallow pieces of meat or other firm foods that are too large to easily travel down to the stomach.

The most common story I heard over time has been that of an obese white male sitting at a restaurant, eating his dinner, usually during a business meeting of some sort, when all of a sudden, he grabs his chest, and his face gets deep red and progresses to a deep blue color before he hits the floor unconscious.

What's happening in these instances is that a large chunk of food has closed off or obstructed the glottis in the upper portion of the larynx, which takes air down into the lungs to exchange gases.

Normally when we swallow, our tongue lifts food up and over the epiglottis. The epiglottis, a tonguelike extension on the front part of the larynx, partially blocks and directs the food into the upper portion of the esophagus and from there down to the stomach. It's worth noting that the diameter of the glottis in the back of the throat is much smaller than the upper portion of the esophagus where the food is supposed to go. Therefore, it's not surprising that when the food gets stuck in the back of the throat, it can completely obstruct the glottis, causing asphyxia.

I think most of the general public is familiar with the Heimlich maneuver. It was initially developed by Henry J. Heimlich and is a procedure for which he has won numerous awards over the years. In the absence of someone being able to perform the Heimlich maneuver, the chances of death increase dramatically.

My first experience with a "café coronary" involved an obese twenty-two-year-old black male from a school for the mentally slow. Our patient had just finished eating lunch in the cafeteria and was told that he couldn't go back and get any extra food. It was late, and he needed to proceed to his classroom. As he walked by the serving table, he reached over, grabbed a handful of sausage patties, and to keep from being detected by the teachers, crammed it into his mouth and tried to swallow it as quickly as possible.

He then took another five or six steps, stopped, grabbed his throat, and passed out, hitting the floor in the hallway of the school. An emergency medical service was immediately called, but the patient had expired by the time they had arrived at the scene of the injury. Although this patient was a relatively young man, the first thing that would come to anyone's mind is that he suffered some type of cardiac event, either a cardiac dysrhythmia or an acute myocardial infraction.

Because the death occurred at a state-sponsored school, an autopsy was required both by school protocol and the medical examiner's office. When the autopsy was completed, I had discovered that the patient had a normal coronary artery pattern, a normal size heart, and no evidence of natural disease. When I started to dissect the neck, however, I was able to discover the large fragment of food sitting on the top of his glottis at the back of his throat. The cause of death was signed out as asphyxia due to obstruction of the airway by a foreign body, and the manner of death was an accidental death, different from the natural death that a diagnosis of heart attack would have rendered.

Sometimes the entities that I examine at work come home to roost. I remember when my second grandson, about eighteen months old at the time, was sitting on the floor across the room, playing with his toys. Instead of laughter, I noticed that he was making a choking noise and that his usual pale complexion was turning a deep blue. I ran over and was able to do a Heimlich maneuver on him, and he shot a piece of broken plastic across the room. I still have that piece of plastic, and I think I'll give it to him mounted in some frame when he graduates from high school.

The experience with these entities can be more personal than even one's immediate family members. It's common at our hospital for physicians to gather in a separate dining room for meals so that we're not interrupted by patients and family members wanting information about their loved ones.

One day, I was sitting in the private dining room with a surgeon sitting on my left, an internal medicine doctor sitting on my right, and a pediatrician seated across the table. For some reason, I got a piece of the roast beef caught in the back of my throat, and I couldn't dislodge it by quietly coughing or choking. I could tell that I was beginning to get anoxic because my vision was starting to blur.

I was making all kinds of motions to the doctors seated around me to try to indicate that I had an obstructed airway, but they were oblivious to my condition, staying deeply engrossed in their discussions. I finally had to get up from my chair, walk over to an adjacent table, and cram my upper abdomen into the rounded corner of the table to imitate a Heimlich maneuver, and after two attempts, I finally got the fragment of meat dislodged from my throat. When I finally caught my breath and came back to the table, the internist looked at me and asked if I just had a piece of food caught in my throat. I felt like causing his death by the strangulation method of asphyxia. Physicians heal themselves.

A person doesn't have to watch much television to realize that there has been a major shift toward shows revolving on the criminal justice system. I used to watch *Perry Mason* religiously as a child. The number and types of programs have exploded to cover all aspects of the judicial process. The investigation of a crime can feature anyone from the small town homicide detective to FBI special agents assigned to specific task forces. All the various types of lawyers have also become stars in various television programs whether they're portraying the humble assistant state attorney or the high-powered federal prosecutors in charge with prosecuting specific types of crime.

The crime scene investigators, and to a lesser extent the medical examiners, have also been victims of television portrayals with a CSI from just about every major city in the country being produced in that extremely successful franchise. I suspect that most individuals involved in the criminal justice system do enjoy having their chosen profession glamorized, but I also suspect that, like me, they become skeptical when they see various cases that, though technically possible, are extremely rare yet presented as an everyday occurrence that any investigator worth his salt should be able to solve in his sleep.

Because of the large number of cable networks broadcasting over the ever-increasing number of channels, there's been a relatively new form of True Detective–type programs being produced. Some producer somewhere discovered that the lay public would watch programs about real crime cases involving real people.

The reality of this concept came home to roost when the country went crazy over the real-time reporting of the O. J. Simpson trial with live television cameras inside the courtroom following the action. One of the pioneers in this form of television programming started filming real courtroom cases that involved someone glamorous or at least controversial. Court TV set the standard in this area and could be seen across the country filming and reporting high-publicity cases as they went through the trial process in real time.

A spin-off of the Court TV idea involved reporting on cases that have already been solved. These shows tell their story by the reenactment of various scenes on location. Interviews with the actual family, police, and prosecutors in the case result in an interesting hour of television programming aimed at the crime groupies. The beauty of this approach from the producer's viewpoint is that those interviewed are paid nothing for their time spent conducting the interviews.

Most law enforcement officers are thrilled to be interviewed on national television in a situation where they can brag about solving an unusual or difficult case. The producer need only pay for his camera crew and their transportation and possibly a few actors for the crime reenactment to generate their television series.

During my tenure as a medical examiner, I've been solicited several times to become involved in a true crime television episode. To be honest, the temptation to be interviewed for a national program is almost impossible to turn down, at least the first time. I've spent my entire professional career located far away from my parents and extended family. The opportunity for them to see me on a television program where they can take pride in my accomplishments was quite an ego trip. Everyone wants their fifteen minutes of fame, and I was no different. I should have known better.

Later, I will discuss my first exposure with the national media when I was interviewed on ABC's *20/20* news program. I felt as though that interview had gone well and that perhaps my fans out there in TV land were ready for another dose of my forensic knowledge; no ego issue there.

What these producers never tell the participants is that the fifteen-minute interview seen on television takes a good four to five hours to record. During that half of a workday, your facilities and any staff involved in the program are unavailable to get any of the routine work done in the office. In fact, in most instances, the morgue facility is where the producer wants to film your interview so that not only are you personally out of pocket, but the whole morgue workday is brought to a halt to maintain an adequate sound stage for the camera. This means, of course, that after the camera crew has driven off in their SUV, the office staff have to spend most of the evening trying to complete the caseload that had been bumped by this moment of fame.

The old "fool me once, shame on you; fool me twice, shame on me" rapidly comes into play. Because the show is usually only broadcast on some obscure cable channel, friends and family will probably never see it anyway. In summary, the whole process isn't worth the time and effort required for me or my office. As a result, I made it my policy to turn down any offers or requests for interviews by these television program producers.

What I had failed to realize, however, was that I wasn't the only local person on the case being interviewed. There was usually a law enforcement officer and an assistant state attorney also on the case. While I was tired of the inconvenience that the interview entailed, this was often the first and possibly only chance for these fellow laborers to see themselves on a national television platform. The producers realized this and would let them know that my refusal to participate was a nonstarter for the filming and that if they were interested in doing the interview, they needed to get me on board with the process. The phone calls that followed usually caused me to give in, but I still felt that the whole process was giving the television producer something for nothing.

One method that I used to get revenge on the television crew was to try to find ways to shock them. Because the interview and reenactments almost always took place in the morgue, it was easy to use their natural unease to scare or gross them out. Some crews are easier to manipulate than others. One of the camera crew's basic video shots involved me doing some routine activity in the autopsy process.

Since it would be unethical to use a real dead body during the filming, it wasn't uncommon for us to take an empty body bag and stuff it with towels and sheets so that it looked like a body on the autopsy table. Because opening the bag would give away the absence of a body, the camera crew suggested that I handle some small pieces of tissue from a previous autopsy. I was asked to stand behind the body bag and with gloved hands told to pick up individual pieces of tissue with a pair of forceps, hold the pieces of tissue up as I appeared to inspect them with a knowing, professional eye, then place them into separate containers. The cameraman recorded the process on video starting from a full panoramic shot of me standing behind the stuffed body bag and slowly narrowing the shot to a close-up shot that showed only my upper chest and face.

With a look of deep concentration coupled with professional curiosity, I systematically began looking at tissue pieces one at a time. While the cameraman was closing in on his video shot, I picked up a clean pair of forceps hidden from the camera and reached into a clean container that I had previously filled with gummy bears. After a quick inspection and while the camera was closing in on my face, I dropped the gummy bear into my mouth and started chewing. I then looked directly into the camera lens and calmly stated, "Tastes like liver." The cameraman screamed, dropped the video camera onto the floor, and ran out of the room to vomit in the men's room. After that particular interview, I was never asked to do another. I wonder why.

Another type of case that many times falls into the masquerade category is police-involved shooting. Although we try to do our job as impartially as possible, we'd be lying if we stated that the job-related friendships that developed during the course of years working side by side with the local law enforcement don't influence or at least render it more difficult to be completely objective whenever the police come under criticism for killing an individual while performing their law enforcement duties.

For the system to work properly, the medical examiner has to treat these deaths the same as any other homicide and let the cards fall where they may. In my experience, even though the victim is an individual who has a long history of run-ins with the police, a long history of alcohol and/or drug abuse, or fathered children by several women but has taken no financial responsibility, once killed by the police, he's suddenly transformed into a saint by the general public.

Forgotten is the fact that the victim had been scuffling with the police officer and firing shots from his own weapon at the time. Instead, there are public hearings and television and newspaper reports all questioning the policeman, the police agency, and the associated sheriff or chief of police. I'm not trying to trivialize the need for a thorough investigation into all shootings, but it does seem a bit ironic that the weight of opinion immediately falls negatively at the feet of the police even though we know that we want that same police agency at our side responding and doing everything possible to protect us. I know I do.

In Florida, when a police-related shooting has occurred, the state law enforcement agency, the Florida Department of Law Enforcement, is required to conduct a complete investigation. This includes crime scene examination and reconstruction, complete autopsy examination, interviewing all witnesses involved in the shooting as well as bystanders, and a complete analysis of any trace evidence collected from the scene. Most, if not all, of these cases are then presented to a special hearing, much like a coroner's inquest, where witnesses are called to testify to the facts of the case before a judge, who renders a verdict as to whether the shooting was justified or unjustified. This court then decides whether the police officer is disciplined, fired, or turned over to the state prosecutor for filing of criminal charges. All these hearings are open to the public so there can be no legitimate accusations of a cover-up.

During my career, I've been involved in at least six police-related shootings. Fortunately, all those cases were deemed either justified or self-inflicted. Although television has overdramatized the cases they present to the public, suicide by cop or police-induced suicides, although not common, are far from rare. These suicides show the same varying levels of intent or forethought seen in all suicides. Some of these deaths seem to be decided on the spur of the moment, while others are preplanned or orchestrated to varying degrees.

I recall one case that fell into the spontaneous side of this suicide subtype. It involved a man wanted by the local sheriff's office for drug-related felonies. He somehow managed to get the attention of a mother who, unknown to the fleeing felon, had her baby riding behind her in a reverse-facing car seat. After realizing that this choice of vehicle and passengers were going to get him even deeper into trouble, he released the mother and child after getting access to a pickup truck located in an adjacent parking lot.

Once released, the mother called the sheriff's office and told her story, giving them the make and model of the pickup truck as well as its license plate numbers and letters. I didn't say this guy was smart. Not long after the mother's call, the truck was reported traveling down one of the busy roadways in Pensacola. The sheriff's office soon had the pickup surrounded by at least ten separate police cruisers in a standoff right in the middle of the roadway on a busy Friday afternoon. Since the suspect was reported to be armed with a revolver, the scene looked like a made for television movie with the sheriff's office demanding that the felon surrender before someone got hurt.

It's been my experience that when a person is surrounded by police with handguns, shotguns, and rifles aimed at him, it doesn't take much for the whole affair to disintegrate into chaos. One nearby sheriff's deputy saw the felon pull out what he thought was a metal object that looked like a gun and heard a single shot fired from within the truck. The vehicle was soon riddled with enough bullet holes to make a block of Swiss cheese jealous.

Once all of the available ammunition had been expended, quiet once again reigned on the busy street. After carefully approaching the truck to assess the condition of its sole occupant, the blood and brain matter noted on the inside roof of the car confirmed that our felon was dead. All the weapons fired were holstered, and I was called out to the scene to help with the investigation. When I was finally close enough to the truck to see both the victim and the vehicle itself, I was amazed at the number and size of the various bullet holes scattered all over the outside and inside of the truck. From the inside, with the late-afternoon sun streaming in, it was like being inside a block of Swiss cheese, yet despite the number of bullet holes into the passenger compartment of the truck, there wasn't much blood inside the cab.

In the meantime, the scene had become a media extravaganza. All the television stations were present with mobile units. There were even local radio stations broadcasting from the site. All types of questions were being asked. "Was it necessary for all of the shooting to occur in a commercial zone of the city?" "Why did so many sheriff's deputies respond to the scene, and who gave the permission for the shooting to begin?" "Was the truck occupant really so dangerous that that level of lethal force should be brought to bear?" The standard answer of "No comment" to an ongoing investigation and "We will have to wait for the autopsy results to answer those questions" were the only responses given to the media; no pressure on me.

It was well into the evening when the body finally arrived at the morgue surrounded by more law enforcement personnel than could comfortably fit into the autopsy suite. We finally had to limit the number of officers to those immediately involved in the investigation being conducted by the Florida Department of Law Enforcement (FDLE). During the examination, I was surprised by the relatively few bullet wounds present on the body and the lack of significant bleeding around the bullet wound tracts. The explanation came when I did the examination of the decedent's head. There was a gunshot wound to the right side of the head with all of the hallmarks of a contact wound (the barrel of the gun actually touching the entrance site).

The explanation for the limited amount of bleeding in the truck cab as well as the limited bleeding of the police-induced gunshot wounds was that before the police could open up with their battery of weapons, our fleeing felon had already turned his gun on himself with a contact gunshot wound to the head. Interestingly, despite the large number of bullet holes in the body of the truck, the victim himself had only a few wounds, none of which would have been immediately fatal.

Once the cause and manner of death was released to the media, all winds of controversy dissipated almost immediately. The sheriff, though pleased that I had solved a controversial case in their favor, was also at a loss to understand how so many of his deputies could shoot so poorly. What started as a suspected homicide by cops turned out to actually be a suicide assisted by cops. The important thing was the case was still a suicide and not a homicide at the hands of the police.

Not long after all the publicity had died down on the case above, I received a call on a Friday night (Why do these cases always occur on a weekend?) to attend a crime scene at a local Firestone tire shop. The information provided when I arrived on the scene was bizarre, to say the least. Lying on the shop's parking lot were two bodies, one belonging to a white male, the other to a white female. Parked nearby was a late-model Jaguar with scattered bullet holes and shattered side and rear glass secondary to bullet holes.

Allegedly, the two victims in the investigation had been on a crime spree that involved robbery at gunpoint at several Circle K stores in the area. Both robberies had been called in to the sheriff's office along with a description of their vehicle. The Jaguar was eventually located by a sheriff's deputy who called in its location and began pursuit. As the sheriff's vehicle began closing in on the speeding Jaguar, the female occupant popped up through the vehicle's moon roof and began firing bullets at the pursuing deputy, blowing out a front tire and causing the deputy's cruiser to crash.

The chase by this time was being continued by other marked and unmarked sheriff's vehicles that eventually were able to disable the vehicle at the Firestone shop. Both the male driver and the female passenger jumped out of the car and tried to run behind the Firestone building. A privacy fence blocked their exit, and soon the police rounded the corner of the building with bullets flying in all directions. Within seconds, both fugitives were lying on the asphalt parking lot, victims of apparent deputy-inflicted gunshot wounds.

The subsequent autopsies were interesting because, despite the number of bullets discharged by several deputies, the male victim died as a result of a close-range gunshot wound to the head coming from the female's gun rather than from the deputies' handguns. The woman in turn died as a result of a contact gunshot wound to the head, with the recovered bullets from both the male and female bodies only matching the female's handgun.

Once again, instead of both of the fugitives dying at the hands of bullets fired from the deputies' guns, the deaths were actually the result of a homicide suicide where the female victim shot her male accomplice prior to killing herself with a self-inflicted gunshot wound to the head. Again, the news of the cause of both victims' deaths deflated the news media's attempt to question the sheriff's office procedures. When all of the publicity had died down, the chief homicide detective from the sheriff's office took me to the side and asked, "Doc, we appreciate all the help that you give us, especially on these complicated cases. But just how many times do you think you can get away with calling all of the police shootings suicides?" He had a smile on his face when he said it. I hope he was kidding. I think he was.

I discovered one interesting follow-up to the case just this last year. The Firestone shop that occupied the building went out of business, and the structure was remodeled and reopened as a compounding pharmacy. One day when I went into the pharmacy to pick up a prescription for my wife, I asked if they knew about the property's past history. When I told them the story, they volunteered that every year, during the month of October, employees have reported seeing a female ghostlike person standing in the middle of the dark parking lot when closing the business at night. When I volunteered that the deaths took place in the month of October after dark, the supervisor's face went pale. She then requested that I keep quiet about the case around her employees, afraid that she would never be able to schedule employees to cover the late shift. I wonder what they're seeing. If the ghost is packing a gun, watch out!

YOU ALWAYS HURT THE ONE YOU LOVE: HOMICIDE AMONG FRIENDS AND LOVERS

Statistics show that the odds are against being killed by a stranger. To be sure, there are cases where an individual is simply in the wrong place at the right time, such as a witness to an armed robbery or eating lunch at McDonald's when someone decides to open up with an automatic weapon, but most people who die at the hands of another know their assailant, many intimately.

At first glance, it seems ironic that most homicides occur between married couples, family members, and friends, yet when you stop to think, it's usually family members who end up as the recipient of our pent-up emotions. I suspect one reason is that familiarity with a person allows us to let down our guard or defense mechanisms to the point that intimate details are shared, and we're more susceptible to being hurt and angered. In the right setting, this anger can escalate until bodily harm results, sometimes ending in death. In most instances, the violent act is instantly regretted, and attempts are made to rectify the injuries.

One such episode involved a young couple living together in Mobile. Allegedly, the couple seemed happy together and shared a downstairs apartment in a nice middle-class neighborhood. Upon arriving at the scene, I saw the body of a nude white male of about twenty-five lying on the bathroom floor. A quick glance at the body revealed a stab wound to the abdomen oozing bloody fluid. Although a small amount of blood was present on the floor near the body, the lack of blood splatters and the neat appearance of the room indicated that the bathroom wasn't the scene of the assault.

Upon examining the bedroom, there was a blood-soaked area on the mattress sheet with impressions on the bedspread and sheet suggesting that our subject had been in bed after sustaining the stab wound. Examination of the kitchen sink revealed the blood-stained steak knife, while blood splatters were present on the kitchen cabinets below the sink. Although the police suspected that it had been the girlfriend who had called the police, she was nowhere to be found. The scene seemed to indicate that the assault had occurred in the kitchen, with death occurring in the bathroom. The blood-stained bed, however, remained a mystery, at least until the autopsy examination.

Back at the laboratory, the only significant wound was the stab wound to the abdomen noted at the scene. When the abdomen was opened, however, the findings helped explain what we had observed at the scene. The stab wound tract into the abdominal cavity measured about four inches. In the process of entering the abdominal cavity, the knife had perforated several loops of small intestines, a usual finding in stab wounds to the abdomen. The unique thing about the stab wound tract was that there were pus and hyperemia (red discoloration due to increased blood to the site) about the stab wound defects. This indicated that the stab wound had been inflicted some time previous to the death, at least twelve hours before.

A probable scenario based on the scene and autopsy findings would be as follows: The subject and his girlfriend were having a fight in the kitchen which escalated to the point that she picked up a steak knife and stabbed him in the abdomen. Probably instantly regretting the act, she then attempted to take care of her boyfriend by helping him into bed, supplying him with medicines and attending to his other needs as best she could. I suspect they both realized that he needed emergency medical care but were afraid of getting the police involved.

With time, he began to develop peritonitis (inflammation of the linings of the abdominal cavity) with fever, nausea, and weakness. It's probable that he felt a need to vomit or defecate, and she helped him to the bathroom where he collapsed and died.

Although uncommon, this type of denial isn't rare. We've seen it before in instances where two drinking buddies get into a fight resulting in a stab wound, and the combination of alcohol and/or reluctance for police involvement keeps the victim from seeking medical attention. In one case, the victim went to a nurse who lived next door for help. She went to great pains to sew up the skin wound with sutures, only to have her patient die from peritonitis.

Another type of homicide between friends and lovers is homicide-suicide. The usual story is that the wife or girlfriend left the husband/boyfriend and in the process let him know that there's no hope for reconciliation. Faced with an emotional loss devastating his ego, the male usually forces a confrontation. This escalates to a point where out of hurt and rage, the husband fatally shoots the wife usually while in a "If I can't have you, no one will" state of mind. Instantly realizing his error, he then, not infrequently, turns the gun on himself.

It's interesting that a large proportion of the homicide-suicide cases involve an older husband who has married a young attractive female, usually after divorcing the older mother of his children. Inevitably, these men are going through a midlife crisis of sorts, and the loss of their new wife or girlfriend is a severe blow to their self-esteem. Because of their mental state, they tend to completely blow the situation out of proportion. Once the impulsive act is completed, the assailant can't tolerate the humiliation or consequences of his act. In this altered mental state, suicide becomes a reasonable alternative.

From a criminal justice point of view, this type of case solves itself in that the individual guilty of the homicide acts as the judge, jury, and executioner. It's unfortunate that in a small portion of these cases, the homicidal acts extend beyond the immediate parties involved, resulting in the death of children, extended family members, and friends unfortunate enough to be present at the wrong time.

Variants of this type of case also include homicides where, instead of killing himself or herself, the assailant tries to escape or cover the homicide. Fortunately, most people do a poor job of covering their involvement in the death. This, coupled with the knowledge that statistically the spouse is the most likely person responsible for a mate's homicide, puts a burden of proof on the surviving wife or husband.

Another variant of this class of homicide involves the suicide component without the homicide. In these cases, for whatever reason, the individual intended to be the homicide victim escapes or is unavailable to the angry mate. In frustration, or as an attempt to hurt the other party, the mate takes his or her own life, usually staged, where the other party will witness or at least find his/her dead body. One of my cases illustrates this point. Allegedly, the wife had left her husband for good and had moved back into her parents' home. One morning, the estranged husband drove into the driveway, parked his car, and walked toward the house, shotgun in hand. Wisely, the wife's parents refused to let him into the house.

While circling the house to gain a portal for admission, he noticed his wife calmly eating her breakfast in front of a bay window. Despite attempts to get her attention, she continued to ignore him, allegedly staring past him out the window. Pushed past some invisible point of no return, the husband leaned over the barrel end of the shotgun and discharged the weapon into his chest in clear view of the wife. Reliable witnesses claimed she continued to calmly look out the bay window, eating her breakfast, oblivious to her husband's suicidal act.

A well-known category of homicide between friends and lovers is the group I call "The Burning Bed Homicides." Like the movie starring Farrah Fawcett, these cases involve a spouse who, after abuse that often lasted for years, reaches a point where, on impulse or premeditation, kills the abusing mate. Most often, the assailant is the wife who perceives herself unable to care for her family without the abusing husband's income. Inevitably, the husband has severe problems of his own, be they alcohol abuse and low self-esteem. Wanting someone around to make him feel superior, the husband continues an ongoing program of brainwashing to convince the wife that she is indeed inferior and dependent on him for her very existence. At some point, for whatever reason, the wife reaches a point where she can stand no more and either spontaneously kills him or begins to plot his death.

One night at about 10:30, I received a call from the Mobile Police requesting that I attend a homicide scene. The address was located in a nice middle-class neighborhood, so I knew immediately this wasn't the usual Saturday night murder. Upon arriving, I was escorted into the kitchen where an elderly white male was lying on the floor having obviously fallen from an adjacent overturned dining room chair. Examination of the body revealed an intermediate-range gunshot wound (there was gunpowder tattooing around the wound) to the forehead right between the eyes. The only other scene finding worth noting was a broken dinner plate on the floor with fragments of food splattered on the floor and wall.

The wife, a small gray-haired grandmotherly looking lady, gave the following story. After stopping for a few drinks after work, the husband had arrived home drunk and hostile. She claimed that this was a common occurrence and that when in this state, he was always argumentative and usually physically violent. This night was no exception. Attempting to pick a fight, he complained about his dinner. An argument ensued, and he finally threw his dish against the wall, food and all. The argument continued to escalate until, fearing physical harm, she left the room. Following her through the house, he continued his verbal assault. Eventually retrieving a .38-caliber revolver from a drawer, he threatened her with the gun.

She ran back to the kitchen to escape, and when the husband reentered the room, he handed her the gun and dared her to kill him. She claimed that he told her if she didn't shoot him, he would take the gun away from her and shoot her. He then grabbed her, and after taking several steps back and warning him, she shot him in the head.

Background investigation by the police confirmed her story. Neighbors and friends stepped forward to relate tales of physical and mental abuse. Their family physician gave dates and injuries he had treated over the years. All of the above information was presented to the grand jury. They refused to issue an indictment, and the little lady never had to go to trial.

I think it would be fair to say that I had a weird job. As a medical examiner, I saw tragic deaths, heart-breaking deaths, unbelievably cruel deaths, freak accidental deaths, a multitude of natural deaths, and some downright bizarre deaths. Webster defines *bizarre* as "strikingly out of the ordinary, usually involving sensational contrasts or incongruities." There are some individuals who might volunteer that most, if not all, of my cases would fit this definition, yet every medical examiner has had those cases that are so far out of left field that they can't wait to have the opportunity to share them with their fellow physicians at the national forensic meetings that occur periodically.

Of course bizarre, just like beauty, is in the eye of the beholder, so one medical examiner's bizarre might not be the next medical examiner's bizarre. Regardless, it usually takes an exceptional case to qualify for a medical examiner's bizarre category. Ironically, these are also cases that friends and family try to pry me of when I'm at social gatherings, hopefully after the food has been served and is well on its way down the digestive tract.

Let me go on record as saying that these social gatherings can be a dangerous trap for the medical examiner. Everyone wants to get their secondhand thrills by hearing about the blood and guts in detail. If the case is big news locally, they want to be in the know so that they look worldly around the water fountain at work the next morning. The problem for the medical examiner is that many of the details of the crime scene and method of killing the victim are intentionally withheld from the public so those details can be used to screen witnesses who might become suspects. If the gory details of the scene are making the rounds at local social events, the investigators lose a valuable arrow from their quiver, and thus, a homicide may go unsolved.

This idea that "loose lips sinks ships" was an issue that Beth, my wife, and I had to address early in my forensic career. I was so excited about my involvement in homicide cases that I would come home and relate all of the gory details to Beth, both to ventilate as well as impress her with how close to the action I was working. One evening at a church social, a wife of a friend came up and started relating some specific details about a recent homicide that she should never have known. When I asked how she had heard those particular details known only to a few from the scene, she smiled and stated that Beth had told her all about it just minutes before. I just about choked on my sandwich.

That evening, Beth and I had a heart-to-heart talk and decided that since she couldn't control what she might say when asked specific questions, it would be best that I didn't tell her anything at all. I lost a confidant but probably saved my career.

My office nearly lost a good investigator the same way. Her mother owned a beauty parlor in a small community that had just experienced a homicide, big news in a small community. My investigator made the mistake of telling her mom specific aspects of the case, and by the end of the next day, everyone in the community knew as much about the case as the homicide detective trying to solve it. The office had to do some fast talking, and she had to do some sincere apologizing to be able to keep her job.

One of the most bizarre cases that I was involved in since coming to Pensacola came out of the blue, just like most of the more bizarre cases do. I received a call from the local sheriff's office requesting that I come out to a death scene. After training my investigators to take appropriate photographs and how to document the information that I would need to interpret the case, I had set up guidelines as to when I needed to be personally called out to a homicide scene. The "you better call me" list included two or more people dead, local celebrity or personality involved, police-involved shooting, death fits ongoing unsolved cases scenarios, state attorney at the scene, and police specifically ask for my presence. The reason that I had established those criteria was that I would otherwise be out just about every night and too tired to do my job the next day. This case fell into the more-than-one-death category and the request for my presence by the police agency involved. I needed to go.

It was a weekday afternoon when I received the call, and after a forty-five-minute drive, I arrived at a double-wide trailer set off a bit from the main roadway. The fire department was present and had been busy extinguishing the trailer fire before I had arrived. I passed an obviously distraught firefighter being escorted to his chief's car. He gave me a strange look before averting his eyes.

As I walked up to the trailer, my investigator motioned me aside to fill me in briefly about the case. Before he could say anything, I asked the investigator what was wrong with the fireman I had seen walking to his chief's car. The investigator smiled and said that the poor guy probably just had the biggest shock of his career. Before I could pose a follow-up question, my investigator walked me over to a body bag and unzipped it. Lying inside was the body of a young white female with two gunshot wounds to her chest. In the bag next to her was the body of a severely charred male. The case would have fallen into a not-unusual scenario of homicide-suicide had it not been for several postmortem injuries to the wife's body.

The background story wasn't uncommon. The couple had been married for several years when the wife found and met someone where she worked. An extramarital affair ensued until the wife was finally convinced that she should leave her husband for the new boyfriend. It wasn't a peaceful separation, even though there were no children. In fact, the wife had just recently filed a restraining order against the husband because of his constant interference and threats to her new life and boyfriend.

For whatever reason, on the day in question, the husband had convinced the wife to drop by the trailer where they had lived as husband

and wife to sign some papers involving the trailer and property to be divided between them. It turned out to be a fatal mistake.

To the best of our ability, we determined that the events of this case unfolded as follows: Against her better judgment, the wife agreed to stop by the trailer on her way home from work with the understanding that she would sign the pertinent papers outside the trailer, then head off to her new apartment. By unknown means, the husband managed to get the wife into the trailer, hoping for reconciliation. It was not to be. Instead, an escalating argument occurred until the husband pulled out a handgun and shot the wife lethally in the chest. Here's where things started to get bizarre.

For unknown reasons, after killing his wife, the husband took out a knife and literally decapitated her. This was either preceded or followed by the husband using a knife to remove both of his wife's breasts and to excise (cut off) her external genitalia much like that seen in a radical vulvectomy surgical procedure. Finally, the husband opened his wife's chest with the knife, cut out her heart, and took a bite out of it before placing it back into her chest.

The husband then proceeded to set his trailer on fire before killing himself with a single gunshot wound to the head. The wife's torso without the head was found in the back bedroom where the fire hadn't had the chance to spread before the fire department had arrived and extinguished the blaze. Upon arriving at the burning trailer, the fireman whom I had seen when I arrived at the scene had gone around to the rear of the trailer looking for potential survivors. Glancing through the bedroom window, he saw the body of a woman lying on the bed. He immediately smashed the bedroom window and grabbed the woman in a fireman's carry over his shoulder. Once the fireman had the body out of harm's way, he flipped her over to find himself looking at a decapitated and mutilated body way beyond any resuscitation that he had anticipated he might have to perform. His fellow firemen still talk about the scream that came from the fireman's mouth when he first got a look at his rescue.

The body of the husband and the head of the wife were both severely burned during the trailer fire. Although it's extremely common for murderers to set a scene on fire after a homicide in the hope that the body will be consumed by the fire or at least be unidentifiable, that's rarely the case. Instead, because of the large amount of water in our body tissues, a typical house fire will char and burn only the external surfaces of the body while the internal parts of the body are turned pink from the combined heat and carbon monoxide released as the body cooks. The analogy would be a large piece of steak put on a grill that can be superficially burned externally but still pink and rare internally.

In this case, it was easy to document a contact gunshot wound to the husband's head indicating a suicide despite the significant burning of the husband's body externally. The two gunshot wounds on the wife's torso proved to be her cause of death. The postmortem excisions to the body were dramatic, but since they were inflicted after her death, they're not technically involved in her cause of death. The same can be said about the decapitation. It was postmortem and not germane to her cause of death.

I'll finish this case presentation by stating two more interesting findings. When I performed any autopsy, it was my routine to always examine the stomach contents. Gastric contents can potentially give the thorough investigator useful information as to previous location of the last meal and even an estimate of the time of death by indicating the length of time since the last meal.

In this case, when I opened the wife's stomach, I found an engagement ring. When I opened the husband's stomach, I found the bitten-off piece of his wife's heart. Although I'll never know for sure what was going through the husband's mind at the time of their deaths, "love" can be an incredibly powerful emotion, and I suspect unrequited love is even more powerful. Although I think I know what went on during that final interchange between the husband and the wife, I'll let you put that all together to come up with your own scenario.

During the career of every medical examiner, there's usually one case that stands out when they review their work history. The case is usually so tragic or professionally traumatic that the mere thought of it causes all the emotions experienced the first time to come back as fresh as when they had first occurred. The case might have been the one that I personally solved in true "made for TV" fashion. Sometimes it's the case where despite my best efforts and the best efforts of others, the true answer to what really happened to cause a death remains always just out of reach.

The true cause of death of Kay Sybers and the mystery that surrounded it is that case for me. It was a case that dragged on over a fifteen-year period with times when I felt certain about what had happened followed by periods of time when I was convinced that I was completely wrong in my assumptions and that I was persecuting or at least contributing to the persecution of an innocent man. It was also a case where I lost my unbiased perspective at times and caused people I admire and respect to be professionally and financially traumatized by bringing them into the case as consultants. It was a case that was embarrassing, frustrating, and humbling.

I became involved in the case by being stupid enough to volunteer. At that time, there were only two board-certified forensic pathologists in our office, Dr. C. F. (Fenner) McConnell and myself. Dr. McConnell was my senior and served as the chief medical examiner of District One Florida. Because of his longevity in the office and his position as chief, Dr. McConnell knew just about everyone in the Florida Panhandle area, including the medical examiner from the adjacent district, Dr. William Sybers, the husband and prime suspect in the death of his wife, Kay Sybers.

Because Dr. McConnell knew Dr. Sybers personally and professionally, I volunteered to take the case when it was referred to our office by the Florida Department of Law Enforcement. It's difficult enough to try to handle a high-profile case when I don't know the suspect personally. When I do, it puts me into the uncomfortable position of having my conclusions questioned not only on a professional level but also on a personal level.

Dr. Sybers was part owner of a private pathology group in Panama City, FL, which served several of the local hospitals. In addition, Dr. Sybers had been appointed chief medical examiner for several county districts including Panama City. Panama City, the county seat of Bay County, is a small city sitting on some of the most beautiful beaches in the country. The county derives a large portion of its commerce from the summer tourist trade, with the local population in the area often doubling during the busy beach season. Kay, his wife of thirty plus years, was a medical technologist by training, but she hadn't worked outside the home for years.

The story began for me on the morning of May 30, 1991. On the previous evening, Dr. William Sybers and his fifty-two-year-old wife had been out to dinner at a local restaurant where they had been seen and greeted by numerous peers from the Panama City Beach, FL, community. Kay was described as being in good spirits, and after they had eaten dinner, they both returned to their home where two of their children, both home for college spring break, were staying.

Allegedly, Kay woke up at four the next morning, May 30, complaining of chest pains and pains radiating down her left arm. Kay had a family history of heart disease, but no documented personal medical problems. Because she was overweight and personally knew all the physicians in town, Kay had refused to have the routine preventative checkups and physical examinations expected for a woman her age. On that morning of Kay's death, instead of dialing 911 and getting her to the hospital to have her heart checked, Dr. Sybers tried to draw blood from her arm, thinking that he would take the sample into the hospital where he worked to have some tests run. Unable to hit a vein during two phlebotomy attempts, he left for work, disposing the used syringe and test tubes in a dumpster on the way. When he arrived at his 7:00 a.m. hospital meeting with colleagues, Sybers mentioned that Kay wasn't feeling well and that he'd been unable to convince her to seek medical help.

Unable to reach anyone at home after his meeting, Sybers asked an employee who was a paramedic and family acquaintance to drive to his home and check on Kay, draw blood, and perhaps convince her to come into the hospital for a medical examination. When the employee arrived at the Syberses' home, he found Kay unresponsive. He and a fellow employee who had accompanied him to the home attempted resuscitation while the children called emergency medical services.

Despite a prolonged attempt, Kay couldn't be resuscitated and was pronounced dead at her home. When Sybers arrived at the scene, he was visibly distraught. As the medical examiner for the district, he was responsible for deciding how the death investigation would be handled. Instead of following routine procedures, he released Kay's body from their home directly to the funeral home, thereby bypassing an autopsy examination or additional investigations to determine the actual cause of her death. The funeral home immediately embalmed the body and began to prepare the remains for shipping to Kay's hometown in Iowa for burial.

In the state of Florida, by statute law, an individual who dies outside the care of a physician who is able and willing to sign the death certificate must be reported to the district medical examiner, who determines whether an autopsy should be performed to determine the cause of death.

In this case, Kay Sybers was a 52-year-old woman with no documented medical condition to explain her death. In my office, she would have been automatically autopsied. This doesn't even bring to bear the issue that there was a real conflict of interest involved when Sybers used his position as medical examiner to bypass the guidelines put in place to keep this very thing from happening. Those individuals at the scene stated that Sybers was genuinely distraught and that his reflex decision to release Kay's body without an autopsy was probably due to a combination of his grief and Kay's wish that she not be autopsied after her death, a not uncommon request among the wives of medical examiners who understand all that an autopsy involves.

Sybers's associates at the medical examiner's office knew that he was making a serious personal as well as professional mistake. They called the Florida Department of Law Enforcement, who has administrative authority over all of the district medical examiners, and got their support in confronting Sybers with the issues. Sybers conceded that he had made a mistake by releasing the body to the funeral home, but by the time the funeral home had been finally contacted, Kay's body had already been embalmed.

Almost instantaneously, rumors began to fly. Panama City is a small community in which everyone knows everything about everything and everybody. Soon anonymous phone calls were coming in to the local police claiming that Sybers had killed his wife. It also became common knowledge that Sybers was having an affair with a younger woman and that a divorce from Kay could have cost him at least half of his estimated six-million-dollar estate.

To add insult to injury, the first call made from Sybers's cell phone as he left his home that morning on the way to his office was to the girlfriend. Although Sybers had claimed to use a syringe to obtain blood from his wife, that same syringe could just as easily been used to inject a poison or drug to cause her death. Although Sybers claimed to have disposed of the syringe at a dumpster down the street, by the time the investigators could find its location, the dumpster had already been emptied. The missing syringe just added more fuel to the rumor fires.

It was at this point that I began my involvement in the investigation. As luck would have it, the autopsy had to be performed on a Saturday that I was scheduled to be off work, so I had the joy of explaining to my wife why I wouldn't be home on a scheduled day off. I'm putting this point in the transcript because my wife demanded that the world should know how she has suffered because of my profession.

At autopsy, Kay Sybers was an obese white female who had bruises about her upper arms and lower legs, probably caused by the paramedics working to get her to a position on the floor or stretcher where they could attempt their resuscitation procedures. Otherwise, the body was unremarkable except for contusions of the arm on the right anterior elbow region (antecubital fossa) that represented the site of Sybers's alleged phlebotomy attempts. The body, as previously stated, had been embalmed with the usual funeral home incisions for arterial and venous access and aspiration ports on the abdomen.

I suspect that most people have no concept of what occurs when the funeral home embalms a body. It's probably just as well, but to understand why forensic pathologists discourage the embalming of a body prior to the autopsy, the reader must at least have a general idea what the embalming process involves.

When a body is brought into a funeral home, getting it embalmed quickly is a priority. The longer the body sits before embalming, the more difficult it becomes to get the embalming fluid distributed evenly throughout the body tissues. I should note that the main purpose of embalming the body is strictly for aesthetics. Our tradition for dealing with death involves having an opportunity to view the deceased at the funeral home while we extend condolences to the family.

To allow this process to occur, embalming to preserve the tissues coupled with nice clothes, hairstyling, and makeup are utilized to make the deceased look as natural as possible. The embalming process, contrary to what is commonly assumed, isn't done for public health reasons. From the funeral home's point of view, embalming allows the funeral home to avoid having a refrigeration unit large enough to hold all the bodies they have in their possession.

The embalming process proper is composed of two separate stages, the infusion stage and the aspiration stage. The infusion component is done first and uses the large arteries and veins of the groin and/or the area above the clavicle (subclavian artery) to pump a formaldehyde solution under pressure to all the different body parts including the head, upper extremities, chest, abdomen, and lower extremities. The pump allows the solution to perfuse the arteries and capillaries of the skin surfaces so that the tint present in the solution can give the skin a lifelike coloration.

Depending on the condition of the body at the time of embalming as well as the length of time till internment, varying strengths of preservative can be used. Prior to infusion, the body is placed in the pose that will be assumed in the casket because once the infusion solution is applied, the body becomes rigid and difficult to manipulate.

Once the body has been infused, the trocar or aspiration phase is performed. The skin of the abdomen is incised one inch long into the abdominal cavity, then long, hollow stainless steel rods are attached to a vacuum device, and the rods are rammed into all the chest and abdominal organs through the skin incision in an effort to aspirate as much blood, body fluids, and excess infusion fluid as possible from the soft tissues and body cavities.

The end result from the forensic pathology point of view is a marked distortion of the internal organs and multiple artifacts that can make injury identification all the more difficult. The infusion of embalming fluid into the blood vessels contaminates or dilutes any blood sample that might be collected post-embalming. Depending on the case in question, the aspiration phase may also involve the infusion of a strong preservative into the body cavities prior to the final aspiration. The initial incision into the abdomen is plugged with a small plastic disc called an aspiration button. Once the embalming has been completed, the funeral home personnel dress the body and do the cosmetics, hair, etc., that the public sees when the body is viewed.

The internal portion of Kay Sybers's autopsy showed no anatomic reason for her death in that there were no massive hemorrhages, no pulmonary thromboembolism, and no infarcts of the brain that would explain a sudden death. By the time I had begun the autopsy, there was already a statewide interest among the medical examiner community. Dr. Joe Davis, the chief medical examiner in Miami, FL, at the time, was considered to be one of the giants in the field of forensic pathology. Because of the size of their office in Miami, they also had one of the best toxicology laboratories in the country.

The Florida Department of Law Enforcement had already made arrangements for the toxicology samples to be shipped to Miami for examination. Since Dr. Davis's area of interest was the heart in sudden death, I agreed to send the heart as well as a complete set of histology slides from all of Kay Sybers's organs to Dr. Davis for consultation.

Since the autopsy failed to show an anatomic cause for Kay Sybers's death, the toxicology rapidly became the focal point in the investigation. At the time of the autopsy, toxicology samples were taken from every body cavity not destroyed by embalming. Samples of clotted blood were taken from inside the body arteries. Fluid from the eyes, hair, and fingernails and frozen tissue samples from the lungs, liver, and kidneys were also obtained. The needle puncture site from the front of Kay Sybers's right elbow was also excised, frozen, and shipped for toxicology. All evidence was packaged, labeled, and released through a proper chain of custody receipt to the Miami medical examiner's office.

Assured that we had collected all the evidence that we would need, the body was released back to the funeral home and subsequently buried in a family plot near Fort Dodge, IA.

Over the next several months, all parties involved in the case awaited the toxicology results. It's common knowledge in the forensic community that the process of embalming either strongly dilutes or destroys toxicology evidence that would otherwise be recovered from autopsy specimens. If we did find a substance that could explain Kay Sybers's death, it would be extremely unusual.

It was no surprise then when the toxicology results from all fluids, tissues, and hair samples that had been submitted came back negative for any substance that would have caused Kay's death. During the weeks following the autopsy, the funeral home handling the burial arrangements for Kay Sybers was anxious for me to sign the death certificate so they could close out their paperwork on her death. I had held up signing the death certificate until the toxicology results had been reported. With the negative toxicology results, I initially signed out the cause of death as "sudden unexpected death due to undetermined natural causes." The FDLE contacted me immediately after the death certificate had been filed, stating that the death was still being investigated as a murder and that the death certificate calling the death due to undetermined "natural" causes would obstruct their investigation. I then amended the death certificate to "sudden unexpected death due to undetermined causes," which made the police agencies happy but upset the attorneys representing Sybers.

From an investigative viewpoint, there were several issues keeping the investigation alive. It became apparent and confirmed that Sybers was involved in an ongoing extramarital affair with a previous employee and that his cell phone records showed that the vast majority of his calls were to phone numbers associated with his mistress. The cell phone call that he had made to the girlfriend immediately after leaving the house on the morning of Kay's death was the most troubling. Additional information suggesting that Sybers had a possible gambling problem was also uncovered. The fact that most of Sybers's assets were either held jointly with Kay or maintained in Kay's name alone brought the issue of how the assets would be divided should the affair have resulted in a divorce. It's quite possible that the majority of the assets that they held in common might be awarded preferentially to Kay should the marriage dissolve.

Finally, in 1993, Dr. Sybers's youngest son died from of a self-inflicted gunshot wound to the head while staying in the family's Wisconsin condominium. According to the investigating police in Wisconsin, prior to his death, he had just called his girlfriend and stated that he couldn't stand to live with the thought that his father might be a killer.

With no smoking gun in terms of concrete proof that Sybers had committed murder, the investigation went cold for several years. The state attorney who oversees the prosecution of criminal cases in Panama City refused to pursue the case. The governor finally had to appoint a special prosecutor to get the case moving forward through the judicial system.

Thus, in 1997, I flew to Orlando, FL, to participate in a roundtable discussion of the Sybers's case in an effort to bring all parties involved up to speed on what the evidence was and to determine if there were other avenues of investigation that should be pursued. The consensus was that in all likelihood, the death had been caused by a poison that would be difficult to detect or would rapidly break down in the body. The two classic examples of this type of poison were potassium chloride and succinylcholine.

The problem with trying to detect these drugs in autopsy specimens is that they're both composed of molecules normally present in the body in large quantities. Potassium is probably the most common element present in the body. The body uses potassium in every cell. It functions to keep excess amounts of sodium, the common table salt element, from getting through the cell membrane into the cell protoplasm, and in the process, it keeps the electrical charge across the cell membrane balanced, making it possible for muscles to contract and the heart to pump blood throughout the body. It's common medical knowledge that an injection of potassium chloride into a vein could cause the heart to go into cardiac standstill. In the drug cocktail used during judicial executions, it's usually the last injection given to stop the beating heart.

The problem with potassium chloride from a forensic viewpoint is that there are vast quantities of potassium located in every cell of the body, and once the cells die, the membranes break down and release the intracellular potassium into the blood and body fluids. Because of this, the finding of markedly increased levels of potassium in the body fluids after death just confirms that the body is indeed dead and has released its intracellular potassium.

Succinylcholine is a drug used in surgery as a muscle relaxer. It's closely related to curare, the drug South American natives place on their darts to paralyze the animals they shoot with their blowguns. The drug prevents the nerves from communicating with skeletal muscle so that the impulse from the nerve that usually tells the muscle to contract is blocked. Although a great tool when it's used in surgery to relax the abdominal muscles so that the surgeon can work inside, it requires that some artificial breathing mechanism be in place because the muscles necessary for breathing on the patient's own are also paralyzed. Anyone injected with succinylcholine would be totally awake but unable to take the breaths necessary to keep oxygen flowing from the lungs to the tissues. The patient would suffocate without someone giving an antidote to the drug or giving them mouth to mouth until the drug had finally worn off. From a toxicology point of view, the drug breaks down quickly into its component molecules, all of which occur in large quantities naturally within the body.

The initial attempt to examine the toxicology samples for potassium chloride showed one of the specimens to contain a high level of the chemical. The problem was that there were no control cases available for comparison, and one high level of potassium doesn't make a poison for the reasons stated above. One thought was that if the body was exhumed and reautopsied, it might be possible to collect samples from different areas of the body and determine whether the one elevated potassium was a fluke or had significance. Since the body was buried in Iowa, the state of Florida requested that an exhumation be allowed on Kay's remains. The family objected and went to court to stop the proceedings.

The circuit court gave permission to exhume, but the appeals court felt that the state of Florida didn't prove their need for more specimens to a level that would override the wishes of the family. Without the exhumation material, the potassium chloride theory of poisoning couldn't be confirmed one way or the other.

It was at this point in the proceedings that the defense asked me to give them the name of a forensic pathologist who would be able to help them prepare for their defense of Sybers. I immediately thought of and recommended my old mentor, Dr. Riddick. It was a big mistake. At the time of my initial recommendation, there was no conflict between what a witness for the defense would say versus what I would say as a witness for the prosecution. I saw the case as a nice opportunity to spend some time with Dr. Riddick while he picked up some extra cash as a defense witness.

This all changed when the prosecution came up with a toxicology result on tissues that I had frozen and preserved at the time of autopsy. Dr. Kevin Ballard, director of Research and Analytic Toxicology at the National Medical Service in Pennsylvania, had found increased levels of succinylmonocholine in tissue samples from Kay Sybers. Succinylmonocholine is the primary breakdown component of succinylcholine, and its presence in the samples was interpreted as proving succinylcholine poisoning.

The first-degree murder trial was immediately converted from a trial based primarily on circumstantial evidence to one where a poison had been recovered. As the main forensic pathology witness for the prosecution, I was put in the position of defending a test result obtained from a laboratory completely unknown to me. Dr. Riddick, as a witness for the defense, was put in the position of having to rebut the toxicology evidence as inaccurate.

When the special prosecutor cross-examined Dr. Riddick on the witness stand, Riddick opined that the true cause of death was an asthma attack. Riddick used histology slides from Kay Sybers's lungs that I had provided to him to make his case. I had examined those same slides and reviewed them with multiple pathologists. We saw no changes of asthma in the tissues. We ended up being on opposite sides of the case with opposing opinions, something that had never occurred in our careers before.

The jury found Sybers guilty of first-degree murder as charged in the indictment. He was given a sentence of twenty-five years in prison. I wish I could say that the verdict ended everything, but the case continued to have a life of its own.

The prosecution had won the case, and Sybers was serving a life sentence. Despite this victory, the special prosecutor refused to let well enough alone. He convinced himself that Riddick and another forensic pathologist witness lied about the autopsy findings. He claimed that at some point their testimony became so untruthful that it went beyond a difference in scientific or medical opinion.

Once I had heard about this claim, I called the special prosecutor and told him that he was opening a Pandora's box. Although I didn't personally agree with the defense's interpretation of the autopsy and I was surprised by their opinion, I would never make the claim that their testimony was intentionally fabricated to help their client win. If I knew nothing else about Leroy Riddick, I knew for a fact that he was the most ethical and honest forensic pathologist I had ever known.

The other point I made to the special prosecutor extended beyond the boundaries of the case under discussion. It was the fact that just the threat of considering legal action against defense witnesses would severely cripple the ability of any defense attorney to obtain expert testimony on future cases. Finally, the special prosecutor had won his damn case, so what was his beef?

Fortunately, although pursued far enough that Dr. Riddick felt the need to defend himself by retaining his own attorney with its associated expenses, the special prosecutor was finally convinced to let the issue drop. Sybers's conviction subsequently disappeared from the headlines for the next two years as the case went through the judicial appeals process.

When a case is going through the appeals process, it's common for the plaintiff to get an attorney with special expertise in that area of law. Sybers had the money, and the case was prominent enough to get a well-known defense attorney from New York City to handle his case. When this happens, the defense reopens aspects of the case in an attempt to find an error in the previous trial proceedings significant enough for the appeals court to overturn the lower court ruling. Part of this process may involve actual testimony in court before a judge to elicit useful facts for the appeal.

The appeal process in the Sybers case was scheduled in another court district. As a result, I wasn't served with the proper subpoena prior to my leaving town for a long-awaited week of skiing in Colorado. Around Wednesday, I received a call on my cell phone, a good reason to not own one. I was informed that I was expected to be in court the next day. I called the prosecutor and explained where I was and that I wouldn't be there to testify the next day. He said he could use transcripts of my previous testimony, but that he would have to clear my absence with the judge and the defense attorney handling the appeal. The judge was fine with my absence, but the defense lawyer refused to release me from the subpoena. My wife just rolled her eyes as we started to pack. My only consolation was the snow was exceptionally sparse that year, so I promised Beth a return trip when there was better snow.

We were actually able to catch a flight that would have allowed me to get to court on time. As we flew into Atlanta (a person can't get anywhere from the panhandle without flying through Atlanta), the bottom fell out of the bucket. Someone had jumped the security fence and was loose in the terminals. The entire airport had to be evacuated, and we in turn had to sit in our plane on the runway until the problem was resolved. I called the defense attorney and told him to look at CNN if he wondered why I was a no-show. I thought my call was clever, but he wasn't amused.

Ironically, my testimony, though delayed, was anticlimactic. The result of the appeal, however, wasn't. The appeals court decided that Sybers should be granted a new trial based on the succinylcholine test results and the prosecution's inability to show that "the test had been sufficiently established to have gained general acceptance in the field."

By this time, Dr. Sybers had already spent two years in prison and was beginning to have significant health problems. Instead of enduring the emotional, physical, and financial trauma of another trial, the prosecution and defense compromised on Sybers pleading guilty to manslaughter with his sentence being limited to the two years already served. William Sybers was once again a free man at liberty to go home to his second wife, the woman with whom he'd been having the affair at the time of Kay Sybers's death.

The final shoe was yet to drop. Later the same year that Sybers walked free, the special prosecutor notified the trial judge that the evidence that had been presented regarding the succinylcholine metabolites found in Kay Sybers's body weren't indicative of succinylcholine poisoning at all. It was a molecule found commonly in decomposing bodies regardless of whether or not the body had been exposed to succinylcholine prior to death. Things got so crazy that the governor appointed a new special prosecutor to investigate the old special prosecutor in terms of how he had handled the case and the subsequent witch hunt involving the defense witnesses. The special prosecutor was found innocent of wrongdoing, but I did find this ironic aspect of the Sybers case refreshing as this final curtain on the case finally fell.

Was William Sybers guilty of killing his wife of thirty plus years? Our legal system is based on the principle that if there is reasonable doubt that he's innocent, he should be judged innocent by society and be free to live his life in peace. If he was innocent, it would make Sybers's manslaughter conviction a compromise accepted by a man who was tired and didn't want to risk the chance that another trial would again find him guilty. If William Sybers is truly innocent of his wife's death, he's at least guilty of being foolish enough to have an extramarital affair, treating his wife's apparent chest pain episode in a nonphysician-like manner and then handling her death in a non-medical-examiner-like fashion.

The question remains as to whether I believe that William Sybers killed his wife, Kay. To be honest, I don't know. I would be dishonest if I didn't admit that there are several things about the case that bothered me. That list would include the lost syringe, the refusal to call 911, the call to his girlfriend as Sybers left his house, and the fact that the girlfriend existed in the first place. Sybers knew that his net worth would have taken a significant hit had Kay filed for divorce.

The fact that he immediately released his wife's body to the funeral home instead of having an outside investigation of her death bothered me because it violated a cardinal rule of ethics as both a physician and a medical examiner. The suicide of his youngest son and his parting message to his girlfriend is equally bothersome.

Finally, who better to know how to kill someone in a way that the existing system couldn't discover than a forensic pathologist? The fact that Sybers eventually married that same girlfriend is more disturbing to me than if she had only been a passing fancy. The seriousness of the relationship would make the need to kill his wife to keep his wealth intact all the more likely.

The bottom line is that William Sybers was either a clumsy, naïve fool or an ingenious killer. If the former is true, I owe Sybers a sincere apology for my contribution to his undeserved pain and suffering. If the latter is true, my only remaining option is to appeal the case to the ultimate judge and await his verdict. My other regret is the unintended grief the case brought on my former mentor, Dr. Riddick. I unintentionally placed him in an awkward position, and for that, I apologize.

In summary, I guess as a death investigator I should be relieved that most homicides involve close parties and are easily solved. Although real whodunits do occur, I suspect that society is equally relieved that Ted Bundys are not a common beast, yet it's still sad to think that in most instances, it's that person in whom the victim, at one point in his or her life, had put his or her highest level of trust and confidence who is most often responsible for his or her homicide.

Although I would like to think that neither I nor my wife, Beth, could possibly get so angry at one another that we would contemplate the other's murder, I always try to avoid going to bed with her angry at me. Because this is often impossible, I've devised an alternate plan. First, I keep no firearms in my house, and second, I've mastered the fine art of sleeping with one eye open.

THE METER GOES 'ROUND AND 'ROUND: DEATH BY ELECTRICITY

If your definition of accidental deaths is chance happenings or "acts of God," then deaths due to lightning would definitely rank high on most people's short. Lightning is responsible for half of all forest fires, resulting in hundreds of millions of dollars' worth of property destruction. It is a major cause of power outages, and it kills at least one hundred Americans per year.

Scientists claim that lightning bolts strike the earth at the rate of one hundred times per second. The lightning that we see is actually channels of pulsating electric energy anywhere from two hundred feet to twenty miles in length. The bolts travel through the air at ninety thousand miles per second and heat the surrounding air up to fifty thousand degrees Fahrenheit (five times the temperature of the sun's surface). It's fortunate for us earth dwellers that three quarters of the bolt's energy is used to heat the surrounding air. Enough energy remains, however, to deliver a 125-million-volt blast to anything unfortunate enough to be between the lightning and the ground.

Although impressive to mankind throughout the ages, it was Ben Franklin in 1752 who demonstrated that lightning was electricity. Although still poorly understood, many scientists believe that lightning is formed in clouds by swirling ice and hail generating electrical charges. In the clouds, positive charges are polarized at the top of the cloud, while the negative charges stay near the bottom of the cloud. The charge continues to accumulate until the one-hundred-million-volt potential necessary for a discharge has accumulated.

When this potential is reached, invisible electrical streamers from the cloud escape toward the positively charged earth. When one of these streamers comes to within thirty yards of the earth's surface, Mother Earth lets loose with an eruption of radiant light that shoots back up the electrical path formed by the streamers. This results in a blazing multichannel stream of light. Thus, what we actually see is not lightning traveling from the cloud to the earth but light or radiant energy traveling from the earth to the cloud. Lightning travels so quickly that it's impossible to tell what direction it's moving.

Because lightning normally strikes the tallest object forming the shortest path to the ground, trees are a common casualty, with the heat generated by a lightning blast causing the tree's sap to boil and often bursting it apart. The human body also makes a good conductor. Because of the massive amounts of energy involved, few people struck directly by lightning live to tell about it. Those instances of survival are probably instances where the lightning had nearly spent itself on grounding trees or other structures before striking the human.

Sometimes, however, the surrounding trees aren't enough to save the involved individual. Such was the case one spring afternoon in Mobile. It was a Saturday and my weekend on call. As I looked out the autopsy room window into the southwest skies, I was taking a small amount of consolation in the fact that a thunderstorm was rapidly approaching and would probably rain out the outdoor projects of anyone lucky enough to be off that day.

Because of its location thirty miles from the Gulf of Mexico, spring thunderstorms in Mobile are particularly violent. The warm, moist air coming off the gulf, hitting the cooler air over the landmass, has been known to result in as much as six inches of rain in an hour. This storm looked to be unusually potent as the pitch-black clouds rapidly rolled in to obscure the previously bright sun. The ensuing rain, lightning, and thunder were dramatic even by Mobile standards. The storm passed over just as quickly as it had come, leaving floods and power outages in its wake.

Later that same afternoon, we had just finished our cases for that day when the Mobile Police called to report two deaths in the University of South Alabama Medical Center emergency room. Allegedly, two boys, ages ten and twelve, had sought refuge from the rain under one of Mobile's live oak trees. Lightning had struck the tree and the boys at the same time. According to the emergency medical team responding to the call, one boy was dead at the scene, while the other was showing agonal respirations. This second boy died soon after his arrival at the hospital.

The autopsy examinations showed the classic injuries associated with lightning deaths. In addition to burns on the body surfaces, there were burns to the items of clothing worn by both boys. The canvas tennis shoes on both victims were burned completely in multiple areas immediately above the rubber soles. The thick sweat socks worn at the time were also burned completely. The shirts and pants of both subjects were torn and charred from the heat and explosive effects produced as the moisture on the body surfaces was instantly transformed into steam. Both bodies also showed a pattern of hemolysis called arborization caused by the rupture of red cells in the blood vessels with leakage into the surrounding skin such that the resulting pattern looks like the branching of a tree immediately under the skin.

All internal organs were congested and had a parboiled feel because of the tremendous heat. In fact, the heat had been so intense that coins in one of the subject's pockets had been welded together. One scary thing about lightning is that it can come out of nowhere. A couple can be having a romantic stroll along the beach, enjoying the warm sunshine and warm fellowship, when *WAM*, the lightning strikes without a cloud in the sky. To this day, I still can't look at lightning without being amazed at the amount of raw energy present in one of nature's most beautiful displays.

Little did I know that I would soon be embroiled in a case where electricity would again be the agent of death. One of the drawbacks with being part of a statewide system of medical examiners is that the office is often called upon to assist in investigations from other state agencies, most commonly law enforcement, but occasionally the prison system. In point of fact, cases from the latter are often some of the most interesting as far as forensic pathology is concerned. It's amazing how resourceful the inmates are at developing weapons for self-defense and at the same time keeping them concealed.

One subtype of death investigation in the prison system that wouldn't ordinary come to mind is the investigation of judicial executions. On second thought, it's obviously in the interests of the society that someone looks at these bodies if for no other reason than to act as an independent observer to verify that the person was indeed put to death and that the death was done within the parameters that the society deems humane. Actually, to be practical, someone has to sign the death certificate.

In April of 1983, our office in Mobile received a call from the warden of Holman Prison in Atmore, AL. John Lewis Evans III, who had been tried and convicted for the murder of a pawnshop owner allegedly while the owner's children looked on, was scheduled to be executed. The warden was requesting our aid in the disposition of the body. Interestingly, this was to be the first execution in Alabama in some twenty years. The Supreme Court had ruled that Alabama's death penalty law was unconstitutional, requiring the state to draft and pass a law within the new Supreme Court guidelines. To add additional stress, this execution would be the first done nationally for some time. Obviously, everyone involved in the case was working to see that all went smoothly. We were going to do an autopsy examination on the body for public record, hopefully to prevent any unfounded rumors about the condition of the body after death.

Even from the start, however, we were put in an awkward position. John Evans, as a last act of penance, had donated his body to medical science. It was to go to the Radiology Department of the University of South Alabama Medical Center here in Mobile. This in effect tied our hands and kept us from doing a complete internal examination of the body. We obviously could have flexed our muscles and gotten overriding authority from the attorney general to do a complete autopsy, but that was hard to rationalize from both a scientific and a public relations viewpoint. It's obviously rare for people doing medical research to have access to a body where the time of death is known so accurately. In addition, we would be put in a position of foiling the attempt of an obviously repentant killer trying to do a humane act, possibly to prove his remorse.

The execution was to take place on Friday, April 22. The actual event was scheduled at midnight. My first thought was that they could have at least picked a more civilized time for those of us who were to participate in the event. After all, we hadn't done anything to deserve punishment. When I voiced my lament to the prison authorities, they rebounded with a reasonable explanation. The dates of executions in Alabama are set by the Alabama Supreme Court. If, for any reason, the prisoner received a temporary stay of execution, say, by a federal judge, lasting for twenty hours, an execution scheduled originally at midnight could still be carried out. If the stay lasted longer than the twenty-four-hour day originally set by the Supreme Court, a judicial proceeding establishing a totally new date for execution had to be set.

I need to interject something at this point. If I didn't, my wife would shoot me. Actually, this wasn't my weekend on call. Initially, I was doing handsprings down the nearest boulevard, thinking not only was I off work for the weekend, but it was probably going to be a "weekend from hell" if there were several cases in addition to the execution, but that wasn't my problem because Dr. Riddick was scheduled for this weekend. Instead, my wife and I had reservations in Gulf Shores, Alabama, to spend the weekend at the beach in a previously rented high-rise condominium.

But fate wasn't on my side. Dr. Riddick was trapped in Montgomery, AL, at a legislative hearing concerning a pending Medical Examiners bill, so not only was I going away from my warm bed that night, I was doing it on my three-day weekend off as well. Needless to say, Beth wasn't thrilled. To this day, when she gets mad at me, she still brings this up.

So at approximately 7:00 p.m., Roy Tex and I left Mobile for the one-hour journey to Atmore, AL, to attend the execution. They wanted us there early to make sure everything was coordinated to run smoothly.

One point worth noting was that all prison officials were a bit nervous over all of this because no one involved in this execution had ever been involved in previous events. With all the delays involved in the overturn of Alabama's death law, all prison officials involved in previous executions had either died or retired from the prison system.

Alabama's mode of execution at that time was the electric chair. The actual electrical system was in good repair. Prison protocol required that prison officials test the system with a dummy resistor load periodically even during the long dry spell. The chair itself was nicknamed "Yellow Mama" by the death row inmates because it was made of thick lumber painted a bright yellow. Allegedly, the chair was made by a prison inmate back in the 1920s. The electrical power to the chair is supplied by a general electric dynamo that produces approximately two thousand volts of alternating current when turned on. In a weak attempt at black humor, I mentioned that the current ad campaign for General Electric was "GE we bring good things to life." I thought they should add another line to the jingle saying, "GE we bring good things to life and put bad things to death." Don't worry, I don't plan on giving up my day job.

The story behind how the electric chair came to be the most common method of execution is interesting. Before electrocution became popular, the most common method of execution was hanging. People don't realize it, but judicial-style hanging isn't as easy as it might appear.

For the process to work as intended, the victim must be dropped through the trap door with enough distance through the scaffold floor to snap their neck when arrested by the rope. If not enough distance is allowed, then the victim slowly strangles to death. Too much distance and they can literally jerk the head off the victim. This is what happened in New York in the late 1800s. Not only did the victim lose his head, but so did the newspapers and the public.

The state decided that they needed a different, more humane way to carry out executions. Someone suggested that the famous inventor Thomas Edison might be able to give advice on the issue. This was about the same time that electricity was beginning to be used to energize businesses and homes in the more metropolitan areas of northeast. There were two competing companies vying for contracts to begin distributing electricity, Edison who owned General Electric and George Westinghouse who owned Westinghouse Electric.

There was an ongoing competition between the two companies not only in getting customers but also on whose technology for generating electricity should be used. Edison's system was a direct current system much like the electricity that comes from batteries. Westinghouse used an alternating current system, the type of electricity that energizes our homes today.

In terms of practical utilization at the time, Westinghouse's alternating current was the better choice. The reason is that direct current is produced by pushing electrons along a conductor to release its energy. The greater the distance the current must be pushed, the more powerful the push must become. Direct current systems at the time were thus limited by the short distance that the direct current could be pushed with the technology available at the time. Alternating current didn't suffer from this issue. Rather than having to push electrons along the conductor, alternating current generators push, then pull the electrons back and forth through the conductor, allowing them to transport electricity over much greater distances than the direct current system. This allowed cities to build their generators at greater distances than the direct current system, which would require that a generating plant be placed in every neighborhood.

When Edison was asked for his opinion on a new method of execution, he recommended that electricity be used. When asked what type of system he recommended, he volunteered that he would use an alternating system to provide the electricity. Why would he recommend his competitor's system over his own?

Edison, in addition to being a good inventor, was an incredibly shrewd businessman. It was indeed true that direct current systems were much safer than alternating electricity. The electrons' back and forth movement was much more likely to cause the heart to go into a dysthymia than the direct current form of electricity. Edison then used the fact that the judicial system was using the alternating current system of Westinghouse because it was more dangerous as an advertising ploy to get cities to buy his direct current system. History shows that despite Edison's publicity trick, the more efficient alternating current systems eventually were adopted to power all our homes and businesses.

Alabama law reads that the inmate dying in the chair must meet his death at the hands of the warden of Holman Prison, so in Alabama, the grisly job of actually "flipping" the switch belongs to the warden. The system is set up so that once the switch is pulled, the dynamo, by means of a mechanical rheostat, sends a set range of voltages through the chair. Initially, the voltage goes to approximately 2,000 volts. It stays there for some twenty seconds. The voltage then drops down to the 500-volt range again for some twenty seconds, and finally, the voltage slowly increases to 1,900 volts, then shuts off completely. This sequence will become important later on in the story.

Well, on the first night, all the preparation was for naught. During our trip up to Atmore, a federal judge in Mobile granted a temporary stay of execution until he could review an appeal by Evan's lawyers. So after sitting for a few hours in the security building at Holman prison, we headed back to Mobile a bit relieved that the back of our wagon was still empty.

Our instructions for the next twenty-four hours were to "be available." The appeal could be overturned at any time. That happened at about seven o'clock the following evening, and we were back on the road to Atmore. The strategy of the prison officials at this point was to get the execution over as quickly as possible before another stay could be granted. This sounds cruel, but during the execution, all the prisoners had to stay in their cells with no recreation and no privileges. The longer that the execution dragged on, the more restless the inmates became.

Our role in the execution was actually minor. We weren't going to witness the execution. Rather, we were going to wait outside the gate to the execution chamber and enter after the witnesses to the execution had filed out. We would then remove the body from the chair, take possession, and transport Evans back to Mobile for an examination before releasing his body to the medical school.

As we waited outside the prison gates with the investigator from the prison, MacArthur Davis, we could see the witnesses file through the gate to the execution chamber after being searched. The group consisted of a few prison officials and three people chosen by Evans: his attorney, a chaplain, and another person I was unable to recognize. The time sitting in our wagon seemed endless.

This time of quiet introspection was interrupted by a prison guard who approached our car and told us we would have to be strip-searched before we'd be allowed into the death chamber. I looked at my investigator while he looked at me. We both then looked the prison guard in the eye and said, "No way." The guard then looked at McArthur Davis, also a prison employee, and stated that by regulations, everyone entering the death chamber had to be strip-searched. We finally looked at McArthur Davis and told Davis to tell him that he had searched us earlier. McArthur then stated that he had indeed strip-searched us earlier and that we should be allowed through the gate. My modesty remained intact.

Both MacArthur and Tex were usually busy cracking jokes, but even they were unusually quiet. Finally, we heard via the state radio that Evans was dead. We sat silently for a few more minutes until the witnesses again filed past us. We could tell they were upset even in the poor lighting outside the death chamber. After they had left, we drove through the gate to the back door of the execution chamber.

As soon as we walked through the door into the hallway outside of the execution room, I sensed there was something wrong. To begin with, there was a lot of smoke and odor in the air. From experience, I knew what that smell was, burning flesh. Having sat in the car for so long, Tex and I had to relieve ourselves. Instead of going through the usual social exercise of introducing ourselves to the prison officials present, Tex and I were standing there cross-legged and bouncing, asking where the nearest restroom was. It was close call, but I made it.

Before I was able to enter the restroom in the hallway, the coroner of Escambia County, AL, who had witnessed the execution grabbed me by the arm and took me to the side. He was upset, explaining that the execution hadn't gone well. Evans, in the process of the execution, had been burned by the electrodes. That explained the smoke and smell in the air. To add insult to injury, family practice physicians from Atmore, AL, were not sure that Evans was indeed dead after the first cycle of electricity. During the first cycle, the electrode to the left leg had caught fire and completely burned through the strap holding the electrode in place. This had resulted in a lot of sparking, arcing, and smoke production.

Evans's attorney was so upset that he demanded that a request be sent to Governor Wallace, bringing the execution to an immediate halt.

Governor Wallace wisely refused to intervene. After rigging the leg electrode to the leg via a strap from the chair, Evans was given another cycle of current. Again witnesses claimed there was a lot of smoke and flame produced by the current. After this cycle, the two physicians again entered the death chamber to examine Evans. One physician felt that he still heard a faint heartbeat, while the other felt that the heart had ceased to beat. With a conflict of opinions, the warden elected to give another cycle of current. After this last cycle, both physicians felt that Evans was dead.

We walked into the death chamber to see a figure with a black hood over his face sitting in "Yellow Mama." He was dressed in white prison clothes. Prison officials helped us remove the body from the chair and place it onto our stretcher. The body was so hot from the electric current that had been sent through him that we were barely able to grip the body with our gloved hands to get it transferred to our stretcher.

At this point, I felt uncomfortable. The radiologist who was to receive Evans's body was a pulmonary specialist. To get the best possible use from the body, he needed the lungs inflated to a normal inspiratory level. Correctly, he was afraid that if he waited until the body arrived in Mobile to inflate the lungs, the degree of postmortem rigor, or stiffening of the muscles after death, would make inflation of the lungs impossible.

Since I was the only person available with the medical background and experience, though it was distant experience, I was elected to intubate Evans and inflate his lungs.

I was nervous about this. I hadn't intubated anyone since medical school. The main pitfall to avoid was keeping the tube out of the esophagus of the patient. The esophagus is the upper tube leading to the stomach. It sits just behind the glottis or opening to the lungs. It's a well-known and dreaded mistake in emergency rooms to get the tube down the wrong hole. If I blew this, the body was worthless to the radiologist. As they laid Evans down on my stretcher, I could feel that he was already going into rigor. I quickly pulled out the laryngeal scope and endotracheal tube and began the intubation. As I started, I could hear the guards muttering in the background, asking what I was doing. I chuckled to myself as I heard one guard say, "I think he's trying to revive him." It was too late for that. On my first attempt at intubation, I had difficulty visualizing the glottis with the laryngeal scope. I pushed the tube down the throat and knew that I was in the esophagus. This did nothing to lower my anxieties. I pulled the tube out of Evans's throat and tried again. This time, I was relieved to see the glottis quite clearly and could watch the tube slip down the correct hole.

Worrying that this had taken more time than it should have, I quickly inflated the cuff of the tube in the airway. This sealed off the airway around the tube, keeping air within the lungs from leaking out around the outside of the tube. My next task was to inflate the lungs. The easiest way to do this was to take a relatively deep breath, blow into the tube, and quickly clamp off the tube before the natural elastic recoil of the chest could blow the breath out of the lungs. In my nervousness and worry to get the body moved, I made a grave mistake. Instead of taking a deep breath before I put my mouth to the tube, I put my mouth to the tube and took a deep breath. In the process, I inhaled all the stale air from Evans's lungs and airways. It had a distinctive charcoal taste.

I usually pride myself on having a strong stomach, but this was one time I could feel waves of nausea rolling through my entire body. It took all the control I had to keep from vomiting on the floor of the death chamber. After a few seconds that seemed like minutes, I regained control of my stomach. I took a deep breath of air, inflated the lungs, cross-clamped the tube, and helped cover the body before placing it in the back of the department station wagon.

After getting the prison officials to sign the release papers, we were ready to leave. Ironically, there was a severe storm blowing through. Driving back was like a scene from an old horror movie with lightning flashing and thunder crashing all around us. Tex, always eager to joke, commented on this and stated that at any second, Evans just might reach out to grab us from the back of the station wagon. I laughed at Tex but also glanced over my shoulder to make sure that Evans hadn't moved.

We were escorted back to Mobile by two state trooper cars. Allegedly, there had been some threats by groups against capital punishment. No one believed anything would happen, but we were relieved to have the troopers with us. All during the drive, rain was pouring down to the point that we were having difficulty seeing the road. It took two hours to get back to Mobile, twice as long as the usual trip.

When we got off the interstate and back onto the streets of Mobile, things got worse. Since Mobile is a port city, it has a relatively low elevation relative to the water table. That, coupled with its high annual rainfall, leads to poor drainage and recurrent flooding. This night was more spectacular than usual. As we took the roads to the hospital, we progressively got into even deeper and deeper water (no pun intended). Water was literally coming into the wagon at the bottom of the doors. One of our trooper escorts drowned out his engine trying to lead us through the streets. All we could do was keep moving. All the while, I kept having visions of having to load our cargo on my back to carry him to dry land, but fate was with us, and our wagon, coughing and spitting, managed to get us through the waters. Where is Moses when you really need him?

We arrived at the medical center to a flood of television lights. Hospital security was present to keep the overanxious reporters from blocking our entrance. After some X-ray studies to confirm that the radiology department was receiving a usable specimen, we took the body to the autopsy facility for examination.

Although I pride myself on being thorough with my cases, this was even more painstaking than usual. I knew that a large number of people would be looking at this report, especially since things hadn't gone as well as expected. In retrospect, the prison officials had probably made one public relations error.

Members of the press corps had been allowed to view the first cycle of current in the execution by closed-circuit television. After the first cycle, the camera was turned off, leaving them in the dark as to what was going on during the subsequent two cycles of current. This, coupled with the understandably distraught testimony given by witnesses representing Evans in the execution chamber, added fuel to the journalistic fires.

Contrary to what the local public perceived from the news media, Evans's body wasn't charred beyond recognition. There were, however, some severe localized injuries to the body most prominent at the site of the electrodes on the head and left leg. These injuries were fourth-degree burns in that they penetrated through the skin to the underlying bone or muscle tissue. On the head, they were localized circumferentially about the head in a hatband pattern. There was severe charring of the surrounding skin. The burning at the site of the other electrode, the left leg, was more focal or smaller in area, but again a fourth-degree burn to the underlying skeletal muscle. These, in my opinion, were arc-type burns. They are formed in the same way as the arc used in arc welding. Instead of the electrode being in direct contact with the grounding object, there is a small gap between the electrode and the ground. If there is enough voltage in the electrode, the current will jump from the electrode to the ground and in the process create a tremendous amount of heat, usually in the thousands-of-degree range. This was more than enough heat to account for the thermal injuries on Evans's body. Actually, aside from the thermal injuries to the body, there was little to report. The toxicology examination of Evans's blood for drugs and alcohol was negative as expected.

One of the aspects of forensic pathology that keeps you alert is that you never know what unanswered questions concerning the autopsy will arise weeks, sometimes months or years, after the autopsy is completed. This case was no exception. Some months later, I received a call from an attorney in Montgomery regarding the execution. It seems that he represented Evans's accomplice in the robbery and murder. His client was also sentenced to die in the electric chair for the crime. In the ongoing attempts at obtaining a new trial or release, an appeal had been offered to the federal court in Mobile. The jest of the appeal was that Alabama's electric chair should be considered cruel and unusual punishment and, as such, would be in violation of a condemned individual's constitutional rights. The core question in the appeal was whether Evans suffered any pain during his execution. Obviously, that question was directed at me and other expert medical witnesses.

To be able to give and adequately explain an answer to this question, the reader must first have an understanding of how electricity kills. Electricity kills by either one of two ways determined by the voltage involved. In low-voltage type of deaths, as commonly seen in household accidents involving 110-volt home wiring systems, the mechanism of death is ventricular fibrillation of the heart. This means that the current traveling through the body causes the heart to go into a dysrhythmia, that is, the normal small electrical impulses initiated in the heart muscle itself and passing through the heart muscle, causing it to contract in a coordinated fashion and thus pump blood, are disrupted. Instead, the electrical current causes different muscles to contract out of sequence so that instead of a coordinated contraction resulting in the pumping of blood, the heart sits there and twitches, each fiber acting as an individual entity, with no blood being pumped. A common sequence of events is that an individual screams out as he/she is shocked, walks a few steps, and falls down dead. The time interval between the shock and death is the time that it takes to lose consciousness from a lack of oxygen. These individuals can often be saved by cardiopulmonary resuscitation.

High-voltage shocks, that is, greater than one thousand volts, usually kill by disrupting respiration or breathing. They do this either by causing the muscles used in breathing to contract and stay contracted or by their heat effect, causing the brain and muscles to coagulate much like an egg being hard-boiled. These high-voltage currents have little effect on the heart. The reason is that the current is so strong that instead of allowing individual heart muscle fibers to twitch or contract independently, high-voltage electricity causes all the muscle fibers to contract at one time and stay contracted. When the body is no longer in contact with the electrical current, all muscle fibers relax from contraction at the same time and allow the normal electrical impulse in the heart to start and travel through the heart by its normal pathways resulting in coordinated contraction and blood pumping. Interestingly, this is the same principle used by doctors when they use those paddles to shock or defibrillate a patient having a heart attack.

This also explains why doctors at the execution kept hearing a heartbeat. When the current was on, Evans's heart was totally contracted by the high-voltage current. When the current was turned off, however, all the fibers in his heart could relax at the same time and initiate a normal heartbeat. Had Evans never received another sequence of electricity after the first, he wouldn't have recovered. The heat damage to his brain was such that the area of his brain needed to initiate breathing was destroyed. His heart would have only continued to beat until it ran out of oxygen. It then would have stopped on its own, probably some five to ten minutes later.

Interestingly, some electrical systems used in electric chairs in other states are designed to avoid this problem. Instead of turning off completely at a high voltage at the end of the cycle, allowing the heart to resume a normal rhythm like the Alabama chair, the voltage is slowly decreased to a level seen in household electrocutions, resulting in ventricular fibrillation as described above. In ventricular fibrillation, there's no heartbeat to hear with a stethoscope; thus, the victim is pronounced legally dead usually after just one sequence.

Did Evans feel any pain from the electrocution? No. The pain receptors in the body transmit electrical impulses to the brain where they're perceived as pain. These fibers transmit impulses at the speed of several yards per second. Electricity, on the other, hand travels at the speed of light or 186,000 miles per second. Electricity to the brain also results in a complete loss of consciousness because the brain transmits from brain cell to brain cell by small electrical impulses. Thus, in my opinion, by the time that a nerve from the scalp could transmit an impulse to the brain screaming pain, the electrical current from the chair traveling at the speed of light had already rendered Evans unconscious. He was unconscious instantaneously.

Much was also made of the fact that Evans's body had received such severe burns. This problem was in the electrode design. Ideally, the electrodes should have a large enough area to transmit all the current to the skin with as little heat generated as possible. The electrodes in the Evans case were made of copper, an excellent conductor. Contact from the electrode to the skin was made by a large saline-soaked sponge, also a good conductor. As the death cap was pulled tight over Evans's head, however, the copper rim of the cap was pulled lower than the sponge. This allowed the copper rim of the cap to rest some inches from the skin of the head. When the high voltage was initiated, it arced across this gap, resulting in the high temperature, fourth-degree burns noted at autopsy. This could be easily prevented in subsequent executions by redesigning the electrodes.

After my testimony in federal court as well as other expert witnesses saying basically the same, the federal judges denied the appeal. The end result was that I had my first opportunity to testify in federal court and had the opportunity to sort out a complex issue.

One embarrassing incident that occurred during the lead up to my testimony in federal court involved a pretrial interview with Alabama attorney general Charlie Graddick. On the day prior to my testimony, one of Graddick's assistants called me to meet with the attorney general to go over my testimony. While on first blush this may sound unethical, in point of fact, it was quite common for the opposing attorneys to go over my testimony prior to my testimony in court. In fact, in many instances it would be considered malpractice for any attorney to go into court unaware of what a witness's testimony would be. In this instance, it was even more important because, unlike a routine case, Graddick was actually defending the state of Alabama rather than prosecuting the case. He was thus a bit out of his element.

The attorney general's assistant explained that they had just arrived from Montgomery that morning prior to the court date the next day. He asked if I could drop by the motel room where they were headquartered and meet with them at 1:00 p.m. He then told me the name and room number of their motel and stated that they would be expecting me.

I was a bit early for the appointment at the motel as I banged on the door to the room number I had been given. On my first attempt, there was no response from inside the room. Assuming that they hadn't heard my knock, I banged harder, then even harder on my third attempt. This time I could hear movement in the room prior to the door opening just wide enough for an unusually large, black male to stick his head out the door and ask what I wanted. Behind him I could see an attractive black woman trying to hide beneath the covers of the large double bed in the room.

When I asked if the Alabama attorney general was in the room the man became obviously scared while his female companion just uttered a low moan.

He went on to explain to me that the attorney general wasn't in his room and had never been there. He then slammed the door in my face as I stood there puzzled by what had just taken place. I went into the motel office and asked the clerk if Mr. Graddick had checked into another room, but was informed that no one answering to that name was in the register.

Since this was before the era of cell phones, I used the motel office phone to call my office and speak to my investigator, Brian Delmas. After I had related my tale of woe, Brian informed me that there was another motel from that franchise located out on the interstate, not downtown where I was standing at that moment.

As I hurried out to my car, I saw the black couple rushing to get into a car parked adjacent to their motel room. When I pulled into the other motel, I found the attorney general and his assistants awaiting my arrival. I suspect that my interview went a bit better than the midday rendezvous that I had interrupted between the boss and his secretary. If he happens to read this story, I hope he will accept my sincere apology. I also hope your wife never found out (I saw your wedding band).

If I were to be honest with myself, even at that point I knew I wouldn't be finished with my involvement in the death of John Lewis Evans. Things remained relatively quiet until the autumn months of 1985. One day, out of the blue, I received a call from the *20/20* news program of ABC news in Washington, D. C. It seems they were doing a program segment on capital punishment to be aired nationally sometime in October. Somehow they had come across my name as the pathologist who had done Evans's autopsy. They were going to be in the Mobile area at the end of the next week and asked if I would be available for an interview. I was caught totally off guard. I mumbled something about being out of town at that time, but that I would check my schedule and get back with them later.

After getting off the phone I immediately talked to Dr. Riddick about the interview. He voiced concerns as to the political implications of the interview as well as concerns about how the interview might be edited. He suggested that I call the state director of our department, Mr. Rabren, for suggestions. Mr. Rabren echoed Dr. Riddick's concerns and suggested that I call our legal consultant in the attorney general's office. The attorney general's office saw no conflict of interest in the interview and felt that the testimony I had given in federal court had actually been favorable to the state's point of view. The bottom line was that it would have to be my own decision.

That night, I discussed the interview with Beth and had pretty much decided that I had very little to gain from the interview but a whole lot to lose. The next day, as I called *20/20*, I had made up my mind to decline. The production supervisor in Washington stated that they were anxious to have my interview and a medical point of view to offset an interview conducted with a neurologist from England. Afraid that my absence from the program would give the neurologist increased credibility for any opinions differing from my own, I agreed to the interview, that is, I now had more to lose by not doing the interview.

The interview itself was to be conducted at our laboratory in Mobile, AL. It was scheduled on a Thursday afternoon after normal working hours so as not to disrupt the laboratory any more than necessary. At the appointed hour two vans and a Lincoln Continental pulled up to our office. The investigative reporter was the legal correspondent for *20/20,* Mr. Tim O'Brian. Also present, in addition to the camera crew, was the producer, Mr. Martin Clancy.

The first decision to be made was the location for the interview. Our office has a nice conference room lined by bookcases. It had always been the site of previous interviews. That wasn't the type background they were looking for, however. They asked to be taken to the autopsy suite. Months before we had even moved into our new building, Dr. Riddick and I had agreed that because of the images associated with the county morgue, we would avoid conducting any interviews in the autopsy suite. When I explained this to the reporter and producer, they responded as though I was trying to hide something. Fortunately, a member of the camera crew came forward and stated that the large amount of stainless steel in the room would make reflections from the TV lights a problem.

At this point, I was beginning to wonder what I had gotten myself into. We went from room to room in the laboratory until they decided that the toxicology lab was a reasonable backdrop for the interview. Knowing that the interview was to be on national TV, I had dressed in my most professional-looking outfit, a dark-blue pinstriped suit. Mr. O'Brian took one look at me and asked that I change into surgical greens and white coat for the interview. Realizing that a person has to draw the line somewhere, I responded that I refused to be interviewed on national television looking like I was in my pajamas.

It seemed like it took hours for the camera crew to get all the lights and sound system set up for the interview. Mr. O'Brian did throw some curves with his questions, but all in all, I felt that he had given me an ample chance to answer and explain my answers. As the Continental and vans pulled away that night, I was relieved that the interview was over. How the interview would be edited was my only remaining fear.

The subsequent months to the airing went by slowly. Finally, however, the appointed hour arrived. In all honesty, I felt that the team did a good job presenting both sides of a complex issue. Although not as eloquent as I would have liked to have been, most of the points I've tried to make in this chapter came across. After hearing the interview of the neurologist from England, I was actually glad that I had agreed to the interview at least to partially offset what I consider to be his scientifically unfounded claims about electrocution.

To say the least, my mother and relatives in St. Louis were thrilled to see their only son on national TV. The only negative outcome has been numerous prolonged telephone interviews conducted by reporters from local newspapers throughout the country on capital punishment by electrocution.

Needless to say, the name John Lewis Evans brings up many conflicting emotions. It's one of the few cases in which I've been put in a situation where my truthful testimony was in defense of a system of killing. I think that I'll always have problems with capital punishment and the liberal public who, instead of really being concerned as to whether the method of execution causes the victim pain, are really concerned that the method isn't repulsive to their own sensitivities when the execution is either witnessed personally or graphically described.

A case before the public eye as much as the Evans execution taught me a lot. It forced me to read any and everything I could find on the subject, in this case the mechanism of death by electricity. The last thing you want to happen is to be confronted with a question you should know the answer to but don't.

Needless to say, by the time all the legal proceedings and public interest in the case had waned, I knew a fair amount about electricity in general and death by electricity in particular. The professional advantage to this is that not only are you able to comfortably document those cases of electrical death which are obvious to everyone involved, but it also raises the threshold of suspicion in terms of looking for the possibility of electricity as the etiology of the death in various situations.

As previously stated, low-voltage-type electrocutions cause death by the mechanism of ventricular fibrillation. Interestingly, the heat generated by the electricity as it passes through its source of greatest resistance in the body, the skin, is only great enough to result in current marks in some forty percent of cases. "Current marks" are localized burns of the skin resulting from the heat generated as the current passes through the skin's resistance. Thus, in 60 percent of the low-voltage deaths, there's no cutaneous evidence to alert the investigating pathologist. The internal portion of the examination is equally nonspecific, with congestion of the organs the only finding. Thus, if the deceased individual has a significant degree of heart disease, he or she may be erroneously categorized as dying from natural disease allowing a potentially dangerous piece of equipment free to kill again or allowing an unsafe method of working on electrical equipment to continue.

A situation similar to this occurred some eighteen months after the Evans execution. A fifty-five-year-old white male electrician and his electrician son were in the process of rewiring an electrical box to be used to run a 440-volt motor. Allegedly, all the wires leading into the box were dead, that is, there was no electricity flowing or potentially flowing through them at the time.

While standing on a suspended grating some fifty feet above the ground, the elder electrician, according to his son standing nearby, let out a loud grunt and quickly slumped to his knees. The son immediately grabbed his father to prevent him from falling. Help was called, and resuscitation began, thinking that the older man was having a heart attack. The electrician was quickly removed from the catwalk and, with the industrial nurse performing resuscitation, transported immediately to a local emergency room. There, despite aggressive resuscitative procedures, he died.

When the death was reported to our office, we immediately raised the possibility of an electrocution. The son who had witnessed the death was also a certified electrician and strongly denied the possibility of electrocution. He maintained that his father was an extremely cautious worker around electricity and went to great pains to make sure that each and every job was done safely.

The subsequent autopsy examination, however, proved otherwise. Located on the web between the thumb and forefinger of his right hand was a raised, dried one-fourth-inch focus of light-brown tissue with a dark core. Interestingly, the remainder of the autopsy revealed a nonspecific congestion of the internal organs and a significant degree of coronary atherosclerosis, or narrowing of the arteries supplying the heart muscle with blood.

Without the current mark, I could have been easily convinced that the coronary atherosclerosis was severe enough to explain the death. Microscopic studies of the questionable current mark revealed the streaming of the nuclei of the skin cells and the coagulation of the surrounding tissue described in electrical current marks of the skin. With this information in hand, I informed the son and the company who owned the job site that in my opinion the cause of death was due to electrical shock and the manner of death was accidental. Because I would be the last person to claim any expertise in electrical circuitry, I called the local Office of Occupational Safety (OSHA) to investigate the scene. He returned with the verdict that, despite the electrician's attempts to make the job safe, there were indeed some safety violations that would confirm my diagnosis.

This category of cases proves as well as any that there's often a significant difference between appearances and reality as it relates to the cause and manner of death. I've often wondered how many cases of low-voltage electrical death I've missed because of the absence of current marks on the body and inadequate background information. Interestingly, in cases such as this, the autopsy on the equipment involved is often as important as or more important than the autopsy of the deceased. In this case, after good background investigation as well as a complete autopsy, the family was eligible to receive benefits from Workman's Compensation as well as benefits from any accidental rider present on life insurance policies' benefits received despite their original denials.

Some bizarre cases are equally tragic. This subdivision of the bizarre usually involves children, and the following case falls within that arena. From a professional point of view, this case also emphasizes the point that many times a good scene examination can keep the investigator from making a terrible mistake. The case in point occurred in Mobile, AL, and involved a twelve-month-old black male who had been rushed to the University of South Alabama emergency room in cardiac arrest. Despite aggressive attempts at resuscitation, the infant was pronounced dead. The body was brought down to the morgue with the clinical history (the best guess of the doctors in the emergency room who attempted the resuscitation) suspecting that the child was a case of sudden infant death syndrome.

On first glance, that wasn't an unreasonable diagnosis. The child was a well-nourished little guy without a mark on his body other than those put there by the resuscitation team upstairs. Since SIDS is a diagnosis of exclusion occurring usually in infants aged four to fourteen months, it was up to us in the medical examiner's office to exclude everything else that could fit the findings and cause the death.

I need to say something here which won't sit well with my medical colleagues. My advice to you or any of your loved ones you care about, try not to go to a teaching hospital for any condition from July 1 until at least Halloween. This is particularly true for serious, life-threatening conditions where the clinical outcome depends on constant physician oversight and input.

The reason for this is that after July first the interns who are given the primary responsibility for taking care of you are fresh out of their medical school training. They don't have a clue about what they're doing. Let me quickly add that the learning curve for a new intern is extremely steep, and it doesn't take long; in fact, it's downright amazing how quickly the intern develops into a competent physician, but the whole intern teaching concept is that of a trial by fire, and if you're the critically ill patient, you don't want to be burned by the process.

The reason I bring up this particular point here is that the diagnosis of SIDS that came down with the body of this child was probably made by an intern who was still extremely wet behind the ears.

Because of the policies of our office at the time, there was no way that this child was going to be released to a funeral home without an autopsy. That fact still didn't mean that the case would be interpreted correctly. The autopsy examination both externally and internally was completely normal except for a small amount of congestion in all the internal organs which could probably be explained by the resuscitation attempts. The follow-up toxicology and bacterial cultures were equally negative. A complete histological examination where I looked at each organ under the microscope after they had been stained was unremarkable except for the congestion that I noticed grossly, but this was the expected findings for a diagnosis of SIDS, an autopsy where both a complete gross examination and a complete microscopic examination coupled with toxicology and bacteriologic cultures are all completely normal. The only problem was that this wasn't a case of SIDS. It was a death due to accidental electrocution.

If the reader at this point is saying to himself or herself that that Cumberland guy must be an unbelievably bright individual, let me refer you to my wife. All kidding aside, the whole key to the correct diagnosis in this case depended on a good, thorough scene examination, something not pursued in all medical examiner's and coroner's offices. Since this death came through the emergency room at our trauma hospital, it would have been easy to just accept the word of the physicians taking care of the infant and follow their opinion down the wrong path of the decision tree to the wrong diagnosis of SIDS. Instead, because I had a group of extremely thorough investigators working for me in our office, they took the time to make the hour drive to the home of the victim and the scene of the incident. That trip moved the case over to the correct branch of the decision tree toward the correct diagnosis.

This is what my investigators found. The location of the infant's home was way out in the boondocks of western Mobile County, AL, almost to the Mississippi line. Extreme poverty was the rule out there, and if the parents were able to work, it was intermittent labor at the farm of a family who was equally struggling to make ends meet. Our family lived in an old trailer that had seen more years than I had lived at the time.

The family was composed of the father and mother as well as five siblings who were stair-stepped in age up from our victim, who had been the youngest. As mentioned previously, this occurred in midsummer when daily temperatures were hitting ninety degrees plus, and the humidity was almost high enough to swim through the air, a typical Alabama summer. It goes without saying that the trailer wasn't air-conditioned.

The father had been without work for some time and stated that about a week previously, the power company had come out and turned off their service to the trailer. To circumvent the power outage, the father had jury-rigged an outlet on the power pole that had previously held the electric meter to the trailer. He used a standard inside electric outlet that he tied into the power line just before the power would have entered the meter. The outlet was energized with 110-volt electricity. To get the electricity from the outside power pole to the trailer, seven separate old light-duty indoor extension cords were connected end to end and finally plugged into a wall outlet inside the living room of the trailer. All the lights, fans, and appliances in the trailer were run off this single string of extension cords.

The potential fire hazard involved in this arrangement would have caused a fire marshal's hair to turn prematurely gray, but fire wasn't involved in the infant's death. To shut the front screen door on the trailer to keep the flies out of the trailer, the father had unscrewed the aluminum threshold to the front door and run one of the extension cords under the aluminum, replacing the screws to allow the screen door to shut tightly. Access to the front entrance of the trailer where the electricity cord entered was achieved by a single, free standing aluminum metal step so that, to enter the trailer, they had to step up from the ground onto the step, then stepped up to enter the front door of the trailer. Over time, the aluminum threshold had cut through the extension cord running under it. This in turn had energized the threshold to 110 volts just like the current running through the extension cord.

So how was the infant lethally shocked while the other family members could use the doorway with impunity? The answer lies in how each member of the family went through the door. If old enough, or rather tall enough, to step from the trailer threshold to the aluminum step without touching the side trim of the trailer's front doorway or without having a foot on both the threshold and aluminum step, there would be no shock because the individual wouldn't be completing a circuit from the energized threshold to the ground.

The key was that the older children and adults never had one foot on the threshold and one foot on the aluminum step at a time, nor were they touching the trim surrounding the door while standing on the energized threshold. The infant, who was just learning to walk, had to hold on to the aluminum doorframe as he stepped from the energized threshold to the aluminum step.

Because he was just learning how to maintain his balance while walking, he would also have had one foot on the threshold with the other foot on the step at the same time while exiting the trailer. By having one foot on the threshold and at the same time having the other foot on the step or holding on to the doorframe, the infant would have grounded the energized threshold through his body and was therefore shocked. Rubber-soled shoes would have also offered some protection, but since it was the middle of summer, everyone was going barefoot. We were quickly able to prove our theory by the use of a voltmeter that we always carried as part of our crime scene kit. A 110-volt potential ran from the threshold to ground.

The scene findings explain the initial story that the mother gave to the paramedics when they arrived at the scene. She had stated that the infant was going out to play with his siblings when she heard him cry out. He was lying on the ground next to the step unconscious when she came running to help. The death was signed out as an electrocution with the manner of death classified as accidental.

This is one of those situations where knowing the truth and getting the right people involved can have a positive result. Once the power company had been notified about the death, they sent representatives out to the trailer and restored their power legally through a charitable program that the company sponsored. The tragedy of the death and its precipitating circumstances allowed the family to gain access to various charitable organizations both private and governmental, so they were soon moved into better housing and received financial help through those programs. It was one of those times when it felt good to be at least partially responsible for making some good come out of tragedy.

SUICIDE: SELF-INFLICTED HOMICIDE

The one category of death that causes the surviving family the greatest anguish is suicide. We define suicide medically and legally as a person taking his/her own life with intent. Most families of suicide victims experience an incredible load of guilt. They feel that there had to be some subtle change in the deceased that, if they had noticed, they could have prevented the death. Frequently, even trivial disagreements between family members assume gigantic proportions in retrospect. There had to have been something they could have done to prevent the unnecessary death. A social distaste for suicide is also echoed in many religions where suicide is considered a sin against the church.

From the forensic pathologist's point of view, suicides can be some of the most emotionally trying cases. Instead of having to convince law enforcement officers and a relatively unbiased jury in court of the cause and manner of death, we instead have to convince a grieving family of the circumstances behind the death. Sometimes this is impossible, and we have to be content that we've convinced only ourselves.

My personal opinion is that everyone has the moral right to take his/her own life. Putting my religious convictions aside, it can be a logical path to follow. Consider the patient who's suffering from a terminal cancer resulting in severe pain not responsive to pain medication. There's no medical hope for recovery, and medical treatments may be continuing to exhaust what little financial resources left to the family. In this instance, suicide might be considered a reasonable alternative.

From a professional point of view, however, those people determined to commit suicide should take time to document their intentions and explain to the family their reasons for this final step. This, however, is not the usual case. In our experience, only about 15 percent of suicide victims leave a note, at least a note that can be found by law enforcement at the time of the investigation.

Most physicians and psychologists also believe that there are degrees of intent to end one's life classified much like the levels of intent used in homicide classifications. Obviously, there are many people who attempt suicide but don't wish to truly end their lives. Sometimes these suicide gestures or attempts go further than the victim had intended. A significant percentage is actually staged so that intervention is at least strongly possible. Most people agree that these attempts at suicide are a cry for help. Telephone suicide prevention programs do much to help these desperate individuals.

Suicide investigation, like accidental death investigations, falls heavily into the medical investigator's lap. In my experience, police agencies tend not to investigate suicides to the same depth that they investigate homicides. The reason for this is simple. Suicides are criminal acts that have solved themselves, that is, the person committing the crime is also the victim. Police agencies would rather expand their energies on unsolved criminal cases. Because the coroner/medical examiner is charged with determining the circumstances behind the death for purposes of death certification, he's equally responsible for being able to defend his conclusions. As previously stated, the headaches come when the level of investigation needed to convince ourselves often falls short in convincing the family.

One case that I'll remember forever occurred on a Friday evening in late winter. We received a call from the Mobile Police requesting that we come to a death scene on the campus of a local university. We arrived some minutes later at the on-campus dormitory comprising the scene. The scene of death was on the first floor of the dorm. The dorm was organized into suites with two large dormitory rooms connected by a shared bathroom. Each dorm room was built to house two students, with a central divider of built-in desks and storage.

We met the police outside of the room in the hallway. Available information at this point indicated that we were investigating the death of a nineteen-year-old coed who was assigned the room as its single occupant. Upon walking into the room, I had forgotten how depressing the painted block walls of a dorm room can be. The body of the deceased was in the far corner of the room in front of a sliding door closet. As I looked at her from a distance, I found myself mentally reviewing all the previous cases of death by hanging that I had investigated. The deceased in this case was an attractive white female dressed in a pullover-type sweater and jeans. The ligature was composed of a pink cloth sash cord from a nightgown or robe. The upper end of the sash was tied to metal handles of a storage area located above the closet. The deceased was standing upright in front of the closet, with her feet touching the floor and her legs slightly flexed at the knees and hips. On the floor at her feet was a leather belt, probably from the jeans that she was wearing. A fiberglass-molded chair, probably used with the desk in the center of the room, was next to the body. A quick look about the room revealed a lived-in look that was cluttered, but not ransacked. The deceased's purse was present in the room and contained a moderate amount of money. Personal pieces of jewelry were still present in the room.

Although I try not to jump to premature decisions about individual cases, my initial impression was that the manner of death was suicide. There are many reasons. First, although homicidal hangings do occur, they're extremely rare. It requires an incredible amount of strength to suspend a body from a ligature. If the person is conscious at the time of suspension, there should be multiple signs of superficial injury on the body of the deceased. Obviously, no one allows another person to take their lives without a struggle. Of course, it's always a possibility that the deceased was dead or rendered unconscious before being suspended. Even under these circumstances, I would expect some sign of struggle on the body, a paralyzing amount of drug in the system of the deceased, or injuries indicative of a manual strangulation of the deceased that would be separate and distinctive from the ligature mark on the neck.

The subsequent autopsy was relatively straightforward. Other than a ligature mark that coursed upward along the sides of the neck, there were no other injuries on the body. If the ligature is tied to an object located above the deceased, hanging-type ligature marks tend to travel upward on the sides of the neck, indicating a suspension at the point of attachment of the ligature to the body. Strangulations with a rope or cord, sometimes called throttling, tend to run horizontally across the sides of the neck as the assailant pulls the ligature tight.

Another point of confusion expressed by lay persons discussing hangings involves the mechanism of death. In judicial-type hangings, the mechanism of death is a fracture of the cervical spine brought about by the dropping of the body through a trap door in the gallows.

The knot of the ligature is carefully placed along the side of the neck so that the sudden jerking of the body brought about when the rope becomes taut literally snaps the neck. In addition to the placement of the knot, the height and weight of the deceased are also variables to be taken into consideration to increase the likelihood of a quick snap of the cervical spinal cord. Allegedly, back when judicial hangings were commonly performed, there were expert executioners who would set up the gallows based on the person to be executed. It was considered bad form for a victim of the gallows to die by strangulation. As previously stated, it was a judicial hanging in New York resulting in decapitation of the condemned man that led to a public outcry, resulting in the development of the electric chair as the common means of execution.

Suicidal hangings, on the other hand, have a different mechanism of death. Instead of a transection of the cervical spine, the mechanism involves the obstruction of airflow to the lungs through the trachea, a true asphyxial type of death. As a result, there's little trauma to the organs of the neck themselves, particularly when the airway and vessels of the neck are as elastic as is normal in a relatively young person. The usual autopsy findings are, in addition to the ligature mark, congestion of the brain and pinpoint hemorrhages in the conjunctivae of the eyes due to the hypoxia and/or the relative, greater compression of the veins draining blood from the head as compared to the muscular arteries supplying blood to the head.

Based on the information available from the scene and autopsy examinations, I felt that the manner of death in this case was best classified as a suicide. The information from the police investigating the case did little to change my opinion. The deceased was from an upper-middle-class family in the Midwest. Allegedly, she had become pregnant after high school and delivered a baby that she subsequently put up for adoption.

After the pregnancy, she had gone through a period of depression that, according to her friends, seemed to be improving. Like most people her age, she was allegedly anxious to be more on her own. Going away to college was an obvious solution. The choice of a college in Mobile was a compromise in that she was out of the Midwest, but near some of her mother's family, originally a native from the area. According to friends, she was unsure of a line of study at college.

I think most people would agree that, based on the background information and autopsy findings, this case, within the limits of reasonable certainty, should be classified as a suicide. The family, understandably, had grave doubts. They had sent their daughter off to college in, by most people's judgment, an improving psychological state only to receive a phone call late one evening informing them that their daughter had taken her own life. Since my initial conversation with the family on the phone that night, I had had interviews with two different attorneys representing the family, one private investigator, as well as multiple phone and person-to-person conferences with the parents.

It soon became obvious that for their psychological well-being, they needed to put this death behind them and get on with their lives. This, of course, is difficult to impossible to do until the cause and manner of death are fully accepted by the family. I would be either a liar or a fool if I purported to know beyond a shadow of a doubt what had happened or what was going through this young girl's mind at the time of her death.

Instead, what we try to do based on experience and training is to classify the death on the physical evidence and background available. Everyone enjoys watching the detective story on television where the police rule the death a suicide only to have the hero private detective come along and prove that the death was a homicide.

Unfortunately, this rarely happens in real life. The best we can do is be as honest and consistent in these cases as humanly possible, knowing full well that, regardless of how hard the investigator tries, he will never convince everyone.

The discerning reader might ask himself/herself, "What real difference does it make whether a family comes to grips with a suicide in the family?" If able to live with the denial in their own minds, that's their business, and the facts of the case shouldn't be pressed to convince them otherwise.

Well, obviously, everyone is entitled to their own thoughts and opinions. One point worth noting, however, is that a suicide within a family unit represents some problem within that family unit. Failing to acknowledge that problem, in essence, indicates that the family is failing to adapt and learn from its mistakes. The continued denial allows the pathology to continue and possibly escalate. The end result may be the dissolution of the family unit or even suicides in other family members.

Whenever this issue comes up, I'll always remember the following cases. I was on call one weekend and was presented with the death of a twenty-year-old white male. The deceased had been found in shallow water off the beach of a gulf island in south Mobile County. According to county investigators, the subject had gone to the island with his girlfriend and another couple. They had planned to camp out on the beach overnight and spend the whole night partying. According to other members of the party, the subject had decided to bring his shotgun along to protect the group from any outsiders who might take advantage of them while alone on the beach.

Allegedly, the campsite had been set up and the partying had begun sometime before nightfall. Later that night, the subject and his girlfriend had gotten into a verbal fight. The subject picked up his shotgun and stormed off to the waterfront to cool off. The fellow campers claimed that they heard the shotgun discharge several times at a distance.

Thinking that the friend was shooting toward the water, they ignored the shots. The three other members of the party finally went to bed thinking that the subject would be back by morning. He never returned. Worried about their friend's safety, they called the sheriff's office the first thing the next morning. The deceased was subsequently found in shallow water off the beach not far from the campsite.

At autopsy, the subject had a shotgun wound to the head. Obviously, everyone was concerned that the subject had been confronted on the beach and shot by another person, making his death a homicide. The autopsy examination, however, revealed that the shotgun wound was a contact-type wound, that is, the barrel of the gun was in contact with the head when the shotgun was discharged. The sheriff's office breathed a sigh of relief knowing more than likely that the shotgun death fell into a suicide category. The family was not nearly as pleased.

Background information on the deceased revealed that he was having all the problems that come to young adults his age. He was trying to decide on a career path and having ongoing problems with his girlfriend. They were allegedly trying to decide whether or not to be married. His past medical history was pertinent. The subject had been involved in an automobile crash that had resulted in head injuries. Although not physically debilitating, his injuries had rendered him susceptible to severe headaches.

Based on the background information and autopsy findings, I felt that the case was best classified as a suicide. His mother disagreed. As we do in most cases, I agreed to an appointment to discuss the autopsy findings. At that time, I discussed all the findings of the case to include the autopsy findings, the tests on the shotgun to prove that it was functioning properly and thus probably hadn't accidentally discharged, and the findings of the blood analysis showing a moderate amount of alcohol in the subject's system at the time of his death. The mother was quite gracious throughout the interview, but by the time she left, I knew she would have difficulty accepting her son's death as a suicide. Over the next several weeks, we discussed her son's death several times by phone.

To be honest, I had pretty much forgotten about the case until one morning, I was confronted with a teenager with the same last name as the above subject. I could tell immediately that his death was due to carbon monoxide poisoning. According to the police report, he had rigged a pipe to the exhaust of his car, then lay in the driveway behind the running auto with his face to the pipe. The autopsy and subsequent blood work confirmed the cause of death as carbon monoxide poisoning. The mother soon called and explained that her younger son had been devastated by the death of his older brother and couldn't come to grips with his feelings about the death. The mother was devastated as she related the information. I've seldom felt sorrier for a person than I did for this lady. I knew there was nothing I could say to console her in her loss.

Some time passed, with both brothers buried in side by side graves in a local cemetery. One afternoon, I received a call that a young female was found dead in that same cemetery. Upon arriving across town, I found a young woman lying over the graves of the two brothers. At her feet was a shotgun she had used to inflict a contact shotgun wound to her chest. I suspected right away that this was the girlfriend of the older brother. A suicide note left in her car nearby explained what to do with her valued possessions. There was no mention of the motivating reasons for taking her own life or any further insight into the deaths of the two brothers.

Obviously, there was something going on in this triangle that I'll never understand, yet I couldn't help but think that the suicide of the older brother was a clue that there were severe problems with this brother or in the family unit. The failure to acknowledge this problem and come to grips with his suicide more than likely contributed to the deaths of the other two individuals.

Acting as an objective investigator and certifier in these types of deaths, we function as a source of objective reality in the emotional process of grieving over the loss of a loved one. Hopefully, this helps the family come to grips with themselves, their family unit, and their relationships in their lives together.

As previously stated, the definition of suicide is the taking of one's own life with intent. Many families are willing to concede that their loved one took their own life, but will balk at the notion that they meant to do so or realized what they were doing. One investigative tool that can help the forensic pathologist live with his opinion in the face of the family's oppositions is the psychiatric evaluation of the deceased, or as it's more commonly known, the psychiatric autopsy. Although this additional evaluation of the deceased will seldom convince the family members, it does allow the certifier to sleep easier at night.

The evaluation is performed by a psychiatrist or group of psychiatrists who, by interviewing family members and people close to the deceased, are able in many cases to develop a feel for the mental state of the subject about the time of his or her death. In addition to helping the pathologist with the certification of the death, the psychiatric autopsy has a distinct beneficial effect on the loved ones who are going through the trauma of their loss. They're given access to a professional in psychiatry at no cost to them under circumstances that, to those observing the interviewing process from inside and outside the grieving experience, have the appearances of investigation into the case and not a personal plea for support or help.

Thus, although the purpose of the interviews is to arrive at a conclusion in the case, by the end of most interviews, the psychiatrist has a good feel for the mental state of the person being examined and whether or not a referral to another psychiatrist for further therapy is needed. The psychiatrist used in our laboratory for these evaluations is Dr. Pam Mussel, a senior resident in psychiatry.

Dr. Mussel has proved her interest and abilities in forensic psychiatry to both Dr. Riddick and myself on numerous occasions. Pam has a nonthreatening approach to the people she interviews and has been rewarded with important insight on many of our suicide cases. She not only aids the departmental investigators in getting needed information but also helps improve their interview techniques so they less frequently come across as police investigators. My interview techniques have also improved under her tutelage.

The following case shows the importance of her input into the investigation. Our office received a call from the deputy coroner of a county in the northern portion of our jurisdiction stating that they had found an elderly white male sitting behind the wheel of his pickup truck with his throat cut. The subject was well known in the community and well respected by his peers. He was a retired local businessman. His wife at the time of his death was away visiting out-of-state relatives. When contacted about her husband's death, she immediately returned home.

Allegedly, she admitted that her husband was undergoing some depression during the past few weeks. He had a fear that the books from a previous business were being audited after his partner's death and that he in turn would be found to owe a considerable amount of money to his partner's estate. This would be money that he didn't have available. He feared that the bankruptcy of his personal estate would be an embarrassment to himself and his family who lived in the same community. This fear had been supported by a letter received from an attorney handling the estate stating that there had been some errors found in the books that would need rectifying before his partner's estate could be settled. The wife had invited the subject to accompany her on the family visit, but he had declined stating he wanted to be at home to receive any news.

Late in the afternoon before his death, the deceased was observed at his bank withdrawing a large sum of money. He was last seen climbing into his pickup truck to leave the bank. According to neighbors, on the evening of his death, three young male strangers were seen in the area. The men were promptly found, questioned, and arrested pending the investigation into the death at hand.

When the body arrived at our laboratory for autopsy, I immediately had an uneasy feeling about the case. As mentioned by the coroner, the deceased had an incised or cut wound to the neck. In addition were two stab wounds to the left lower abdomen. The incised wound to the neck, however, didn't look like homicidally inflicted cuts to the neck that I had examined previously. In most cases when a person slits another person's throat, he/she pulls the head back and cut with one deep stroke. It's not unusual for these cuts to completely transect the larynx (voice box), trachea (windpipe), and the upper esophagus (muscular tube leading to the stomach). Often the arteries and veins leading to and from the head are cut with the incision extending deep enough to cut into the bony spine in the neck.

In this case, the incised wound to the neck began on the right and became deeper as it progressed to the left. Although the skin and neck muscles had been cut, resulting in a large amount of bleeding, the incision to the larynx was relatively superficial, not even extending into the lumen of the airway. In addition, along the right margin of the wound were multiple small superficial cuts which I interpreted as hesitation marks. Presumably when a person cuts himself, the fear or presence of pain is such that it's difficult for him or her to make one deep cut. Instead, he/she tends to cut themselves superficially at first to either build up his/her nerve or test the amount of pain he/she will experience.

The stab wounds in this case were equally interesting. Although there were two stab wound defects to the skin surface of the abdomen, internally there were five defects to the front of the stomach, three defects through the back wall of the stomach, and two stab wounds that traveled slightly upward to pierce the underside of the left lobe of the liver. The stab wounds were such that, once the knife had pierced the anterior abdominal wall, the knife was then probed about internally, stopping when the pain became too great, only to move the tip of the blade and try to push inward. The multiple attempts were successful when the knife blade finally incised an adequate number of small arteries and veins resulting in enough internal bleeding to cause shock and death.

Although I thought the wounds had the appearance of self-inflicted injuries, investigators at the scene remained convinced that the death was a homicide. Supposedly the large sum of money that the subject had withdrawn from the bank was missing. To add credence to their suspicions, at autopsy, the deceased had multiple small cuts on the fingers of his hands, commonly called defense-type wounds. These occur when the victim attempts to grab the knife being thrust at him or her.

Because of the unanswered questions from the scene investigation as well as the defense-type cuts to the hands, I felt that the death was best left undetermined from a certification point of view. This would allow a death certificate to be issued and at the same time wouldn't handicap any subsequent homicide investigation.

Some weeks later, Dr. Mussel and I were talking and I mentioned the case to her in passing. I stated that although I felt that the case was probably a suicide, I just didn't have enough information to defend my viewpoint. She volunteered to look into the case.

Her subsequent interviews with the wife cleared up the ambiguities. After a few sessions with the wife, Dr. Mussel was able to get the wife to fully open up to her. She admitted that she felt that the death was a suicide and had even found a note left to her by her husband explaining his state of mind over what he thought would be his impending bankruptcy.

The money initially thought to be missing was subsequently found in the house. The police had already discovered this information and had released the men originally arrested. It seems all agencies involved in the case knew more than we did, at least until Dr. Mussel talked to the wife. Interestingly, Dr. Mussel was the only person in whom the wife had confided concerning the suicide note. This in part probably explains why so few notes are recovered from suicide scenes. Based on Dr. Mussel's interview, I was able to amend my report to classify the death as a suicide. In addition, she allowed me to gain some confidence in my opinions based on relatively subtle findings noted at the autopsy.

Sadly enough, the letter from the attorneys representing our subject's estate finally arrived some ten days after his death. Indeed, there had been an error in the company books, but instead of the subject owing his partner's estate a large sum of money, a check for several thousand dollars was enclosed, representing the money that the partner's estate owed our subject.

In many instances, suicides committed with a gun are usually straightforward, except when they're not. I say that they can be straightforward because in many or most instances, the gunshot wounds to the body of an individual committing suicide are contact wounds where the end of the barrel is in contact with the skin surface when the gun or shotgun is discharged. When inflicted over a bony surface like the side of the skull, there tends to be a stellate tearing of the skin around the wound caused by the gases being produced by the explosion of the bullet dissecting between the bone and skin around the entrance defect. This is also usually accompanied by abundant burned and unburned gunpowder granules which can give the entrance defect a dirty appearance.

Contact gunshot wounds located over skin without underlying bone usually result in a small wound of entry, the edges of which are charred and abraded as the bullet passes through. In addition to the hole, however, there's often a patterned abrasion on the skin surrounding the entry hole that we call a muzzle imprint. This forms when the gases produced by the gunpowder explosion follow the bullet through the entrance wound, causing the underlying soft tissues to balloon up and literally slap the skin surface against the muzzle of the gun giving a superficial abrasion of the skin. Often this abrasion has the same configuration as the end of the discharging gun muzzle. Some terminal ballistic experts also call this a muzzle tattoo.

When a medical examiner sees either of these two wound types, although he can't diagnose the wound as resulting from a definite suicide, he knows that the gun muzzle was close enough to be considered a possible suicide. This, combined with associated scene and background findings, can give the examiner a level of comfort with a suicide classification.

Of course, there's always the possibility that the gunshot wound was inflicted by another person in an execution type shooting where the victim is being restrained or controlled such that the assailant can put the muzzle on the skin surface prior to discharging the gun. This happened in one of my cases.

After a prolonged hospital stay, a young married woman died as the result of a gunshot wound to the right side of her head. The police investigation revealed that the woman had been severely depressed for some months prior to taking the hand-gun and shooting herself in the right side of the head, a common placement of a self-inflicted bullet wound in a right-handed individual. The husband claimed that he had come home from work to find her lying on the kitchen floor with the head wound. There was no note. My autopsy examination confirmed that she had died from a contact wound to the head.

Based on the autopsy finding of the contact gunshot wound, the history of depression confirmed by the deceased's psychiatrist who had the patient on medication for depression, I signed the case out as a suicide and went on to the next case. Some three months later I received a call from the district attorney asking whether the wound that the women had could have been inflicted by her husband. I explained that I could say with absolute confidence that the gunshot wound was a contact wound, but that I couldn't swear that the wound hadn't been inflicted by another person.

The district attorney went on to explain that during the hospitalization one of the nurses taking care of the deceased overheard the husband whispering in the patient's ear that he was glad that he had killed her and that he looked forward to taking her life insurance money and finding a real woman who knew what a man wanted and needed. The nurse claimed that she was able to exit the room without being seen and had been afraid to contact the police with the information until after the woman died because of what the husband might do to her as the sole witness.

The police reopened the investigation and found that there were multiple life insurance policies on the wife and that the husband's version of a loving, happy relationship was instead an abusive and degrading marriage. This was confirmed by close friends and family of the deceased who, once the truth began to percolate to the top, were finally brave enough to tell the truth despite the possibility of having to face the husband's retribution.

With the additional information and the limitations of my ability to tell the difference between a contact wound inflicted as a suicide versus an execution type homicide, the husband was convicted of murder and sent to prison. During the trial, I had the fun of having to admit my error in classifying the case as a suicide and allowing the husband's defense attorney make me look ridiculous on the witness stand. The truth is the truth even when stating it makes me look incompetent. Of course, my wife says that there have been many occasions in our marriage when I've looked worse.

Telling the difference between an entrance gunshot wound and an exit gunshot wound is an area where the medical examiner has more expertise and experience than just about any other medical specialty. The reason for this is simple. We're the only medical specialty that, as part of our training, have studied the differences between the two and know how to tell them apart. There are numerous studies in medical literature that have tested the ability of the different specialties to differentiate entrance from exit wounds. Neurosurgeons and emergency room physicians are only slightly better than fifty-fifty in telling the difference. They might as well just toss a coin and call heads for entrance and tails for exit wound.

The common rule of thumb used by clinicians is that the exit wound is always larger than the entrance wound. For many gunshot wounds this is true, but not all. As you probably recall from the above example, contact gunshot wounds to the head have an entry wound much larger than the exit wound because the gas from the bullet dissects between the skull and the skin, causing the stellate or starlike tearing of the skin. This makes the entrance wound much larger than the exit wound and there have been many an emergency room physician who's been completely fooled as to entrance and exit wounds because of it. I've been on the receiving end of the fallout from this mistake and it's never fun.

The case that brings this point home is one involving a twenty-four-year-old black male who was home on leave from the service and was having girlfriend trouble. Allegedly, he'd been having an ongoing argument with the girl because she wanted to break off the relationship while our subject had been hoping to get engaged to her while on leave. Everyone who witnessed the interaction claimed that the dispute was escalating in both volume and physical interactions. The last time the two were both seen alive was outside with our subject sitting in the driver's seat of his car while the female was standing outside the driver's side window. They were both involved in a heated, escalating argument.

According to the young woman, the deceased stated that if she broke up with him he didn't want to live and would kill himself. To emphasize his point, he allegedly picked up a .38-caliber revolver from the driver's seat to his right and pointed it at the woman, then put the gun to the right side of his head before discharging the weapon, instantly killing himself. The young woman saw the gun and fell to the ground before it discharged.

The paramedics were called, and the victim was rushed to the hospital where despite aggressive therapies, he expired in the emergency room. The father arrived at the emergency room only to find that his son had been pronounced dead. In talking to the emergency room doctor, the father was told that his son died from a gunshot wound to the head with the bullet entering the left side of his head and exiting out the right side. It was a mortal wound regardless of how soon and how much medical care he could have received.

Later that same day, I autopsied the young man and found him to be in overall excellent health, with his death having been caused by a contact wound to the right side of the head. The entrance wound was classic in appearance with a large stellate tear of the skin surrounding the entry type hole in the skull, abundant gunshot residue around the entrance, an abrasion collar around the wound edges, and a beveling pattern in the skull that indicated a right to left wound path. I finished the case and drew appropriate toxicology samples to be submitted for alcohol and drugs.

The toxicology screen came back negative, so some two weeks after the death I completed my report and signed the death certificate certifying the death as a suicide due to a contact gunshot wound to the right side of the head.

Life went on in the office as usual when I received a phone call from the father of the deceased young black male requesting an appointment to go over the autopsy findings. On the appointed date at the designated time a tall burly black male introduced himself as the father of the deceased. We went into an adjacent conference room to have some privacy to discuss the autopsy results.

The father sat there quietly as I discussed the autopsy results and why I had classified the case as a suicide due to a gunshot wound to the head. He then quietly asked why I didn't consider his death a homicide with the girlfriend shooting him in the head during a fight.

I explained that the gun belonged to his son, he was right-handed, with the gun found lying by his right side in the car, the same side as the gunshot wound entrance. When I put all the information together, the findings were, in my opinion, more consistent with a suicide rather than a homicide. It would be hard to explain how the girlfriend reached into the car far enough to shoot the son in the right side of his head. I also explained that, since his son was as large and strong as he was, it was hard to see how the petite girlfriend could have manhandled his son to inflict the head wound.

The father then hit me with a bombshell. He stated that the emergency room doctor had told him categorically that the entrance wound on his son was located on the left side of the head, and he believed that she shot him as he sat in the car through the driver side window. I silently cursed the fact the emergency room physician had given the father bad information and that despite a prolonged search the expended bullet couldn't be found in the car or in the surrounding scene location.

At this point I tried to diplomatically explain that if the emergency room physician had stated that the entrance wound was located on the left side of the son's head that he had misspoken. I stated that although the emergency room doctors are trained to take care of people who have been shot, they didn't have the level of training that I have to correctly determine which side of the head was entrance and which side was the exit wound.

His final response to me was who was he supposed to believe more, a doctor who takes care of living people or a doctor who is only allowed to work on dead people? I had to chuckle to myself because I didn't have a convincing answer to that point, and there was some common sense logic to his statement.

Before I could respond to that question, the father reached across the table, grabbed me around my collar and tie, and with one arm lifted me out of my seat. I was soon choking as my body was suspended in the air while my feet were kicking trying to get back onto the floor. Although I'm short and was much smaller than the father, I had been raised in a relatively rough area and had learned to take care of myself when needed. Having said that, I reared back with my right foot and kicked the father in the groin just as hard as I could. The air went immediately out of his lungs, he dropped me to the floor, and I was able to breathe again.

With the father on the floor trying to regain his breath through his pain, I stepped over him and met the office personnel at the door as they rushed in to see what was going on in the conference room. As I straightened my tie I asked them to please call hospital security.

Security soon arrived, and as the father finally began to stand, the security officer asked if I wanted to press charges against the father. I stated that that wouldn't be necessary, but I did want the security officer to sit down with both the father and myself as I again tried to explain why the autopsy and death certificate were signed out as written. I don't think I was able to change his mind about the death of his son, but I knew that at the least, I had managed to get his attention. I know he had gotten mine.

One issue that comes to the fore in the medical examiner's world is the cases of suicide where the victim has been shot multiple times. I've personally had several cases that fall into this category, and there's no doubt that having multiple gunshot wounds and calling the death a suicide requires a stronger level of proof than the case of a single gunshot wound to the head with a suicide note next to the body explaining how and why he/she took his/her own life.

In my personal experience, all of my multiple shot suicide cases have involved smaller caliber handguns, usually a .22 caliber. In addition, common sense dictates that if multiple wounds have been self-inflicted, then their location must have been in areas of the body where immediate debilitating injuries wouldn't occur. That usually includes the abdomen and lower extremities where, although vital organs can be compromised, the individual has the time to shoot himself or herself again before consciousness is lost.

It's also been my experience that those who commit suicide in this fashion tend to have significant mental disabilities, but there are exceptions. Early in my career I was called to a death scene involving a young white male who had died from an apparent gunshot wound. When I examined the body at the scene, the deceased was in a previously secure house lying on the floor of his bedroom with a .22-caliber revolver lying on the floor next to his right hand. A quick look at the body revealed a contact gunshot wound to the center of his forehead. The wound had an abrasion collar around its edges and gunshot residue under wound defect proper. There wasn't the prominent stellate tearing of the skin commonly seen with contact wounds over bone, but that's not uncommon in small caliber wounds.

I left the scene thinking that I was dealing with a gunshot wound suicide in a young male who had recently been separated from his wife and family because of his domestic violence issues. He was depressed knowing that he had lost his family due to his own bad behavior and wasn't going to get them back. He decided that life wasn't worth living and shot himself in the head.

When I was back in the office getting dressed to start the autopsy, one of my investigators called me back to the autopsy suite by stating that we had a problem. When I examined the nude body of our victim there was a contact wound to his chest in addition to the contact wound to the forehead. I immediately began silently kicking myself for not doing a more thorough examination at the scene. I decided to start the autopsy immediately so that if this was indeed a homicide rather than a suicide, the police could get going on the homicide investigation immediately that same day.

As I opened the chest to examine the heart and lungs, I saw immediately that there was an accumulation of blood in the sac surrounding the heart. This bleeding was due to the bullet piercing the front of the pericardial sac before perforating the left ventricle of the heart, the main pumping chamber of the heart that pumps blood to all of the organs of the body after being oxygenated. Although not immediately fatal, this gunshot wound was in and of itself lethal, probably killing the victim within minutes. Examination of the skin around the wound as well as the tissues immediately below the skin confirmed that this was indeed a contact gunshot wound.

The big surprise came when I began dissecting the scalp away from the bony skull in the forehead region. Located just below the skin surface, pancaked on the outside of the bony skull was a completely flattened bullet which hadn't penetrated the skull or entered the underlying brain tissue. The only internal finding in the head was a small nondisplaced fracture of the frontal bone and a small amount of bruising on the brain surface that didn't involve the brain tissue below its gyral surface. This gunshot wound wouldn't have killed the patient and was probably not severe enough to cause unconsciousness. I'm sure that it probably hurt when inflicted.

The probable sequence of events in this scenario was as follows. The victim, depressed and wanting to take his own life, placed the gun barrel onto his forehead and discharged the weapon. I suspect that he blinked and wondered why he wasn't dead. Convinced that suicide was still his best option, he then turned the gun on himself and fired a bullet into his chest. The second attempt was successful.

I need to emphasize to the reader that to diagnose suicide, the evidence must show that the individual took his/her own life with intent. This added hoop that we must jump through, and the denials commonly encountered from grieving family members make these cases much more challenging than even homicide cases. The medical examiner was obviously not present when the death occurred, nor does he know what was going through the deceased's mind at the time of the death. Instead, we try to take the background information, autopsy findings, and medical history and, using our education, training, and experience, do our best to correctly classify the case. I'm sure that we are sometimes wrong and we make mistakes just like all other humans.

DRUGS: DYING SOONER THROUGH MODERN CHEMISTRY

There's little doubt that the use and abuse of drugs has infiltrated all levels of our society. No longer just a problem among college age young adults trying to find themselves, drug abuse now extends from the elementary school student convinced to partake on the playground during recess to adults in the highest levels of government and industry.

No subset of our society seems exempt. While on one hand federal and local governments commit larger and larger portions of their budgets to law enforcement agencies in an attempt to stop the flow of illegal drugs, the volume of drugs available continues to increase by leaps and bounds.

As you might suspect, drugs are involved in a large percentage of medical examiner cases. In fact, most forensic death investigations would be considered incomplete without a complete toxicology screen for drugs of abuse.

Toxicology has always played an important role in death investigations. It's become even more important over time as our society has become more and more involved with legal and illegal drugs to either treat a specific medical condition or for recreational purposes. It would be a fair statement that in my personal experience drugs are a contributing factor in some 60 percent of unnatural deaths. In at least 15 percent of unnatural deaths, drugs are the primary cause of death. I should quickly add at this point that when I speak of drugs I also include ethanol as a drug that's abused. Although legal to use under well-defined statutory limits, it's still a substance that causes demonstrable changes in behavior and affect. Because it's legal to use and readily available, ethanol plays a role in a large percentage of violent deaths.

When I first entered the field of forensic medicine, the limiting factor in getting the death investigation case completed was nearly always waiting for the toxicology results. The analytic tools available to analyze blood and urine samples for drugs and alcohol were extremely time consuming. Because of these time constraints there was always the temptation to eliminate the toxicology examination to get the case report finished. I suspect that in some cases we missed important drug and alcohol findings that could have better explained the cause of death or even changed the cause of death. The computer age did much to change all that.

Most people think about the personal computer revolution in terms of what the PC and its associated technology could do for them with word processing and spreadsheets. There's no doubt that the popularity of the PC changed the home user's way of doing things forever, but that pales in comparison to the PC's impact in the world of basic and applied sciences. Once the computer programmers and developers jumped onto the band wagon, the same PC technology that allows you to do word processing at home could be harnessed to do the complicated calculations necessary to automate and calculate the data fed to it by analyzers in both the clinical laboratories and research laboratories around the world. The result was a more accurate result obtained at a much quicker rate.

The piece of equipment that when coupled with the calculating abilities of the personal computer made the biggest impact on forensic toxicology is the gas chromatograph mass spectroscope (GC-MS). The beauty of the GC-MS is that not only does the instrument have the ability to separate and analyze an unknown substance, but it can also positively identify the unknown substance by comparing the generated results to a library of known substances. If that weren't enough, the onboard computer can calculate the amount of the unknown in the sample submitted.

The GC-MS is actually two instruments in one. The gas chromatograph has been around for decades and was already a workhorse in the clinical and basic science laboratory. The methodology of the gas chromatograph when coupled to the mass spectroscope is as follows.

The initial step involves injecting a small sample of the unknown being analyzed into the entry port. The GC then heats it to three hundred degrees Celsius to change the sample from a liquid to a gas. This sample gas is mixed with an inert carrier gas (usually helium) to transport it through the separation process. The resulting gas mixture is then put through a thin glass tube column that's about thirty yards long (turned back on itself multiple times to keep its size reasonable) and has been coated internally with a special polymer that variably attracts the molecules of the sample and separates those molecules based on volatility. In general, the column separates the various molecules of the sample and allows the smaller molecules to go through faster than the larger molecules.

Once the molecules have been separated by the gas chromatograph, they enter the second phase of the analysis, the mass spectrometer. As the separated molecules enter the mass spectrometer, they're bombarded by electrons which cause the molecules to ionize or become positively charged. The ionized particles of the sample are then passed through an electromagnetic field called the filter which filters out molecules based on their mass or weight.

The instrument operator determines the amount or level of filtration needed based on the type of analysis being conducted. Once sorted by the filter, a detector measures the number of ions based on their specific mass. That information is then sent to a computer which analyses the data and generates a graph depicting the number of molecules of each mass that's been detected. The graph generated is called a mass spectrum of the unknown sample. The computer then takes the data from the unknown mass spectrum and compares it to a library of known substances to determine its identity.

The computer, based on the height of the individual ion peaks in the generated mass spectrum, can take the peak information and compute the amount of the unknown in the sample. We now know both the name and the amount of drug present in the small sample analyzed. Although not all drugs can be analyzed and quantitated by the GC-MS method, it's taken a big bite out of the time previously needed to get toxicology results on a death case.

The toxicology results obtained from the blood, urine and vitreous samples obtained at autopsy are highly dependent on the abilities of the toxicologist who's operating the equipment and overseeing quality control in the laboratory.

The toxicologist is without a doubt the unsung hero in death investigations. The confidence that a medical examiner can place on the toxicology results in drawing his conclusions is dependent on the education, training, and experience of the toxicologist performing the analysis. The good toxicologists have usually earned a PhD in toxicology from an accredited university. This means that after college, they've completed an additional four to six years of university-supervised research and training. They must then take and pass a national examination to become certified toxicologists.

In addition, the good toxicologists know that to get a truly accurate answer often requires a consultation between the medical examiner and the toxicologist. The exchange of clinical and pathologic information gives the toxicologist the information that he or she needs to choose the appropriate tests for drugs and toxins. This in turn helps produce a report that can withstand the scrutiny of all the parties involved in the death investigation.

The general public probably doesn't realize that it's impossible to test for every drug or poison in every case that comes to a medical examiner's office. Despite what the TV shows demonstrate, there's no analyzer available that allows a toxicologist to inject a drop of blood and in turn get a report that includes or excludes all the known drugs and toxins.

Instead, multiple analyzers are necessary to check for even the common drugs of abuse. Because of time and financial constraints, most medical examiner's offices develop a panel of tests that look for those drugs commonly associated with misuse or abuse in the forensic literature or in the jurisdiction of the medical examiner's office.

Most offices routinely screen for some ten to fifteen drugs of abuse as well as alcohol in most if not all of their death investigation cases. This screen commonly includes opiates, stimulants, diazepams, marijuana, and ethanol as a minimum. Although a routine screen will find some 95 percent of drugs causing or contributing to a person's death, it's this remaining 5 percent of cases that requires the consultation between the pathologist and toxicologist to solve the common riddle.

In some instances, only specialized reference laboratories have the equipment necessary to analyze for the more unusual drugs and toxins.

The medical examiner depends on the expertise of his or her toxicologist to help him or her navigate through the difficult toxicology case. It's the toxicologist who knows the limitations of his equipment and has the knowledge of concerning other laboratories available to analyze specimens for the esoteric substances.

Forensic toxicologists make life easier for medical examiners in another important way, court testimony. The toxicology results are often important in those cases going to either the criminal or civil courts. A good defense attorney looks for every opportunity to put uncertainty into the minds of the jury. Because the medical examiner is not a true expert in the fine details of the toxicology analysis, the defense will often attempt to use this lack of expertise to confuse the medical examiner or at least confuse the jury. When there's a board-certified toxicologist present and able to answer all the technical questions that a defense attorney might pose during his cross-examination, the medical examiner can concentrate on the testimony that involves his area of expertise knowing that the questions concerning the toxicology will be answered correctly and appropriately.

I've been fortunate in my career to be associated with two excellent forensic toxicologists. During my time in Mobile, AL, the State Department of Forensic Sciences had a PhD toxicologist in their Mobile laboratory named Matthew Barnhill. Barny, as we all called him, knew his stuff and could not only do the analysis on the fancy computer-driven equipment but also knew how to do the basic toxicology sometimes necessary to get the results that fell between the powerful analyzers. I'll always be grateful to Barny for his willingness to teach this chemistry-challenged pathologist what little toxicology he knows and for keeping him out of trouble during those years in Mobile.

When I moved to Pensacola, FL, I didn't have the pleasure of having toxicology services in the same office as I did in Mobile. Instead, after several disappointing attempts, I was able to locate an excellent forensic toxicology service at the University of Florida. Again the toxicology service was manned by a well-trained PhD in toxicology who could and would consult on the tricky cases that I encountered over the years. Dr. Bernstein proved himself to be an extremely good forensic toxicologist of immeasurable value to our office.

Toxicology results are useful in just about all forensic death cases, but are indispensable in some. Obviously, they're important in drug overdose cases, but they're also invaluable in those cases where they help explain the mental state or irrational actions of a victim at the time of his death.

In addition to the drug ingestion–related cases, the underground marketing of the highly illegal yet highly lucrative drugs brings in distribution issues that are usually controlled by the criminal elements of our society. The end result is those individuals killed while selling or buying the drugs. On one occasion, I had the job of examining the bodies of four young black adults found bound, gagged, and stripped naked, lying on the floor of their apartment dead as the result of contact gunshot wounds to the back of each head.

It doesn't take an investigative genius to figure out that their deaths were the result of their superiors or competitors in the local drug trade. Usually, in addition to eliminating the individuals causing the problem, a death scene staged like this is used to send a message to other members of the drug selling community.

The more common scenario in this subcategory of drug-related death cases is the personal use purchase that goes sour. The buyer, usually not expecting trouble, goes to buy his drugs from the local dealer. For whatever reason, a misunderstanding occurs resulting in a death, usually of the buyer. In most instances, the surviving family is not only shocked to find that their relative is dead but must also suffer the shock of learning the circumstances of the death. This pain is once again suffered when the murder suspect goes to trial and the news media covers the proceedings.

Cases where toxicology is often extremely important are the suicides. The suicidal overdoses are usually a perplexing group of cases. As previously stated, to truly classify a death as suicide, there must be evidence that the subject intended to take his/her own life. In cases where a suicide note is found or a history of previous suicide attempts is discovered, a suicidal manner of death is probably a reasonable conclusion, but few of these cases are that straightforward. Instead, one finds an individual with a recent history of depression taking multiple drugs, usually prescribed by multiple physicians. Family members usually deny the possibility of suicide, and the investigator is forced, in turn, to patiently wait two to four weeks for the toxicology results.

One method used by the medical examiner to decide the subject's intent in these cases is the amount of drugs still present in the stomach at the time of autopsy. Usually if an individual intended to take his/her life, there is a large amount of the drug still in the stomach and intestines, as though the person wanted to make sure they had taken enough drugs to do the job. This indicates intent. The accidental overdoses usually have little if any excess drugs in the stomach. In nonsuicidal overdoses, it's not uncommon to find multiple drugs in the blood at levels near the lower level of each drug's lethal range, the implication being that for whatever reason the deceased on this one occasion simply took too much of the drug or drugs. Most medical examiners would classify this type of case as an accidental overdose. One personal observation I've noted is that it's unusual to find an individual committing suicide by an oral drug overdose with food in the stomach. It's as if the victim doesn't want digesting food competing with the drug for absorption.

Although "T's and Blues" and heroin have given way to crack cocaine and crystal methamphetamine as the most common street drugs, in terms of a medical examiner's caseload, alcohol is still king. As one of the few psychoactive drugs that can be obtained legally without a prescription, alcohol's use and abuse permeates all aspects of our lives.

From the medical examiner's viewpoint, alcohol plays a significant part in just about all types of violent deaths, not to mention its acknowledged role in traffic fatalities. In my experience some 75 percent of homicide cases and a large percentage of suicide cases involve alcohol use. Alcohol tends to depress the more inhibitory control areas of the brain, resulting in an intoxicated individual more likely to speak his mind, something that probably wouldn't have happened had the individual been sober. As you might imagine, this loss of control predisposes the individual to react to situations of escalating hostility differently than might be the case in a sober state. This commonly leads to violence and death.

As with any depressant drug, if taken in sufficient quantities, alcohol will kill in and of itself. Most people who overindulge in ethanol reach a point where their bodies revolt and they begin vomiting to rid their stomach of any alcohol waiting to be absorbed. In some individuals, for reasons I don't clearly understand, instead of vomiting the excess alcohol, they pass out with the excess ethanol in their stomachs. Over time, it's absorbed into the blood. If sufficient ethanol is absorbed the individual's brain becomes more and more depressed until coma and death occur due to the loss of brain function necessary for breathing.

Usually in these cases the blood alcohol level is in the range of .40 gm percent or about four times the legal limit allowed by most states to drive a motor vehicle (.10gm percent)

As a substance toxic to the body, ethanol also results in forms of natural disease. Cirrhosis of the liver is just a scarring of the liver as a reaction to the death of liver cells caused by alcohol poisoning. Over time, the death of these valuable liver cells interferes with the liver's ability to detoxify absorbed food, produce proteins for the blood to use in clotting, absorb fatty foods from the intestines, and excrete harmful drugs and toxins from the body. Other diseases associated with ethanol abuse include cancer of the stomach, cancer of the pancreas, cancer of the liver, and loss of brain cells (cerebral atrophy.)

Although I'm not naive enough to advocate a return to prohibition, neither am I naive enough to think that the answer to illegal drugs is increased law enforcement. Although both are done with the best of intentions, it seems that neither method has proved effective. In my opinion, education is our only hope. As long as there's a demand for drugs, there will be individuals willing to take the risk necessary to profit from the demand. Only by educating the children from kindergarten upward can we hope to eliminate the future markets of the drug kings. In my opinion, the education should also include learning a more rational use of prescription drugs and legal drugs like ethanol. At some point, we as a society need to decide if we're indeed living better or dying sooner from modern chemistry and pharmacology.

Toxicology cases can be especially trying to the medical examiner when they involve an unusual poison or a poison that requires a special test to discover its presence. It's fortunate that no matter how well a homicide is planned and executed, there are usually incriminating clues that can still be gleaned. When pursued, these clues will usually direct the investigation through the steps necessary to solve the mystery. The clues can only be found through a complete examination of all the facts of the case, including the crime scene, and a medical and background investigation. The following case not only shows the need to systematically cover all of the bases but also shows how cases can slip between the cracks despite the best intentions of everyone involved.

Serial killers are rare individuals. There are those like Ted Bundy who are motivated by deviant sexual desires. These are the cases that get the most press and are thus better known. They're usually attractive, but almost always charming males who move about the country leaving the bodies of young attractive females behind. They're motivated by their perverted sexual desires that ironically involve control and sadism as much as they do sexual lust. Many of the victims are picked during a chance encounter where some physical characteristic of the victim attracts the killer. This unpredictable victim selection makes this type of serial killer all the more feared by the public simply because they seem to snatch their victims at random and there's no way to predict who will be next.

There's another type of serial killer who isn't driven by sexual desires but is instead driven by the desire for money and what that money allows them to do. These serial killers are much more subtle than their sexually motivated counterparts because their method requires patience. They must first choose their victim and develop a relationship, which, in most instances, progresses to marriage so that they can eventually inherit the partner's assets or life insurance proceeds.

In many instances, the monies obtained from the previous marriage are used to set up an appearance of financial independence that makes the predator more desirable to the next victim. One might wonder how someone gets away with multiple killings before getting caught. The answer, particularly in this subset of cases, is mobility. These killers tend to stay on the move, changing localities after each murder and often legally changing their names. After they are established, they begin to hunt and attract a new mate.

Once the relationship is established, they convince their new lover or spouse to make them the beneficiary of a new or old insurance policy. They then wait so as not to draw undue attention to themselves before they kill the spouse. The killer is usually pretty or handsome and tends to have the outgoing-type personality that makes him/her attractive to the opposite sex. They seek out a victim who will fall in love with them and are naïve enough to not identify their true motives. Their prime victims are those who have never married or have a low self-esteem. This makes the romance seem all the more wonderful.

The most common method for killing the spouse is poisoning; however, an occasional instance of causing an accidental death has been seen. Using the right poison increases the odds that the death will be classified as a natural disease event and will in many jurisdictions escape an autopsy examination or toxicology screen. They often use a family physician who knows the patient and will naively sign the death certificate. This decreases the odds that the medical examiner or coroner will become involved. Finally, the really devious killer will use a poison that mimics a natural disease process but is undetected on the routine toxicology panels of both hospitals and medical examiner's offices.

In the present case, an attractive middle-aged white female named Judy graduated from a reformatory high school in Albuquerque, NM. She soon moved to Roswell where she worked as a nurse's aide. While in Roswell, Judy had a son out of wedlock but soon met and married James E. Goodyear USAF. Five years later, the Goodyear family moved to Orlando, FL, where the couple opened a child care center. Though James had no known history of significant illness during his military service, on September 15, 1971, he suddenly became acutely ill, was admitted, and died in the local US Navy Hospital. Judy, the wife, surrendered three separate life insurance policies that had been taken on James, with her as the only beneficiary. That same year, Judy received $90,000 as a homeowner's insurance settlement following a house fire.

Claiming the need for a change of scenery, Judy moved to Pensacola, FL, with her three children by James Goodyear. She purchased a house in Pensacola, which she and her children shared with a new beau named Bobby Jo Morris. After a four-year stay together in Pensacola, Bobby Joe moved to Trinidad, CO, where he took a better-paying job with the local water company.

In July of that same year, 1977, Judy's Pensacola residence caught fire, and she once again collected homeowner's insurance. Soon after the fire, Judy and her three children moved to Trinidad, CO, to be with Bobby Joe Morris. The makeshift family seemed to be doing well until January 4, 1978, when Bobby Joe Morris was immediately admitted to San Rafael Hospital in Trinidad. Although the picture of health some twenty-four hours previously, on admission to the hospital, Bobby Joe was vomiting profusely, complaining of severe abdominal pains, and producing copious amounts of egg shell–colored diarrhea. He had the classic signs and symptoms of shock with resulting metabolic acidosis, acute renal failure, and congestive heart failure. The clinical impression from the attending physician was suspected acute alcohol withdrawal syndrome with associated delirium tremens, acute pancreatitis, and alcoholic hepatitis. The precipitating cause for the acute presentation was never clearly determined.

After some eighteen days in the hospital receiving supportive treatments, Bobby Joe was released home to Judy's care with a follow-up appointment scheduled in one week. Two days later, Bobby Joe collapsed at the dinner table and was readmitted to San Rafael Hospital again showing gastrointestinal distress and signs of shock with multiple organ failure. Five days later on January 28, 1978, Bobby Joe died from cardiac arrest and metabolic acidosis.

Because the cause of death remained obscure, an autopsy was performed by a Denver pathologist. At the time of the autopsy, the body had already been embalmed, and because of the "rush to get the body shipped back to Bobby Joe's hometown of Brewton, AL, the autopsy was conducted with the body in the casket. With all these handicaps, the autopsy findings were inconclusive for an anatomic cause of death. The next month, Judy surrendered three life insurance policies on Bobby Joe Morris. His body was laid to rest in a family plot in Brewton, AL.

Although never married to Bobby Joe, Judy had assumed the last name of Morris throughout her time in Colorado. After Bobby Joe's death, she legally changed her name to Judias Buenoano, the Spanish equivalent to Judy Goodyear. After settling all of her affairs, Judias packed her belongings and moved to a house in Gulf Breeze, FL, across the bay from her previous residence in Pensacola.

Sometimes people just don't know when to leave well enough alone. Although she owned a busy nail spa, Judias's lifestyle required ongoing infusions of cash to maintain herself at what she deemed an acceptable level. Had she walked away with the insurance money she had collected on both James Goodyear and Bobby Joe Morris, there was a fair chance that she would never have been discovered. The problem was that Judias had to always be the big shot with plenty of excess money. In addition, she had to buy herself the best of everything, all the while trying to impress everyone by lying about her accomplishments. She was particularly vocal about her educational achievements, claiming at various times that she was a medical doctor, had a PhD in biochemistry, and had a master's degree in nursing when in fact a high school diploma was her highest educational accomplishment. She loved to live and vacation extravagantly and needed additional money to finance that lifestyle.

Let's not forget that to this point, Judias had been incredibly successful. She had already cashed in on multiple life insurance policies from the two men she had killed and collected fire insurance claims on two different homes. If pride comes before the fall, then Judias Buenoano's pride pushed her to believe that she was smarter than the system and would never be caught. In fact, her behaviors showed many attributes of a sociopathic personality. Allegedly, the disorder allows the subject to dismiss many notions of right and wrong, those mental rules that allow the normal person to keep unacceptable behaviors in check.

I realize that it's only a matter of degree, but it's still hard for me to believe that any mother would kill her own child for money; then again, Judias Buenoano was no ordinary woman. Michael Arthur Schultz, Judias's oldest child, was born out of wedlock on March 30, 1961. Judias married James Goodyear in January 1962, and he adopted Michael in 1966. Michael began school in Orlando, FL, where he was described as a disruptive child with a slightly below average IQ. Following evaluations, Michael was placed in a residential treatment center for disturbed children. When his father's military benefits expired, Michael was reevaluated and eventually placed in a foster home with ongoing psychiatric therapy. Those times when Michael was living at home proved that Judias had neither the interest nor the patience needed to control Michael.

In 1977, Michael moved to Trinidad with the family, all the time receiving outpatient psychiatric care. After Bobby Joe Morris's death, Michael returned to the Pensacola area with the family where he attended Gulf Breeze High School before dropping out in the tenth grade. In June 1979, Michael joined the US Army where his physical examinations on entry described him as in excellent health. After basic training at Fort Leonard Wood, MO, Michael was sent to water purification school before being stationed at Fort Benning, GA, starting November 6, 1979.

Before beginning his station at Fort Benning, Michael was alleged to have stopped to visit his mother in Gulf Breeze, FL. By the time he arrived for duty at Fort Benning on November 6, 1979, Michael was already suffering from classic symptoms of heavy metal poisoning. After six weeks of hospitalization, Michael's legs and arms had atrophied to the point that he could neither walk nor use his hands. Doctors at Walter Reed Hospital found that Michael's body contained seven times the normal levels of arsenic. The army suspected that Michael had ingested arsenic during his water treatment schooling.

Because he would never recover from the peripheral neuropathy and muscle atrophy, Michael was placed in some sixty pounds of braces to aid in his mobility. Despite support from the braces, Michael was unable to walk and had no control of his extremities below his knees and elbows. In March of 1980, Michael was transferred to the VA hospital in Tampa, FL, pending medical treatment for permanent disability. On May 12, 1980, Michael was discharged to his mother's care in Gulf Breeze, FL.

Two days after returning home, May 14, 1980, Michael drowned in the East River near Milton, FL, when the canoe in which he was riding overturned, sending him and his sixty pounds of braces to the bottom of the river. His mother, Judias, and younger half-brother James were also in the canoe when the mishap occurred. James was slightly injured, but not hospitalized, and Judias survived the plunge without injury. Judias collected over $90,000 in private insurance money as well as $20,000 from a military life insurance policy. The death was investigated and deemed a tragic accident.

She wasn't done yet. John Wesley Gentry II first met Judias at a Pensacola female mud wrestling bar. John got her phone number and called her the next day for a lunch date. He claimed that she wasn't that attractive but "knew how to use what she had been given." The relationship was initially a whirlwind romance with John moving into her house after about six months. They lived a fairly extravagant lifestyle until John had a case of severe abdominal pain requiring two-week hospitalization. He thought his illness might be related to the vitamins Judias had given him and refused to take them. Judias exploded in anger. Gentry claimed that after this, Judias and he basically lived separate lives in the same house.

Early on in the relationship, John had borrowed several thousand dollars from Judias to open a wallpaper outlet store. It had been pretty successful, and because "Judias is so funny about being owed money," he made it a point to pay her back as soon as possible.

In late June of 1983, Judias threw John another curve by claiming that she was pregnant. She wanted to get married on a cruise they had planned. John was actively trying to disenfranchise himself from Judias.

He later found out that Judias previously had a tubal ligation, so the pregnancy was just another lie.

Such was the state of their relationship when one day, John left his car home so that James, Judias's son, could install new speakers. He had agreed to meet Judias later that evening at a local restaurant to attend a going-away party for one of Judias's employees. Judias was adamant in telling John where to park his car when he arrived at the restaurant.

He drove to the party, stayed a while, and then made his excuses to leave early. He went out to his car, started the ignition, and was greeted by the explosion of a bomb that had been placed in the trunk of his car. John survived the bombing but had injuries severe enough that he required several days of hospitalization at Sacred Heart Hospital. When it was time to be released from the hospital, John Gentry stated that he wanted to finish his recovery at his mom's home in Pensacola.

Although he had to face Judias's anger, standing firm on that one decision probably saved his life. Incidentally, Judias had taken out a $500,000 life insurance policy on John Gentry, claiming that they were partners in his wallpaper outlet business and that they had decided to take out life insurance policies on each other should something untoward happen.

Things finally started to unravel for Judias. Although initially trying to divert the blame to others, a tenacious homicide investigator and an aggressive assistant state attorney collected enough evidence to charge Judias with the murder attempt of Gentry. The investigation and arrest resulted in a domino effect in that suddenly, the accidental drowning of her son as well as the suspicious deaths of her two previous husbands came under scrutiny.

The state attorney's office and the local police department did the extensive research and interviews necessary to charge Judias with the death of her son and fraud for claiming the money from his life insurance policies. In addition, the death investigation into the suspicious death of her first husband, James Goodyear, was reopened, and she was again charged with murder. Over the intervening years, she was systematically tried on all of the cases and found guilty of the murder of her son and her first husband in the Florida Panhandle and in Tampa, FL, respectively. She was sentenced to death by electrocution in the Florida electric chair.

My personal involvement in the Judias Buenoano case was peripheral. As a state medical examiner in Alabama, our office was involved in the exhumation and reautopsy of Judias's second known victim Bobby Joe Morris, who had been buried in Brewton, AL. Our examination confirmed lethal levels of arsenic throughout Morris's tissues, hair, and fingernails. The autopsy was performed under the auspices of the Trinidad, CO, state attorney's office with the information obtained for use in a murder trial planned to take place in Colorado. Because of the three convictions and subsequent death sentence obtained in Florida, however, the trial in Colorado was continued indefinitely.

One question that probably jumps out of this narrative is how can both husbands be autopsied and both fail to reveal the true cause of death? The general lay public, most law enforcement officers, and trial lawyers still think that all autopsies are alike. As you know by now, that's not the case.

The hospital autopsy and the forensic autopsy are actually looking at different aspects of the death. The hospital autopsy tends to place emphasis on looking for the natural disease processes that would explain the clinical history and laboratory findings noted while the patient was being treated. Because it usually plays little or no role in the patient's clinical history, toxicology is rarely obtained in the routine hospital autopsy. This is particularly true if the autopsy reveals natural disease processes that could explain the clinical findings. Thus, even though both autopsies failed to show a convincing cause of death, there was no effort extended to check the body tissues for toxins and poisons.

Remember, there's a big difference between the cause of death and the mechanism of death. In this case, the mechanism of death was indeed the multiple organ failure diagnosed in both the hospital autopsies, but the true cause of death remained undetermined; what was the disease or injury that caused the multiple organ failure and deaths?

It's interesting that in this case, the toxin of choice was arsenic. Arsenic has a storied past as an agent of homicide. It's even been given the title of "the king of poisons" because of its use during the Middle Ages to rid the kingdom of one monarch so that a more desirable candidate could assume the throne. Arsenic is actually an element found in the periodic table that hung in your high school science class. It has metalloid properties that can be combined with both inorganic and organic molecules, making it useful for various applications. It's the inorganic form that's most toxic to humans and other animals, and it's the inorganic form that has historically been used in various poisons to control insects and rodents.

In the human, arsenic interferes with the energy production that occurs on the cellular level in the Krebs Cycle, the one that we all hated in college biochemistry classes. The most common symptoms described in poisoning cases are related to gastrointestinal cramping and diarrhea. Depending on the amount and timing of acute arsenic poisoning, the death can occur relatively quickly or can linger over days or weeks. Acute arsenic poisoning is a medical emergency requiring dialysis, blood transfusions, and chelating to have even a chance of survival.

From a killer's point of view, arsenic has attributes that they find useful. Particularly in the past before more specific agents became available, arsenic was easy to obtain from sources that sold insecticides and rodent control poisons. Arsenic also has the advantage that the symptoms it causes in the victim are basically the same symptoms that are seen clinically in self-limited illnesses like viral gastritis and food poisoning. Usually by the time the symptoms have lasted long enough that a family clinician would begin to consider a more serious diagnosis, the patient has reached a point of no return. Because arsenic poisoning wouldn't be found on routine hospital clinical laboratory tests or found on routine toxicology drug panels, it's a poison that must be considered early on in the clinical course so that the specialized tests required for its identification can be ordered.

From the death investigator's point of view, arsenic has attributes that are helpful to us. Because of its chemistry and the body's inability to excrete arsenic at any significant level, it tends to remain in the body, present in most tissues. Because of its metalloid character, arsenic can often be found in even severely decomposed bodies. It tends to concentrate and remain at discernible levels in samples of hair, fingernails, and toenails, three tissues that usually maintain their integrity despite decomposition.

Although our involvement in the case was somewhat anticlimactic, we all had visions of a free trip to Colorado to testify in the trial. The end result was that Bobby Joe Morris's death certificate was amended to list arsenic poisoning as the cause of death, with the manner of death reclassified as a homicide. Obviously, nothing that we did could in any way bring back Bobby Joe, but I hope that knowing the truth has allowed the family to work through their grief and has given them the satisfaction of knowing that justice, though too long in coming, had finally been done. In fact, that justice was consummated at Starke prison on March 30, 1998, when a small, scared Judias Buenoano was led to the Florida electric chair and became the first woman executed in the state of Florida in over 150 years.

FORENSIC PATHOLOGIST: GUARDIAN OF YOUR PUBLIC HEALTH

One function of the medical examiner's office that gets little publicity but at times can be important is its function in terms of the community's public health. The duty to investigate cases that may pose a public health hazard is defined by most medical examiner's statutes. Although investigations of public health–related cases make up a small proportion of the caseload, they can often have a profound impact on the living.

Far and away, most public health cases revolve on the exposure of family or friends to those dying of a communicable disease. Most of these are cases of bacterial meningitis (bacterial inflammation of the membranes surrounding the brain) commonly seen in young children. Although most cases involve bacterial organisms that are essentially noncommunicable (can't be transferred from one person to another by contact), occasionally, an organism called meningococcus, a bacteria that can be easily transmitted between individuals, is identified. All people who have been in contact with the infected person, from family members to funeral home personnel, are located and put on prophylactic antibiotics (antibiotics given to an individual to prevent coming down with a disease.) Although most people dying due to meningitis do so in a hospital, it's interesting that there's a small percentage of the population with a high pain threshold that dies before they can be hospitalized and diagnosed. In these cases, it is the responsibility of the medical examiner to make certain that appropriate cultures are obtained so that a specific diagnosis can be made and the appropriate treatments given.

Historically, the infection responsible for a considerable morbidity (illness) and mortality (deaths) earlier in this century was the bacteria responsible for the disease tuberculosis. Mycobacterium tuberculi, the name of the bacteria responsible for the disease, is a waxy, slow-growing organism. Its ability to grow slowly in part explains why the organism is so difficult to destroy in the body.

Most antibiotics kill bacteria by catching them at their most vulnerable moment, at reproduction, when an individual bacteria is splitting into two organisms. By blocking a step in this reproduction or preventing them from building a new protective wall about themselves, antibiotics kill or at least render a bacteria susceptible to the body's defenses. By growing and reproducing at a slow rate, TB makes it difficult for an antibiotic to work.

Thus, it requires large doses of antibiotic over long periods of time to sterilize the body of TB. TB's waxy coat also causes havoc. This coat is so effective in protecting the organism from adverse environmental conditions that individual bacteria can survive for months in dust or formalin fixatives. In fact, its ability to resist drying out is the reason some communities have laws against spitting on the sidewalks.

TB's ability to withstand formaldehyde has been proven by growing the organism from autopsy specimens of TB stored in formalin for greater than fifty years. The waxy coat is also responsible for the body's inability to destroy the bacteria when engulfed by neutrophils and macrophages (mobile cells in the body responsible for removing foreign materials by engulfing them and digesting them with naturally produced enzymes.) The waxy coat also causes an immune reaction in the body partially responsible for the disease tuberculosis.

The disease called tuberculosis is divided into two phases called primary and secondary tuberculosis. In the primary form of the disease the TB organism is inhaled into the lung where it lodges, usually in the mid aspects of the lung tissue. The body's immune cells composed in this case of lymphocytes and macrophages attack and attempt to destroy the bacteria. In the process, the immune system recognizes the TB's waxy coat as a foreign substance and begins to produce lymphocytes (a form of white blood cell) that are specifically made to react only with molecules contained in the TB's waxy coat.

Because the initial exposure dose of TB is usually composed of relatively few organisms, the body through its protective immune system is usually able to control or destroy this first exposure. The result of this immune response to the primary dose of TB bacteria is the presence of activated lymphocytes which form the basis of a positive skin reaction to purified tuberculin proteins in a TB skin test.

In many people, the second exposure to this organism is more costly. As in primary TB, one route of acquiring the second exposure is by inhaling the TB organism. The more common route involves reactivating TB organisms still in the body to produce disease at a time of decreased immunity.

Once lodged in the lung, the body's previously formed lymphocytes specific against TB's waxy coat begin the attack. This secondary form of TB usually lodges in the top or apical regions of the lungs where there are increased oxygen levels. The specific lymphocytes attack the TB by inducing increased numbers of macrophages into the fight as well as getting killer lymphocytes involved. The immune response causes the macrophages to produce increased quantities of digestive enzymes and to act more aggressively.

The end result is the death of many immune cells which in turn release their digestive enzymes, causing digestion of adjacent lung tissue in an attempt to control the infection. This necrotic or dying lung tissue is what forms the cavities commonly seen at the top of the lungs by X-ray in cases of secondary TB Ironically, the TB organism's response to this battle is to sit and smile. Nature has given him a natural built in defense, his waxy coat. Although this immune battle does restrict the spread of tuberculosis to a large extent, the trade-off is loss of lung tissue through scarring and necrosis (cell death).

The outcome of the disease can be quite variable with the secondary disease becoming asymptomatic, eradicated, or slowly progressive with lung destruction and spread to other organs. Fortunately, in all but those with advanced disease, treatment with antibiotics can usually arrest progression and effect a cure.

Because of the immune system's vital role in arresting progression of the disease, tuberculosis flourishes wherever there's poverty, malnourishment, and lack of medical care. Such appeared to be the case involving a seventy-year-old white male living in a rural portion of Mobile County. The report of the death came from the Mobile County Sheriff's Office and indicated no evidence of foul play. However, because there was no physician to sign the death certificate, it automatically became a medical examiner's case. Upon receiving the body into the medical examiner's office, I noted the deceased had a wasted appearance. We use this term to describe individuals with little or no fat or muscle on the body that gives them the appearance of World War II concentration camp victims. As this is a usual finding in patients dying of terminal cancer, I had the investigators attempt to locate medical records documenting a previous cancer diagnosis or treatment. There was none to be found; in fact, the elderly white gentleman was, according to family members, last seen by a physician at a veteran's administration clinic some twenty years previous.

Because there was no medical history of any disease capable of causing death and the deceased had the appearance of a malignant disease process, I elected to do an autopsy. I ended up being glad that I did. Still expecting to see a lung cancer or similar tumor, I was surprised to find fibrotic cavities at the top of each lung partially filled with necrotic cottage cheese appearing pus. In addition, both lungs had small white areas of pneumonia, giving the lungs an appearance of leopard spots where the spots were white instead of black. Examination of sections of the lungs under a microscope confirmed my naked-eye impressions.

This man died from tuberculosis with pneumonia type spread to both lungs. In cases such as this, it's extremely important to prove definitely that the TB organism is present in the tissue. This can be done by culturing the tissues and waiting for them to grow identifiable organisms or by staining microscopic slides of the tissues with acid fast stains that will preferentially stain the TB organism for identification. In this case, the TB was readily seen on microscopic examination so that tissue cultures, which may take weeks to grow cultures sufficient for identification, were unnecessary.

Because tuberculosis is a communicable disease, it also is a reportable disease. This means that confirmed cases must be reported to the local board of health for investigation and follow-up. Because the immediate family members had had contact with the dying grandfather, they were all given TB skin tests. About half of the family members had positive skin tests, indicating that they had the TB organism in their bodies. Chest X-rays performed on all family members were negative, indicating that no one had yet developed secondary TB. All the skin positive family members were put on an extended course of antibiotic to arrest and eradicate the disease.

The end result was a family and community saved from a possible tuberculosis outbreak and a medical examiner's office that could be proud in fulfilling its role in helping monitor the community health. Before I break my arm trying to slap myself on the back, it's humbling to think that it's just as possible that in this case an autopsy would never have been done. In a seventy-year-old male, it's easy to rationalize heart disease as a cause of death and never do an autopsy. One key to avoiding this pitfall is the issue of past medical history. A lack of documented disease should always cause a medical examiner to stop and think. Although it's always possible for an elderly person with heart disease to also develop a disease like tuberculosis, it would certainly be rare for such a disease not to be discovered in an elderly person being seen regularly by a family physician for heart disease. The word "autopsy" literally means "to see for one's self." In most cases, that's really the only way to know for sure why a person dies.

Few people would disagree that more has been written in the medical and lay journals and magazines about the acquired immune deficiency syndrome (AIDS) than any disease in history. The medical blitz has been so thorough and detailed that it hasn't been uncommon for my nonmedical friends to know more about the latest breakthrough than I've known. It has occasionally been humbling to have them fill me in on the latest details in AIDS research.

I think it would also be fair to state that no disease in modern times has stirred up as much anxiety and resulted in as great a polarization of opinions as has the issue of AIDS. This was particularly true at the early stages of the disease when we still didn't know how the disease was transmitted, what organism or substance caused the disease, and how the disease could be prevented or cured. Since that time, we've identified the contagious agent and known a lot about how the agent is transmitted and how the disease can be prevented. Unfortunately, there isn't, at least at this writing, a cure or even a hope for a cure in the near future.

In June 1981, the initial report of Pneumocystis carinii pneumonia (a rare protozoan pneumonia only seen in severely immune compromised hosts) from Los Angeles marked the recognition of what is now known as AIDS.

In retrospect, the responsible agent had already been in the United States for some five years at this time, the actual disease for some three years. By 1984, a human retrovirus was isolated as the cause of AIDS. Initially called HTVL III/LAV, its name was subsequently shorted to HIV (human immunodeficiency virus). Since its discovery, cases of AIDS have been reported from all fifty states, the District of Columbia, and some two hundred foreign countries.

Like all viruses, HIV reproduces itself by entering the cells and using the infected cell's DNA to make copies of itself for subsequent release to infect other cells. Studies of HIV show that the virus's genetic material becomes an integral and permanent component of the DNA of the infected individual. Thus, the infected individual is likely to be a carrier of the virus for the rest of his life as well as probably capable of transmitting the virus to others.

The presence of antibodies to HIV doesn't indicate that the tested individual has the disease AIDS. A positive antibody test only indicates that the individual has been exposed to the virus and is probably or at least potentially infective to other people. To be diagnosed as having AIDS, the disease itself, the patient must have a positive, confirmed antibody test plus an opportunistic infection like Pneumocystis carinii pneumonia, Kaposi's sarcoma, or other unusual infection not seen in individuals with a normal immune system. AIDS-related complex (ARC) is a diagnosis based on the findings of two or more symptoms (night sweats, fever, lymph node or gland swelling, etc.) and two or more laboratory findings suggestive of an otherwise unexplained immune deficiency consistent with AIDS. In reality, ARC is probably an intermediate step in the progression from asymptomatic antibody positivity to the full-blown AIDS disease.

Does a positive blood test for AIDS mean that an individual will always develop AIDS? We don't know absolutely. The latency period between antibody positivity to AIDS disease averages four or more years in the adult. Many researchers believe that everyone who has the antibody will eventually develop the disease. The same is true for ARC; however, the truth is that we just don't know.

How does this particular virus reap such a profound havoc on the human body when compared to all of the virus types to which we're continuously exposed? The answer lies in the particular cells that the HIV attacks. The human body was designed to protect itself from outside invaders, be they viruses, bacteria, or toxins, by two separate armies, each with their own type of soldiers and their own weapons and firepower. Everyone has been to the doctor and has had blood drawn and analyzed. The most routine of these blood tests involves counting the cells that circulate in the liquid portion of our blood. The most common are the red cells, or erythrocytes, which are responsible for carrying oxygen to all cells of the body. Less numerous but also important are the white cells, which the body uses to fight off the various bacteria and viruses that are continually trying to use us as a food source.

The most common white cell normally found in blood is the neutrophil. Its job is to immobilize and devour bacteria that have slipped into the blood or body tissues. The pus associated with a wound is predominantly composed of dead white cells of this type. Another type of white cell circulating in our blood and located in lymph nodes, tonsils, and the intestines are the lymphocytes. There are two types of these lymphocytes with totally different functions.

One type called the humoral system is composed of B lymphocytes (white blood cells.) When exposed to a foreign substance, B lymphocytes are stimulated to produce proteins called antibodies. The antibodies produced react specifically with the foreign substance and attach to its surface preferentially in a specific lock-and-key-type mechanism, that is, specific receptors on the antibody attach to specific molecule patterns on the foreign substance. This specificity prevents the antibodies from attaching to substances at random and thus from destroying useful or important body cells and structures.

Once the antibody is attached, it does several things to the foreign substance. Antibodies attached can initiate a destructive sequence called complement fixation where proteins of the body attach to the antibody and result in destruction of the foreigner. The antibody attached to the foreign substance can also signal amoebalike macrophages, a white blood cell with a voracious appetite, to attack and destroy the foreigner by devouring and digesting it.

The other division in this battle against invaders is called cell-mediated immunity. In this division, the main regiment is composed of T lymphocytes (similar to the lymphocytes of humoral immunity but with different functions). These lymphocytes are further divided into helpers and cytotoxic groups. The cytotoxic group of lymphocytes, like antibodies produced by their humoral cousins, is specific for groups of molecules on cells or tissues and attaches only to these specific foreigners.

Once they attach, they're capable of punching holes in the cell membrane, allowing the cell's protoplasm to leak out and thus killing the foreign cell.

The lymphocyte helpers, when stimulated by specific substances recognized as foreign, secrete a group of substances which attract other lymphocytes, macrophages, and various white blood cells to the field of battle. This allows a concentration of troops in areas where they are needed. Helper lymphocytes amplify or increase the conversion of cell mediated or T lymphocytes into killer versions. These helper cells also perform the same function with their antibody-producing lymphocyte cousins. Helper cells thus function as a sort of lymphocyte army boot camp changing easygoing lymphocytes into battle-ready killers and antibody producers.

As you might imagine, the role of T lymphocyte helper cells is crucial to any immune battle. As stated, the helper cells convert circulating lymphocytes of both types of immunity into active forms. They also secrete substances which recruit lymphocytes and other white cells to the scene of battle. As you've probably guessed by this time, it's the helper subtype of the cell-mediated lymphocytes that's attacked and destroyed by the AIDS virus. The end result is a depression in the body's ability to fight off invaders through the loss of the body's cell-mediated portion of defense. Although crippled to some degree by the loss of the amplifying helper lymphocytes, the humoral cells are still able to respond, though not as quickly or aggressively.

Thus, organisms like bacteria, fungus, and protozoa which were previously kept easily under control by the cell-mediated immune system can now get an upper hand and take over with a resulting severe infection. Indeed, one of these easily controlled organisms must set up such an infection to make a positive diagnosis of AIDS.

The real problem, of course, is how do we go about fighting such a lethal opponent? Because the possibility of an immune vaccine or antiviral medication effective against the AIDS virus is years away, the only real weapon available to us is prevention. The problem with this method is that it requires the active participation of all of us to control the spread.

Although various groups of the population are statistically at greater risk of becoming exposed to HIV; anyone who is gay, an IV drug abuser, or has unprotected sexual intercourse with multiple partners is at increased risk. Also at risk are infants born to HIV-positive mothers. It's only by educating IV drug abusers on the need for sterilized needles and syringes as well as educating both the homosexual and heterosexual populations on the risk of multiple sex partners and the need for the routine use of condoms outside of a faithful relationship between two HIV negative individuals that we have a chance to avert the death of untold millions.

The medical examiner has both public and private concerns in investigating the death of AIDS victims. As an agent of the public he's required by law to certify the cause of death in all cases as accurately as possible. Unfortunately, there's no room in this responsibility for protection of the family and friends left behind. As a result, I've had to certify deaths as due to AIDS against the wishes of the family and close friends. The publicity over the death of Liberace is an example of what we can all expect to see in the future if this is not followed strictly.

Another aspect of the medical examiner's responsibility in AIDS cases involves the health of all persons who come in contact with the AIDS victim's body, in particular the embalmer at the funeral home and the person who has assisted at the autopsy. Because available studies have shown that HIV is transmitted only by body fluids, doesn't appear to survive long outside of the living body; and is readily susceptible to disinfectant agents, in particular a 10 percent solution of liquid bleach, much of our initial anxieties about exposure to the body of an AIDS victim has diminished.

Evidence also shows that, though extremely rare, HIV can be transmitted through a needle puncture or cut, events quite common during the course of a year on the autopsy service. Because of this possibility, all autopsy participants must take extreme care. In addition we use special equipment which provides extra protection of those body areas susceptible to trauma during the autopsy of an AIDS case.

Many friends have asked me whether I'm willing to conduct autopsies on known AIDS cases. I always answer by saying that it isn't the known AIDS cases that bother me. It's the HIV-positive cases that are not identified as such that worry me. As already stated, there's a latency period of four years or more between contracting the HIV virus until contracting the disease; thus, asymptomatic people capable of transmitting HIV can go about their business oblivious to the viral time bomb in their system. If that business includes violence of any sort, there's a good chance that they'll end up on my autopsy table. I then do an autopsy on this same individual with no way of knowing that he can infect anyone who cuts themselves or sticks themselves with a needle.

An obvious option would be to run an antibody test on all bodies coming to autopsy. Initially, it took at least three days to get the results back, and the cost is still prohibitive. The reasonable compromise is to treat all cases as though they were HIV positive and wear protective garments, face shield, and thick gloves for all autopsy cases. This is, in fact, what we do.

To date, there are no reported cases of a pathologist or pathologist assistant contracting AIDS from an autopsy exam. Although my wife may raise a skeptical eyebrow, I do try to be careful during all of my cases. I don't want the honor of being the first autopsy-contracted AIDS patient. When asked by close friends what special measures I take doing autopsy exams in this age of possible AIDS exposure, I jokingly reply that I've stopped licking my fingers after autopsies. They usually change the subject.

If a pathologist is really honest with himself, the real fear is not contracting AIDS from an autopsy; it's getting hepatitis from an autopsy exam. Of the various viruses responsible for hepatitis, the hepatitis B and C viruses are the types most commonly associated with autopsy-related cases.

Unlike hepatitis A, which is transmitted predominantly by a fecal-oral route, hepatitis B and C have a transmission pattern similar to the AIDS virus with most infections acquired by parental (needle sticks) and sexual contact with an infected individual. To make matters worse, only 1/1000 of a drop of blood is needed for a successful transmission of hepatitis B. This makes transmission possible with even trivial accidents at autopsy.

While only 0.5 to 0.9 percent of the US population are potential infectious carriers of the hepatitis virus, the rate is much higher in the IV drug abuse population that makes up a large percent of the medical examiner's client population. Of individuals who develop hepatitis, 1 to 2 percent will have an acute fulminant type, often resulting in death. Ninety percent of individuals who develop hepatitis recover without problems. Ten percent, however, have a slow smoldering infection called a chronic carrier state, often causing progressive damage to the liver and continued potential infection for contacts.

Fortunately for the health-care population, there are now hepatitis vaccines that give a great deal of immunity to the hepatitis viruses. Not wishing to sound cavalier about the real possibility of contracting an infectious disease from an autopsy case, it's quite frankly one of the risks of the job. Although I take every precaution to avoid accidental exposures, there are, nonetheless, cases where the need to know why an individual died must take priority over the fears and personal wellbeing of the individual performing the autopsy.

To keep this discussion from sounding melodramatic or self-serving, let me add that this same philosophy is put into action every day by the police and firemen of our respective communities. In their roles as public servants, they're expected to risk life and limb on a daily basis as part of their routine duties. This type of self-sacrifice obviously makes the occasional risk of infectious disease by the forensic pathologist seem rather trivial. From a practical point of view, there are other reasons.

I've learned through experience that attorneys will take advantage of any weakness in a case and exploit it to their client's advantage. This point was brought home to me in a civil case involving a forty-year-old female. According to witnesses at the scene, the subject was driving her car erratically down a county road. Allegedly, she passed a county garbage truck parked on the side of the road, barely missing the parked vehicle. According to the witnesses, our subject then turned her vehicle around and again passed the parked truck. On her third pass, she plowed directly into the rear of the garbage truck, killing herself instantly.

At autopsy, in addition to noting the injuries responsible for her death, she had severe liver changes suggesting viral hepatitis. Although witnesses described erratic driving suggesting that our subject had alcohol or drugs in her system at the time of her crash, I elected to hold my toxicology specimens until I could run the serology tests to eliminate the possibility of a potentially contagious disease. The laboratory results came back strongly positive for hepatitis B. Because no criminal charges were being filed in the case, I elected to withhold the toxicology samples permanently. My rationale was that little would be gained by exposing the toxicology section of our department to hepatitis when for all practical purposes the investigation was being dropped by the police. I signed the case out as a single-vehicle crash fatality with the only real question in my mind being whether the driver had committed suicide by crashing her car.

I had completely forgotten about the case until I was called by an attorney asking questions. Thinking that perhaps the question of suicide was being raised by some insurance company, I was surprised that my inquirer had been retained instead by the family of the deceased. I explained in detail the risks of infection due to hepatitis as the reason for omitting the usual toxicology studies. I was particularly puzzled when he communicated his pleasure about the absent toxicology. It seems that the family members of the driver were planning to sue the county for her death. This was being pursued despite the findings that the truck was parked safely off the road and that the subject had allegedly been driving erratically and had even passed the stationary truck twice before the crash.

He indicated that the lack of toxicology would help his case considerably because, despite her long history of alcohol abuse, there would be no scientific evidence to support that hypothesis. When I got off the phone, I was violently angry. My Good Samaritan act was going to be turned against me in civil court and could possibly result in a large monetary award to a family who cared little for their relative during life but saw her death as a potential gold mine. In addition, it would be my tax money that would be used to pay the award should the county lose the court battle.

Needless to say, this case taught me a valuable lesson. Never again would I allow a potential contagious exposure to prevent me from doing a complete job. Although I make sure that all persons handling tissues and fluids from the cases are appropriately warned and that the tissues and fluids are appropriately labeled as to infectious agent, I never again want to be in a position where I've allowed public health concerns to compromise my work. It just isn't worth it.

DEATH OF A CHILD:
TYPES OF PEDIATRIC DEATHS

Probably no category of cases causes a forensic pathologist to think, rethink, and expend more emotional energy than those cases involving the death of a child. One subtype of these cases includes those falling into the sudden infant death syndrome or crib/cot death. These cases are more difficult when your own child is less than one year of age. When Sarah, my daughter, was that age, every case of SIDS looked like her.

Even more taxing, however, are those cases involving a fatally abused child. From a human point of view it's hard to understand how an adult can inflict so much injury on a person who's obviously so much smaller and helpless, although I must admit there have been times in the wee hours of the night when Sarah has made it seem more within the realm of possibility.

To be honest, I thought that getting married had really changed my life (for the better, dear), but it doesn't even begin to compete with the life changes that accompany that first bundle of joy. After you're married, the major change is that everything costs twice as much when you go to the movies or go out to eat.

When a baby arrives, doing anything spontaneously is impossible. My wife had to make sure that she had a reliable babysitter before going to a movie. After the movie, going out to eat can't occur because you the babysitter has to be home. I won't even mention the anxiety that parents experience when the children get sick. When it's my kid who is sick, all of my medical training goes out the window. I am every bit as anxious and paranoid as any other parent. Don't get me wrong. I love my children to death and love my grandchildren even more, but they have a way of completely changing my life in ways that I'd never considered.

From the pathologist's point of view, a fatally abused child is the one category of case where we have to be willing to call the parent or guardian a liar and state that the child hadn't died as the result of a tragic accident but had been killed by another person. Obviously, it's rare for parents to present themselves to law enforcement personnel stating that they've just killed their child.

Instead what usually happens is that the parents present the child to an emergency room with a story of an injury that at first seems reasonable. It's only by a careful examination of the body at autopsy, coupled with an equally careful examination of the scene, that a pathologist can come forward and say that the injuries are too severe to have been the result of the story given. This isn't usually done without some sleepless nights and some real soul-searching.

One case that springs to mind immediately involved a nine-month-old black male who was delivered to a local hospital. The mother of the infant was a divorced black nurse who was dating a white male employed by the city. Allegedly, Mom and her boyfriend had planned a date out that night, but she was unable to get a babysitter. Their plans ruined, they had decided to stay at home for the evening, have a nice home-cooked dinner together, and babysit the child. The mother left the house to go to a local grocery store to pick up steaks and assorted goods for the meal.

While the mother was gone, the boyfriend had allegedly placed the child on the sofa in the living room with a bottle. He then left the child and had gone into the kitchen and was in the process of getting dinner started. While in the kitchen, the boyfriend claimed that he heard the baby let out a loud scream. Afraid that the child had fallen off the couch, he came charging into the living room at a full gallop. As he entered the room and rounded the couch, before he could compensate, he claimed that he stepped on the child in the chest/abdomen region.

He then immediately picked up the child and tried to console him. Within minutes, however, he realized that something was seriously wrong with the baby. He continued to cry and refused to accept a bottle. The boyfriend claimed that he then picked up the child and rushed him to the grocery store to find the mother. From there, all three rushed to the emergency room where, after an attempt at resuscitation, the infant was pronounced dead. The emergency room physician, feeling that something was wrong, contacted the juvenile division of the city police.

After multiple interviews, the boyfriend maintained his story. The body was transferred to the county morgue where an autopsy would be performed to determine if the story was compatible with the injuries noted at necropsy. Unfortunately, I was the pathologist who had to make that decision.

At autopsy, the infant was a normally developed, normally nourished black male who appeared to be his reported age of nine months. Externally, there were no injuries of significance other than the tubes and needles placed in the child for resuscitation.

Internally, however, it was a different story. The abdominal cavity was full of blood. This was the result of a longitudinal tear of the liver, that is, a tearing running from the direction of head to toe. In the chest cavity, there were fractured ribs on both sides at the back. There was an additional finding which gave me reason to pause. One rib fracture on the left side was older than the other fractures, at least two weeks old. This was sobering. It indicated that the child had had other episodes of severe trauma, at least one episode severe enough to fracture the relatively elastic rib of an infant.

The information brought in by the city police was even more discouraging. This child had been admitted to different hospitals on two previous occasions for injuries, all within the last six months. One was for skull fractures, and the other was for a questionable fracture of a tibia or lower leg bone. Based on this information, in my opinion, this child represented a fatally abused child, a variant of the child abuse syndrome. This means that the child had received multiple severe injuries inflicted by an adult or adults over a period of time. With this information in hand, I signed the case out as a homicide, with the cause of death being blunt force injuries to the chest and abdomen.

This case proves that nothing is as easy or as straightforward as it first appears. In my mind I felt that if ever there was a straightforward case of a fatally abused child, this was it. That confidence lasted for some fourteen months until the case was being readied for trial.

One day in early February, I received a call from a Mr. Ion Gaston, defense attorney for the boyfriend. It was the first of many conferences we were to have in the pretrial interval. Mr. Gaston was, to say the least, an impressive attorney. It was obvious from each ensuing conference that he was doing his homework in terms of background information on the child abuse syndrome in general and our case in particular.

From the defense point of view, the crux of the defense revolved around whether the injuries could have been inflicted as described in the scenario so strongly maintained by the boyfriend. I would be less than honest if I didn't admit that I was sorely tempted to reply in the negative. Whether a pathologist will admit it or not, it becomes easy to get emotionally involved in a death under investigation. This is particularly true when the death is that of an obviously defenseless small child.

I suspect that from a social point of view, the senseless death of a child is repugnant to all of us at a visceral level. In addition, it's also easy to be swayed to the side of the defendant's guilt by the relatively biased information received from the police as they work their investigation. This, in my opinion, is one of the main reasons that the coroner or medical examiner must be a separate agency and politically unattached to law enforcement or local government.

In point of fact, I answered that the injuries were indeed consistent with the story given. I answered in the affirmative because quite honestly, I couldn't look at the injuries in this child and tell how they had been inflicted. All that I could say with certainty was that the injuries had been inflicted with a large degree of force by a relatively blunt object. This object could have been a shoe, a fist, or even a concrete block falling from an upper floor. The real question, as I related to Mr. Gaston, wasn't whether the injuries were consistent, but whether I believed the story. It was because I didn't believe the story that I had called the death a homicide.

I didn't believe the story for the several reasons that I related to Mr. Gaston. First, even though the child was only nine months old, he had already had several admissions to the hospital for severe trauma. One was for a fractured skull and one for a questionable fracture of the leg. If this had been a child just learning to walk or actively running about the house, it would be easier to rationalize the injuries, but this was a child who wasn't even actively crawling. Second, it was hard to believe that an adult would step down or stomp down on a child inadvertently. My reason for this was strictly nonmedical.

My wife, Beth, is and always has been an avid cat lover. As a result, since our marriage, we've had at least one and up to four cats around the house. At the very best, my relationship with the cats can be described as peaceful coexistence. Although compared to a dog, cats are relatively easier to care for, I seem to spend a large proportion of the time that it takes to get ready for work brushing cat hairs off my suit jacket and pants, but since Beth has made it perfectly clear that I would be booted out of the house before the cats were required to leave, I've learned to coexist.

One annoying habit that the cats have, however, is a tendency to want to sleep either on the bed or at least near the bed at night. I suspect it's a sign of their devotion to my wife or else they enjoy having all night to lie there watching me sleep, plotting all types of scenarios for doing me in, while at the same time making the event look like an accident. Regardless, on more than one occasion, feeling the urge to go to the bathroom in the middle of the night, I've had the misfortune to inadvertently step on one of the cats. Out of reflex, as soon as I subconsciously realized that I wasn't stepping on the carpeted floor, my reaction was to throw my weight off the cat in some other direction. This has quite often resulted in scraped knees, bruised elbows, and lumps on the head.

Talking to fellow indoor animal owners, I found the response was universally the same. It was reflex to avoid stepping on the sleeping animal even at the cost of bodily harm to the person doing the stepping. A local vet agreed with my analysis. It was thus difficult to believe that an adult entering a room at full gallop to check on a child would inadvertently come down on the child with all of his weight, in my opinion the amount of force needed to inflict the degree of injury noted at autopsy.

Interestingly, these points didn't seem to bother the defense attorney. I suspect that he realized that all that he really had to prove was the question of reasonable doubt. It was the prosecuting attorney's problem to prove intent to inflict harm.

Over the ensuing weeks, I had several meetings and telephone conferences with Mr. Gaston. It was one of the few times that I felt good about a defense attorney's ability to understand and interpret my testimony as it related to his client. If any defendant had a shot at proving his innocence, Gaston was doing the homework needed to do it.

A week before the case was to go to trial, I had my first conference with Mr. Galanos, Mobile County's district attorney. This conference did much to allay what reservations remained in my mind concerning the case. Mr. Galanos had several pictures of the home where the injury had taken place. Interestingly, the end of the couch where the infant had been placed was some two to three feet from the entrance that the boyfriend had used to enter the room at full gallop. For him to have stepped on the child lying in front of the couch, he would have had to enter through the doorway, turn sharply to his right, then sharply to his left. Only after these maneuvers would he have been in front of the couch where he stated that the child was lying. Unless this guy was a Walter Payton, in my opinion, he would have had difficulty maintaining a high rate of speed into the room while at the same time negotiating his way around the couch. In my opinion, coupled with the evidence already known, I felt secure that the infant's death was not an accident.

Although I'll obviously never know what really happened, I suspect that the boyfriend was a bit upset that this child kept getting in the way of his relationship with the mother. In a moment of anger, he stomped the child with his booted foot. Probably instantly regretting the act, he attempted to console the child. Realizing that the child was in trouble, he rushed him to his mother and subsequently to the hospital. The injuries, however, were too severe, and the child died.

Interestingly, after a trial of many days with testimony from other experts in forensic medicine, the jury convicted the boyfriend for murder. He's currently spending time in a state prison. I'm told that the mother of the infant initially believed that her boyfriend had killed her child but eventually became convinced of his innocence. She strongly supported his innocence throughout the trial with her moral support and testimony.

I suspect that many who finish this story will comment that justice has been done or that our judicial system, at least in this case, did work. Even though I realize that I had limited access to all the information available in the case, and even though in the rational side of my mind the scene and autopsy examinations pointed to a nonaccidental type of death, there's always a small nagging voice that wants me to believe that the death was an accident.

Unfortunately, there's no revelation from heaven after a trial is finished telling everyone involved what really happened. In my experience, most convicted murderers don't admit their guilt after the trial. Perhaps it's just as well not to know the whole truth and let that little nagging voice continue to give a suspected killer the benefit of the doubt until the facts of the case drown it out.

The other type of infant death that the forensic pathologist has to deal with is those deaths from the sudden infant death syndrome or, as the British refer to them, crib or cot death. These deaths usually occur in infancy during the first year. It's extremely important to remember that the diagnosis of SIDS can only be made in cases where death has occurred in an infant who was apparently healthy prior to his or her death. In addition, a complete autopsy examination to include bacterial cultures of the blood and cerebral spinal fluid (the fluid that surrounds and cushions the brain in the skull) and a microscopic examination (small pieces of tissue cut thin and stained so that they can be studied through a microscope) are all negative for disease or infection and a toxicology screen negative for drugs and poisons.

The importance of this rather strict criteria for the SIDS diagnosis is that the syndrome has become well known to the general public and lay coroners, and it has become easy to certify a death in infancy as SIDS. After all, the public was well aware of the syndrome, and it was a socially accepted explanation for the death of an infant. It also allowed everyone involved in a case to circumvent the possibility that the infant had been fatally abused.

Consider this scenario. A mother and father bring their infant child to a busy hospital emergency room. In the emergency room at the same time are multiple injured victims of a three-car pileup on the interstate highway. The overworked emergency room physician examines the infant in one of the examining rooms only to find that the child is dead. He quickly looks at the external surfaces of the infant and notes no signs of trauma. In an attempt to console the parents, he states that the death appears to be a case of sudden infant death syndrome and that there was nothing the parents could have done to anticipate or prevent the death. He then asks, without too much urgency in his voice, if the family would like to have the child autopsied. The mother breaks into tears and states that she can't stand the thought of having someone cut on her child. The doctor states that he understands completely and sends the child to the hospital morgue until the family can decide on a funeral home. He assures the family again that it was a SIDS death and that he'll sign the death certificate accordingly.

After the child is buried and the death certificate signed, the mother of the wife goes to the police. She feels that the father of the child was responsible for his/her death and wants the police to do something about it. Over the next week, rumors are flying and gaining momentum. Finally, a local judge, at the request of the prosecuting attorney, orders an exhumation and autopsy on the infant. Although the body had been previously embalmed making some subtle findings difficult, it's determined that the child died as the result of a fractured skull with bleeding into the brain and multiple fractured ribs with bleeding into the chest cavities. These findings were present in the complete absence of signs of external injury. The death certificate is thus amended from SIDS, a natural type of death, to blunt force injuries to the head and chest, in this case ruled a homicide.

When confronted with the facts from autopsy, the father breaks into tears and admits that he had lost his temper at the child after a long, hard day at work. The father had convinced the mother to keep quiet about the matter or her only source of income would be in prison. She had other older children to think about. The mother, out of guilt, had leaked the story to her mother, and the grandmother had gone straight to the police. Obviously, this doesn't happen every day. The majority of infant deaths classified as SIDS without an autopsy are probably just that, cases of SIDS; however, it is only with a complete autopsy that we as a society can be sure.

Another reason for confirming an infant's death as being a case of SIDS, though less emotionally dramatic, is that there's a considerable amount of money going into SIDS research. Obviously, we need good, accurate statistics to determine the true incidence of the syndrome and follow the impact of various modes of intervention.

From my perspective, there are few categories of death that can be more emotionally taxing than SIDS deaths. Here is a couple who has just had a baby together. They have had sufficient time to develop strong emotional ties with all of the resulting hopes and dreams for the child's future; then one night, the child is put to sleep just as he or she has been put to sleep every other night. The parents usually wake up late, wondering why they weren't rudely awakened in the middle of the night by a hungry baby. They go to the baby's bed to find him cold and stiff. Not knowing what to do, they call the paramedics to help resuscitate the child, but it's much too late for that. The police come to the scene and ask a few questions. They in turn call the medical and legal authority to aid in the investigation. That's where we come into the picture.

These death scenes are always tough. Walking into the house, the mother and father are usually assembled in a room together with family members who are trying to console them. To be honest, I try to avoid contact with the parents until after the examination of the baby. I want to have at least an initial impression of the circumstances of the death so that my response to the family is as appropriate as possible. If after examining the child the circumstances make the death appear as a SIDS type of death, I talk briefly with the mother and father, usually asking questions about how the baby was acting, about the baby's delivery, and about the baby's health record in general. If after this discussion I still feel comfortable with the SIDS classification, I explain to the parents that the death appears to be a SIDS type of death, but that a complete autopsy will be necessary before a definitive cause of death can be given. I promise to call them with the autopsy results as soon as possible and usually try to have a conference with the family after the entire report is completed.

The autopsy examination that follows in the true SIDS case is by definition completely negative for any abnormality in the organs that would cause death. The only usual findings are petechial (pinpoint) hemorrhages on the outside surfaces of the lungs and thymus (an organ responsible for formation of a subtype of white blood cells in the blood.) All blood and fluid cultures from the body must also be negative for disease-causing organisms and drugs.

Although no one knows the exact cause for SIDS, most people feel that it's really a group of disorders, with the final mechanism of death being disruption of breathing. Although much money has been spent trying to prove some rather far out explanations, no one has, to my knowledge, offered a reasonable all-encompassing explanation. Most authorities feel, however, that SIDS is not an inherited problem, so the loss of one child to the syndrome shouldn't discourage a family from having another child. One interesting subgroup has, however, been described. These are infants who die while in the same bed with the parent or parents. It's been hypothesized that some of these cases are actually the results of the parent rolling over and smothering the child during sleep.

From the forensic pathologist's point of view, it's difficult to impossible to differentiate between a SIDS-type death and an intentional asphyxiation of the infant. Adults tend to put up a good fight when someone attempts to cut off their air. At autopsy, we usually see signs of this struggle in the way of scratches, bruises, or even fragments of the assailant's hair or skin beneath the victim's fingernails. In children less than one year of age, however, there is no struggle. In fact, it's not unusual for the infant to remain asleep during the asphyxia. Only occasionally will there be facial scratches to indicate forceful airway obstruction. These cases can only be solved by a spontaneous confession of guilt by the responsible parent.

Fortunately, this type of case probably represents the vast minority. The family of true SIDS victims needs to be reassured that there was no way to predict the infant's death and that there was nothing they could do to prevent the death. This information is particularly important to emphasize in those cases where the infant was totally under the care of one particular parent at the time of death. In addition, most areas have support groups available to grieving parents. These groups allow access to families who have gone through the same crisis. In my opinion, the role of the pathologist in these cases is not only to confirm the diagnosis by a thorough autopsy but also to reassure the parents as much as possible. Again, only if all members of a family can fully understand the death are they in a position to put the death in perspective and begin to rebuild their own lives as individuals and as a family.

One interesting trend has occurred in the recent past. Some eighteen years ago, the number of SIDS cases in our medical examiner's office dropped by about 40 percent. The next year, it dropped an additional 20 percent. It has since maintained this markedly lower number over the intervening years. What happened?

The year before the first drastic drop in SIDS, the American Academy of Pediatrics published a paper describing a lower rate of SIDS in children who were placed in their cribs on their backs. As a result, the pediatric community began to immediately pass this information on to the new and repeat parents in their practices, and the rest is history. From just a common sense point of view, a discerning person would automatically assume that by laying the infant on their backs in their cribs would cause an increased chance of aspirating acid and food from the stomach into the infant's lungs. That in turn would lead to possible chemical pneumonitis or plain old bacterial pneumonia. This is not the case, and my personal experience with the subject confirms the studies. Of course, the Native Americans already knew this, and as a result, their populations have always maintained a historically lower SIDS rate.

Although I believe that every citizen should have the right to own and bear arms as a constitutionally guaranteed freedom, along with this right comes a responsibility to maintain and store these weapons safely. Another case that causes me great personal anguish is those involving the death of a child due to the unsafe storage of a firearm. Unfortunately, in this line of work, we get to see these tragedies firsthand. I personally have had the grim task of investigating some ten deaths involving children killed with firearms. Most of these deaths were caused by handguns kept in the home for protection and were simply misstored and thus easily accessible to the children, usually between the ages of eight and twelve. In our jurisdiction which combines both metropolitan and more rural territories, I've also investigated pediatric deaths where rifles and shot guns have been involved.

One case that comes to mind involved an eleven-year-old male who had ready access to a 410 shotgun which he used for hunting in the woods near his home. He had come home one afternoon shotgun in hand. He entered the front door and, according to his testimony, was in the process of unloading the gun. The shotgun discharged, with the pellet load crossing the living room and entering the kitchen. His five-year-old sister was standing at the refrigerator in the process of getting a glass of milk. The buckshot hit her in the left chest, exiting from her right flank. In the process, the subsequent autopsy showed, the pellets had struck her heart and severely torn her liver. The mother, sitting in a nearby room, heard the discharge, ran into the room, and immediately rushed her daughter to a nearby ambulance company. The twenty-minute ambulance drive to the nearest hospital wasn't quick enough to save the child.

One repeating scenario in these senseless deaths involves a young friend or sibling who knows where the family's loaded handgun is stored, be it in a closet, bedside drawer, or under the parents' mattress. Either to scare friends or to show off, the youngster gets the gun and in the process of playing, discharges the weapon critically wounding or killing a fellow playmate. In one of my cases, a young boy was using the father's handgun to play cops and robbers with his sister. The sister died as the result of a gunshot wound to the head. I could go on and on.

Obviously, for every tragedy, there are hundreds of families who keep weapons in the house without mishap. Diehard gun addicts claim that the answer is a combination of education for the children and common sense by the parents. Children in the home where guns are kept should be taught about their dangers and probably have the weapon's potential destructive capabilities demonstrated at a firing range. In my opinion, a loaded gun should never be kept in the home. The weapon should be stored out of the reach or ready access of all children. A bedside drawer or between mattresses, in my opinion, isn't a good location. In addition, ammunition should be stored separately preferably locked in a site separate from the gun. Some might argue that this makes access to the weapon during a burglary difficult, but in real life, the chances of needing access to the weapon that quickly are improbable. I keep my handguns in a locked box where only my wife, Beth, and I know the combination.

Quite possibly even the greater tragedy in these cases involves the youngsters who are holding the discharging weapon responsible for the death of a sibling or friend. I'm sure that the event scars their life and dreams for many years. Although some might maintain that my perspective is skewed, in my opinion, it only takes one look at my daughter, Sarah, playing after I've finished a case involving this type of death, to make any reason for keeping a loaded gun in the home insignificant.

Infanticide is yet another form of pediatric death encountered by the forensic pathologist. These are the deaths of newborn, or at least newly born, infants at the hands of another, usually a parent. The death can take an active form where the adult actually causes the death by physical means, or it can be a passive form where death is the result of a failure to supply basic needs such as food, water, and shelter.

From strictly an autopsy point of view, these cases are difficult to prove beyond a reasonable doubt. There are several reasons. First, in most states, the burden is on the prosecution to prove that the child was born alive and capable of sustaining life on his/her own independent of the mother. To prove live birth in many cases is a feat in itself. To qualify, the infant must be totally expelled from the mother and show evidence of respiration on his/her own. These facts can be proven by finding food in the infant's stomach, evidence of lung expansion at autopsy, or evidence of vital reaction at the site where the umbilical cord is severed. (Anytime there's injury, the body reacts to that injury by increasing blood flow to the site accompanied by white cells. Once the body dies, this no longer occurs. If present, we know that the injury was inflicted when the person was still alive.)

Finding food in the stomach is obvious evidence that the child was alive at least long enough to eat. Although the finding of pus cells and hemorrhage at the site where the umbilical cord was cut is good evidence of life after birth, in many of these cases, the placenta and cord are still attached to the baby. Although historically the determination of live birth can be established through examination of the lungs for signs of expansion, many forensic experts are skeptical about our ability to predict whether or not breathing has actually occurred.

The methods used to make these lung determinations involved the use of both gross and microscopic tests. In the gross portion of the test, the lungs were simply dropped into a solution of 10 percent formalin. If the lung had been expanded such that all or most of the individual alveolar air sacs were opened and filled with air, the lungs should float in the formalin solution. If, on the other hand, the lungs hadn't been expanded with air, they tend to be denser than the formalin solution and sink. Thus, floating lungs indicate extra uterine life, while sinking lungs tend to indicate stillbirth.

The microscopic test, though appearing more sophisticated, is actually a variation on the same theme as floating. In this case, however, thin stained sections of lung tissue are examined under the microscope to determine if the small alveolar air sacs and small tubes leading to the sacs are expanded and open or collapsed and closed. The findings would indicate live birth and stillbirth, respectively.

As with most tests in medicine as well as life in general, neither of these tests prove to be absolutely reliable. Premature infant lungs have been noted to flunk both tests despite surviving for days after birth. Postmortem decomposition with gas-producing bacteria may expand the air spaces even though the child was born dead. If anyone attempts any sort of artificial respiration on the child at the time of birth, it becomes difficult or impossible to separate the resuscitation-induced artifact from the true findings of the case itself.

Proving that the child was capable of sustaining life on his/her own with only the aid of basic supports like food, water, and shelter is no less a feat. In cases where the question of neglect with malnutrition involves a live child, the pediatricians have a distinct advantage. In these cases, they need only to hospitalize the child and feed him nutritious meals and see if he improves. If the child does improve, a case for intentional neglect is proven. If the child doesn't improve, the parents or guardians are exonerated, and the reason for the failure to thrive can be investigated and probably corrected.

In the child found dead with signs of malnutrition and neglect, the problem isn't so easily solved. For in addition to proving there's no major birth defect responsible for the condition of the child, the pathologist is also forced to attempt to prove there were no metabolic or absorption problems responsible for the death. Because many of these problems are the results of genetic abnormalities manifested on a subcellular or biochemical level, they're impossible to prove or disprove in a deceased child. Thus, no matter how thorough an autopsy examination, there are literally hundreds of diseases which can't be eliminated after death. As a result, proving that a malnourished child died as a result of neglect after birth is often impossible.

Fortunately, the circumstances surrounding the death as well as good background investigation can often fill in the gaps left by the autopsy. I had one such case that occurred in Mississippi. I had been asked by a coroner in a nearby county in Mississippi to perform the autopsy of a deceased, newborn baby delivered in his county. According to the coroner, the morbidly obese mother had arrived at the hospital in labor and was severely ill from a medical complication of pregnancy called eclampsia. She was taken to the delivery room where she produced a stillborn baby girl. Realizing that the mother was also in grave danger, the obstetrician anxiously waited to deliver the placenta or afterbirth. To his surprise, the placenta was actually composed of two fused placentas. Examination of the umbilical cords showed that the other cord had been recently cut, but where was the other baby?

The coroner was contacted. Accompanied by local police, the coroner went to the mother's home to look for the other baby. He claimed that he was just about to give up his search when the other baby was located in a dirty clothes basket in the back of a closet. The child had been wrapped in the bloody sheets, probably stripped from a bare mattress in one of the adjacent bedrooms. Trying to decide if he should take the whole dirty clothes basket for examination or just the baby and sheets, he brought the whole clothes basket to our laboratory for examination. I was glad he did.

After examining the two babies and twin placenta, I knew I would have a difficult time proving live birth in the basket baby. As I talked to the coroner, we both began going through the clothes basket, looking for any helpful clues. What we found was infant skeletons, three in all, each wrapped in separate sheets at different levels in the basket. Obviously, this had become a regular ritual for our mother. She probably delivered her babies at home and wrapped them in a sheet which was placed in the back of the closet where the baby wouldn't be heard and could soon be forgotten. She probably had attempted to do the same this time but had gotten into trouble because of the twin pregnancy. Had she not been rushed to the hospital this time, there's no telling how many more babies would have ended up in that clothes basket.

The story continued to play to its sad ending. While the mother continued a stormy medical course in the hospital, the husband was interviewed by the police and coroner. The husband denied knowing that his wife had ever been pregnant, a possibility given her morbidly obese state. He volunteered that they had both agreed that because of their financial condition, raising a family at this time was out of the question. They had decided to start a family when they could better afford it. He claimed that his wife had been on birth-control pills since their marriage five years earlier.

The legal problems remained. Should the district attorney charge the mother with infanticide? He felt that he had a strong case based on the findings of the newborn skeletons despite the obvious problems from the autopsy's inability to prove live birth in either twin. He was probably right, but the legal questions soon became academic. The mother subsequently died in the intensive care unit of their local hospital, the result of complications from her twin pregnancy.

The one case involving a fatally abused child which to this day haunts me most occurred not long after I had moved to Pensacola, FL, to work as an associate medical examiner. One evening, I received a call from my investigator, Eric Huter, stating that he thought that I should come out to a scene. When he explained that the case was an apparent fatally abused child, any reluctance on my part quickly drained away. Fatally abused child cases were always the most difficult and emotionally trying. The more information that I can glean, the more likely I would be able to handle problems that were sure to arise.

The history available to me when I arrived at the scene was that the deceased white male infant was the child of a young couple who had been married for a little over a year. They had been high school sweethearts since middle school and had married shortly after both had received associate's degrees from the local junior college. They both planned to eventually finish their undergraduate degree as time and money permitted.

Both parents worked full-time at entry-level jobs in the community. The wife worked nights at one of the local hospitals, while the husband worked days at a car dealership.

It was the police officer's understanding that although the baby came as a surprise, both parents were thrilled to have their own family started. In fact, the mother had switched from her day shift at the hospital to the evening shift so that one of them would always be home to care for the baby. In addition, both sets of parents lived in town so they had help available as needed.

According to the police, on the day of the incident, the husband had come home from work after a "normal day." The wife was home with the four-month infant baby boy and had already fed him his bottle, changed his diaper, and prepared him to be passed over to the father's care. A short time later, the mother kissed her husband and baby goodbye and left for work, just another normal day.

According to the father, the early evening went well with another bottle and a clean diaper being all that was necessary to keep his son happy. There was no history of colic or other chronic conditions with the child. The father stated that around 9:00 p.m., the baby awoke and started crying nonstop for the next three hours. The father stated that he tried everything that he could think of in an attempt to calm the child, but nothing helped.

At this point, the father lost his temper, jerked the child out of his crib by his ankles, and smashed his head against the wall, the side of the crib, and the baby's changing table. At the scene, there was blood and brain fragments splattered everywhere on the floor, walls, and ceiling. The dead, brutalized baby was quietly lying in his crib when I arrived at the scene.

Immediately after the incident, the father walked out of their apartment, got into his pickup truck, drove to the sheriff's office, and turned himself in. Initially, the sheriff's deputy who the father contacted at the sheriff's office didn't believe the father's story. The gelatinous fragments of blood and brains still on the father clothes made him change his mind.

So why did it happen? That's been the question that has plagued me over the intervening years. The father was a man without a previous mental problem and a negative history of drug and alcohol abuse. He had a loving wife and extended family yet was able to commit the most grotesque crime imaginable. I think what scared and still scares me most is the fact that I've been in that same place with my own children. If I've learned nothing else from this case, I've learned that when children or grandchildren push the adult to the breaking point, they must learn to make themselves walk away and allow themselves the time to cool down and put things into perspective. Ironically for this young man, he was only a phone call away from extended family support. Why didn't he call?

I suspect that you can now understand why pediatric death cases bothered me most. Without a doubt, it was the cases that involve children as victims. The most horrific are the fatally abused children, but cases of accidental deaths in children closely follow. Sudden infant death syndrome victims were also emotionally draining for me, especially when I had to meet with the parents to explain the findings of my examination. How do I explain to parents that their normal, healthy baby suddenly died without a good medical explanation?

The major reason for the stress involved in these cases is the fact that they always made me reflect on my own children and how lucky I've been to have them survive into adulthood. Although I could statistically hope that my children would be spared an early death by the hands of another, the accidental deaths that occur in children make me realize how easily it could have been me mourning the death of my own children from some freak accident or SIDS, but despite the multitude of pediatric deaths that I've investigated over the years, it's extremely rare to have a medical examiner case where the victim was an adult while the perpetrator or perpetrators were children. In November 2001, I experienced my first and only case.

In 1986, twenty-one-year-old Terry King met seventeen-year-old Janet French. There was an immediate attraction between the two, with Janet seeing the older Terry as fun and exciting while Terry was attracted to Janet's natural beauty. They fell in love, moved in together, but were never officially married. Two years later, their first child, Derek, was born and followed one year later by the birth of their second child, Alex.

After the birth of their two children, their marriage began to suffer. Terry, with only a high school diploma, had difficulty financially providing for the family. Janet, a young attractive nineteen-year-old became progressively depressed with her boring life as a stay-at-home mom with two young boys and no social interaction due to a lack of money. One day, while looking together for jobs in the local newspaper's classified ads, Terry was depressed to find that he wasn't qualified for any of the jobs listed. They both noted a classified ad promising big money fast with earnings of $1,000 weekly. The ad was seeking new attractive young women to work as exotic dancers for a local men's club.

Although the job violated both Terry's and Janet's sense of morality, they desperately needed the income. Janet interviewed for the job and was hired. While Terry became a stay-at-home dad, Janet became an exotic, topless dancer and soon found herself immersed in a party lifestyle that she found appealing. She never made the $1,000 per week that had been advertised, but she made more than Terry was able to provide.

As Janet became more and more involved in the party life at work, she was soon coming home later and later, finally culminating in not coming home for days at a time. Terry was left at home with the two boys, while Janet, unbeknownst to Terry, had become the girlfriend of the club owner. The club owner eventually became jealous of the attention Janet was getting as a dancer and demoted her from exotic dancer to a waitress, with her income dropping as a consequence. She became pregnant with twin boys that Janet eventually confessed belonged to another man. Terry accepted both infants as his own without hesitation, hoping that the act would solidify his relationship with Janet. It didn't work.

Janet, meanwhile, continued her relationship with the club owner, but her decreased income wasn't enough to provide for a family with four growing boys. Terry needed to go to work again, but he would also need child care for his four children. Janet was simply not home enough to take care of the children, so Terry solicited help from Janet's previously divorced parents.

Janet's mom and stepdad agreed to take five-year-old Derek while her father and stepmother agreed to take four-year-old Alex into their respective homes indefinitely with custody until Terry was financially able to provide for them. Janet elected to take the twins and moved in with the boyfriend. It took Janet only two days to return the twins to Terry because they bothered her boyfriend.

Eventually, all four of the King boys were placed in a privately funded "home for troubled children." The boys were just becoming adjusted to their new life when after eight months, the home ran out of funding and had to permanently close their doors. The twins were put up for adoption and went to a good permanent home.

Alex couldn't adjust to foster care and soon went back home to live with his father. Derek went to live with a local family in a foster parent–type arrangement. Derek, despite being placed in a stable, loving environment, continued to have emotional issues that slowly escalated until the foster family finally had to return Derek to his father.

Shortly before Derek returned home, Terry had begun working two jobs, one at a printing shop and another at a local flea market. The flea market job introduced Terry to a local business man who befriended him and leased him a small home in Cantonment, a rural area near Pensacola. Reliable transportation continued to be an issue for Terry. The problem was solved by Ricky Chavis, a white male in his late thirties who had converted his yard into a mechanic's paradise. Ricky befriended Terry and allowed him free access to his tools and equipment.

Terry and Alex would often stay late at the Chavis residence and occasionally they would sleep over if Alex had already fallen asleep. Anxious to have his family reunited, Terry welcomed Derek's return home in September 2001. Terry was thrilled to be with his two boys in a place that they could call home. It was impossible at this point for Terry to realize that there were still big problems ahead. The first problem was that, unknown to Terry, Ricky Chavis was a convicted pedophile who had converted his home into a video game heaven to entice children into his home. He had even dug a hiding place under his bedroom floor to help hide runaway children should his home be searched. The second was that Terry's relationship with Ricky Chavis would lead to his death in the upcoming month.

Not long after their reunion as a family of three, Alex began acting strangely. He progressively became more subdued and wouldn't participate in the church activities that he had previously relished, all the while continuously complaining and acting out with his dad despite their previous close, loving relationship. In the weeks leading to their father's death, both Alex and Derek decided to run away from home. After a several-day community-wide search, both boys were safely located.

Ricky Chavis, Terry's good friend, was the hero who both found the boys and brought them back home. Despite a safe reunion, things weren't well in the King family. Terry was deeply disappointed in the boys' attempt to run away, and the boys in turn were afraid that their dad was going to physically punish them for their act of defiance, something that Terry had never done before.

On the night of Terry King's death, November 26, 2001, Terry and the boys were home alone. The boys had been restricted to their room as a punishment for running away. Terry elected to sleep in the living room where he would hear the boys should they try to run away again. While asleep in his recliner, someone came up behind him and struck him hard on the head at least three times with a blunt object subsequently determined to be an aluminum baseball bat. He never knew what hit him and died while continuing to sit comfortably in his living room recliner. The house was then set on fire, with the alarm reported at 1:39 a.m. Some 40 percent of the house was destroyed by the fire despite attempts to extinguish it. The sooty, charred body of Terry King was recovered from the rubble. The two boys were nowhere to be found. The fire investigation showed that the fire had originated in the bedroom area of the small house. Evidence of an accelerant was found.

The initial question was where were the two boys when all of this was occurring, and what, if any, was their involvement in Terry King's death? The search for the boys on the first day after the fire was fruitless; the boys were nowhere to be found. On November 27, the next day, the boys were brought into the Escambia County Sheriff's Office by Ricky Chavis, who claimed the boys had called him and that he had convinced them to come to the sheriff's office.

Both boys were individually interviewed by homicide detectives in the sheriff's office, and both separately confessed to their involvement in their father's death. They calmly admitted that Derek had smashed his father on the head with an aluminum baseball bat, while Alex claimed credit for masterminding the idea.

After killing their father, they had used lighter fluid to start the house fire in the hope of destroying any evidence. The legal circus surrounding the case started immediately when both boys, Derek, thirteen years of age, and Alex, twelve years of age, were charged as adults for the first-degree murder of their father, Terry King.

From this point forward, the case began to get confusing. Although the brothers had initially claimed complete responsibility for their father's death, during their subsequent grand jury testimonies, after talking to their court-appointed attorneys, they instead claimed that Ricky Chavis had come to the house to pick them up, and while they hid in the trunk of Ricky's car, Chavis had killed their father and set their house on fire. He then took them back to his trailer where they stayed until Ricky Chavis had taken them into the sheriff's office.

Allegedly, Ricky Chavis had used the time between the house fire and their surrender to the sheriff's office to have the boys memorize and polish the confession that they had initially given to the homicide investigators. As you might imagine, the story soon caught the attention of the national media, and television personalities began arriving in town to report on the unfolding drama.

The change in Alex and Derek's testimonies during the grand jury quickly transformed Ricky Chavis from the hero who had found the boys to the perpetrator who had kidnapped the boys and killed their father. He was arrested without bond and placed in the Escambia County jail pending trial.

Who was really guilty of the murder of Terry King, and logistically, who would stand trial for King's death? The prosecution found itself in a "Damned if you don't, damned if you do" scenario. With little or no physical evidence on which to base his prosecution, the state attorney had to mainly rely on testimony that was conflicting in terms of who actually committed the murder.

If Alex and Derek had actually planned and murdered their father as they initially confessed, then Ricky Chavis might be tried and possibly convicted for a crime that he didn't commit. If Ricky had indeed been the murderer, then the boys shouldn't be tried for a death in which they were mere pawns used by a sick man. Since all three of the defendants had been indicted for the murder, how should the court choose the order in which the three are tried and how do you keep the earlier verdict from influencing the verdict that will follow?

After much debate between all parties concerned, the trials were conducted back to back, with Ricky Chavis being tried first and the two boys to follow. To prevent the first verdict from influencing the second verdict, the verdict from Chavis's trial was sealed and held until the second trial was completed, and then all three verdicts were to be read together. The fact that Chavis was tried first placed the prosecutor in the awkward position of trying to convince the jury of Chavis's guilt while being personally convinced that the boys were really the guilty parties.

Both trials were conducted amid a flood of media lights and cameras. The Chavis trial revealed to the jury and community that Ricky Chavis was a sick man who preyed on young boys to get his sexual kicks. The defense attorney representing Chavis was in the enviable position of defending his client against a prosecutor who, because of the trial to follow, was pulling all of his punches so as not to contradict his prosecution of the subsequent trial. The first trial was finally completed and the jury's verdict rendered and sealed, allowing the next trial to go forward.

Both the prosecution and the four defense attorneys, two for each brother, were much more animated during this second trial and the level of media coverage much more ubiquitous with representatives present from the national outlets as well as Court TV.

I was called by the prosecution to testify to the autopsy findings. The use of color prints of the autopsy wounds was guaranteed to capture the interest of all the parties present. I wasn't disappointed. After describing the wounds and explaining the photographs for the jury, the prosecution asked me if the description of the sounds that Terry King made after being struck by the baseball bat were consistent with what I would expect to hear. Alex had described his father making breathing noises that sounded like he had a stopped-up nose, with the breathing process causing his face to expand slightly with each breath. This type of breathing pattern is commonly noted in brain injury cases when a partial obstruction of the airway by traumatized soft tissues results in what physicians call a death rattle. The ballooning of the face would also be consistent with air escaping from the victim on exhalation being trapped by the fractured bones and swollen soft tissues of the face, causing it to expand with each outward breath. The description was too close to what would actually have been observed in the room at the time of Terry King's death for me to believe that Alex hadn't been present to experience it up close and personal.

The trial continued with all five lawyers calling multiple witnesses to give dramatic, heart-wrenching testimony, both for the victim and for the boys accused of his murder. After equally dramatic closing arguments, the defendants and attorneys from both sides as well as the Pensacola community expectantly awaited the jury's verdict. On September 6, 2002, the juries read their verdicts.

Derek and Alex were found guilty of second-degree murder without a weapon as well as both guilty of arson. One hour later, Ricky Chavis was escorted into the same courtroom where his jury rendered the verdict of not guilty on both the murder and the arson charge; he would be tried separately on charges of obstruction of justice and pedophilia.

Things started to get really crazy. The local newspaper had interviewed several of the jurors from the King boys' case who stated that they had dropped the charges from first-degree to second-degree murder because they believed that it had been Ricky Chavis who struck the actual blows to Terry King's head and set the house on fire, but because they believed that the boys had opened the door and allowed Chavis into the house, it was a preplanned effort involving all three defendants. They had convicted both boys of the lesser charge assuming that Ricky Chavis would be found guilty of first-degree murder to go with the boys' second-degree verdicts. The Ricky Chavis jury, on the other hand, claimed that they felt that Ricky Chavis was guilty of being involved in the murder, but that the prosecution had failed to give them the proof or the direction they needed to render a verdict to convict him.

The media circus got out their three ring tent and had a heyday interviewing defense attorneys, family members, jurors, and friends of the family, baiting them to become more and more outraged by the injustice they perceived to have occurred in Pensacola. Because there were few newsworthy events occurring at the time, the Terry King trial continued to cause a feeding frenzy with the news organizations at all levels. The publicity became so intense that Alex and Derek's mother became involved in the mounting protests, assuming the role of the weeping mother who only wanted justice for her boys. This was despite the fact that she had made no attempts to visit her sons prior to the trial.

Finally, it came time to have the King boys' sentencing. The judge began by criticizing the prosecutor for handling the two cases in such a way that he presented two different scenarios with different perpetrators for the same homicide. Because of the way the trials were handled, it had been possible to end up with two different first-degree murder verdicts based on the two separate scenarios that the prosecution had presented to the separate juries in the two trials. This could have put the judge in the unenviable position of having to set aside one of the murder convictions by overriding one of the jury derived verdicts. That was unacceptable to the judge, and in his opinion, it kept Derek and Alex King from having a fair trial.

As per routine, the defense attorneys for the boys presented after trial motions requesting that the judge set aside the jury verdict, allowing their defendants a new trial with a new jury. This is only rarely done, but in this case, that was exactly what the judge decided to do. The judge granted the defense's motion and overturned the verdicts on both of the boys.

This was obviously good news for Derek and Alex's defense team, but the overturned verdicts didn't mean that the boys were deemed innocent in the case. It only meant that the defendants had won the right to a new trial. In this instance, the judge had another surprise up his robe sleeve.

He ordered the case to mediation so that, instead of a new trial, both legal teams were required to sit down and come up with a compromise acceptable to both sides, enough punishment given that the prosecution felt justice had been served yet a light-enough sentence that the defense felt that their client had not been offered up as a sacrifice. Although mediation is a common method of arriving at a compromise in civil and family law issues, it has rarely if ever been used in a first-degree murder case.

In mediation, both sides start by announcing what they want the verdict to be, then an unbiased court-appointed mediator goes between the two camps seeking areas of possible compromise. Both sides usually have issues on which they refuse to compromise, and it's the mediator's job to soften them up on these tough issues in an attempt to end up with a final result that no one really likes but that they are willing to accept.

In this case, the final result was that both boys would be given a third-degree murder conviction if they both wrote letters to the judge confessing to the murder of their father and if Alex agreed to testify against Ricky Chavis, who was soon to be tried for obstruction of justice and pedophilia. In return, Alex would spend seven years in prison while Derek would serve eight. Neither side was happy with the mediation, but on the other hand, no one wanted to risk the outcome of another trial.

As previously stated, Ricky Chavis was found not guilty for the murder of Terry King. His second trial for the charges of kidnapping and child molestation began on February 11, 2003. Chavis was being charged under a state statute that a person is guilty of kidnapping if he confines a victim under the age of thirteen without the consent of his legal parent or guardian for the purpose of committing a crime. Even if the child consented, it was still a crime. Since Derek had been thirteen at the time of the offense, only Alex's confinement could be pursued under this statute.

The prosecutor in this trial was the same individual who had handled both Chavis and the King boys' previous trials. Because of the outcomes of the two trials, he had taken a beating both professionally and personally. He went from being the prosecutor who handled and won the difficult murder cases locally to being investigated by an attorney ethics board. He was also enduring the media blitz judging his legal abilities, his ethics, and his moral integrity. As a result, he was probably not at his best during the Chavis kidnapping and molestation trial.

Although he'd been given permission to use the testimony of previous Chavis sexual victims, the prosecution did a poor job of showing Chavis's history of pedophilia and the damaged lives that he had left in his wake prior to his molestation of Alex King. The prosecution was so focused on confirming that Alex had indeed been the person who murdered his father that he failed to convince the jury that Alex King was also a sexual victim of Chavis.

The end result was that the jury failed to convict Chavis on the kidnapping and molestation charges. I suspect that the state, by trying to convict Chavis on the verdict that would guarantee him the longest time behind bars, failed to convince the jury that Chavis met that higher level of guilt. The jury instead convicted Chavis of false imprisonment, a much lesser charge that allowed only a maximum five-year prison sentence compared to the life in prison with an additional 170 years that the kidnapping charge allowed.

Fortunately, Chavis wasn't yet completely out of the woods legally. There was yet another hurdle that Chavis and his defense attorney would have to clear before the legal system was finished with him. Chavis had also been charged with being an accessory after the fact in the murder of Terry King and tampering with evidence of the murder by washing the boys' clothes after the murder.

This trial began on February 24, 2002, and unlike the previous three trials, it moved along quickly. Derek King took the stand and basically knocked out all of the props from under the defense attorney's attempts to prove that Chavis was merely trying to be a Good Samaritan by taking in the boys and washing their clothes. After a short time to reflect on the evidence given, the jury returned a verdict of guilty on both the accessory to first-degree murder and tampering with evidence. The judge quickly handed Chavis the maximum sentence possible.

So was justice served when all was said and done? In my opinion, those parties guilty in the murder of Terry King were punished. Although we'll never really know who actually swung the bat to kill Terry King, I feel confident that the three punished were the three involved in his death. In addition, the testimony that Alex gave the court in terms of the sounds that his father was making after the blows to the head as well as the sounds made when the blows were being inflicted convinced me that Alex was at least in the room when the murder occurred. Did Alex have the strength necessary to swing the bat and inflict the wounds that I noted at autopsy? Having coached a Little League baseball team composed of young men of a similar age, my answer would be yes, quite capable.

Of course the real villain in this awful case was Ricky Chavis. He, in my opinion, had brainwashed the two boys into believing that their father was abusive. He convinced Alex that he was a homosexual and used their relationship to satisfy all of his own perverted desires. He had convinced both boys that by killing their father, they would be able to spend the rest of their lives with him at his fun-filled trailer with endless video games, alcohol, and pot.

Whether Chavis actually swung the bat himself or merely convinced the boys that killing their father was the right thing to do, Ricky Chavis was the real murderer in this case. His thirty-year prison sentence rendered at his second trial guaranteed that he would be on the receiving end of sexual abuse for years to come. Pedophiles are among the favorites of the homosexual prison population because even they think that sexual abuse of children is wrong. There is a concept of justice, though perverted, in prisons.

Despite all that Chavis will have to endure while in confinement, it's still not nearly enough punishment for a man who knowingly used young boys in such a self-serving destructive way. Of course, there are many who would agree with me that there's an entity called ultimate justice and that Chavis is yet to stand before the Ultimate Judge, one who knows all the evidence and renders judgment righteously. Thirty years in prison may end up being just "a walk in the park" when compared to that judgment to come.

DEATH IN THE SUMMERTIME: DECOMPOSED BODIES

Probably the one category of cases where few people would argue that the forensic pathologist really earns his money is those involving decomposing bodies. Most forensic pathologists agree that these cases are job security. There's something basic to the human animal that makes the sight and smell of a decomposing body repulsive. Even funeral home personnel and police officers who are exposed daily to dead bodies will turn green about the gills at the first sight or whiff. I would be lying if I stated that decomposed bodies don't bother me. As I've already stated I've been blessed with a fairly strong stomach, so most of the time I'm able to cope. Personally I've found that if I psychologically prepare myself for what to expect, I do fine. If, however, I walk into a scene not expecting a badly decomposed individual I tend to have to fight the nausea along with the rest of the folks at the scene.

An example of this occurred right after I had started with the department. It was a case known to Beth and me as the maggot man. Brian Delmas and I were called by the Mobile County Sheriff's Office to a scene at a chemical plant in the north section of the county. We arrived to find a middle aged white male lying in the woods off a service road just inside one of the gates to the plant. Examining the body at the scene was no real problem. Admittedly, he was beginning to decompose.

We estimated that he had been dead for at least two days. Initial impressions as to the cause of death were equally obvious. The victim had been stabbed several times in the chest and hit about the head with a blunt object. It was in the middle of June at the time and terribly hot. As we examined the body at the scene I did notice a few maggots beginning to work about the head area of the body, but I was surprised that with the degree of decomposition, the infestation wasn't more advanced. I did note a lot of yellow-tan sawdust-like material over the neck region, but this was no more than a passing mental image.

Because of the incredible heat at the scene, we hurriedly got the body into the ambulance and en route to our body cooler located at the hospital. As it was late afternoon and both Brian and I were hot and tired, we elected to do the autopsy early the next morning after the body had had a chance to cool down in the morgue.

I arrived at the hospital a bit earlier than usual the next morning hoping to get the external portion of the examination finished before the autopsy assistants arrived. The body was still covered with a sheet as I rolled it into the autopsy room. I then turned on the lights and pulled off the sheets.

What I saw at that point will be firmly etched in my mind until I die. Instead of the body as I remembered from the scene, the head and neck region was a moving mountain of maggots. They were so thick that I had to scrape them off the surfaces of the body to convince myself that I was looking at the same body. Waves of nausea came over me and I was glad no one was present to witness my performance. As I attempted to wash the maggots from the body, they would dive head-first into the tears and cuts on the head and neck. When they did this they had the appearance of parallel strings of pulsating pearls. Once the water was directed elsewhere they would come back out only to retreat back into the body when intimidated.

I have to admit that my embryonic forensic pathology career came close to an end at this point. Not only was I physically repulsed by the body, I was equally convinced that I had destroyed my career by allowing the maggots to destroy any evidence from the body. I did, however, manage to regain control and finish the autopsy.

I learned several important lessons from the experience. First, once the process of decomposition begins, it's difficult to impossible to stop it. I now strive to do these cases as soon as possible after they're found. Second, the saw dust that I remember in passing on the body was actually fly eggs. I go to great pains to get as many of them as possible off the body immediately. Third, I've come to hate maggots more than any of the various creatures God in his infinite wisdom decided to place on this Earth.

It was ironic that that very evening my wife was taking me out to dinner at the fanciest restaurant in Mobile to celebrate having just finished my anatomic and clinical pathology residency. As we sat at the table looking at the menu, the waiter volunteered that the specialty of the house was a baked chicken with rice dish. I had a well done steak and asked Beth to pass on the rice dish. When she asked me why, I told her I would explain later.

People have asked me what type of mask I use to block out the odor when I autopsy a decomposed body. I don't use any type of mask. I've found that the best method is to get into the enclosed room where the autopsy is being done and remain there until the autopsy is completed. If I stay in the room, I get used to the smell after about ten minutes. If for some reason I have to leave the autopsy and return, I have to acclimate my nose to the smell all over again.

I guess a good analogy would be a visit to the bakery. When you enter the store, your sense of smell is flooded with all the delicious aromas of freshly baked bread and cakes. Once you have been in the store for a while, however, you no longer smell all the mouthwatering odors, so that at least in the case of decomposing bodies, this process of acclimation where eventually the sense of smell no longer registers a consistent odor is a real blessing.

During my twenty-three years in the field, I've seen various attempts at avoiding the distinctive smell of decomposition. Some people use surgical masks dipped in wintergreen or peppermint oil to avoid the smell. At one scene the Mobile Police arrived with the self-contained breathing equipment used by the fire department to avoid the smell. One of my favorite episodes involved a Mobile homicide detective who used a gas mask at one decomposed scene. The mask was held tightly in place with four separate rubber straps.

As we walked into the scene together and approached the body, the detective suddenly began retching and heaving. He loosened the mask straps as quickly as he could, but not before he had vomited into the gas mask still tightly secured to his face. I ended up laughing so hard I was afraid I was going to vomit from sheer laughter.

Brian Delmas, the chief investigator in our office, probably has the strongest stomach of anyone I know. Brian could walk into the foulest smelling scene and slowly go about his work oblivious to the environment. Many times this gift proved to be a mixed blessing because Brian would often be assigned the scenes that the fainter of stomach investigators simply couldn't tolerate, yet every statue at some point shows clay feet, and I'm afraid Brian was no exception.

One hot July afternoon Brian and I were called to the scene of an apparent natural death. The subject, an obese elderly female, hadn't been seen for seven to ten days. A relative finally broke into the non-air-conditioned, tightly closed house to find the decomposing lady sitting in her rocking chair. After arriving, Brian and I carefully walked into the room. The varnished hardwood floors were covered with a one fourth inch film of liquid fat that had seeped from the subject's generous subcutaneous fat stores.

The liquid fat was so slick on the polished hardwood floor that as I took a step toward the body, I had the sensation of slowly floating toward the body completely unable to stop my forward movement. In fact, it also became equally difficult to keep my balance. The last thing I wanted to do was to fall into a pool of liquid, decomposing fat. It made me a firm believer in wall to wall carpeting or at least area rugs.

As we went about the scene, Lamar Whitten, one of the identification officers, volunteered that he had recently read about a technique to rid a scene of the smells of decomposition. He then poured ground coffee into a big iron skillet on the stove and turned on the gas burner below. Before long the odor of burning coffee grounds filled the air and, at least in my opinion, obscured the decomposition odors.

As Brian and I examined the body, I noticed that he was pale and sweating. We hurriedly placed the body into a body bag for transportation and stepped outside. Once in the fresh air, Brian's color returned. He volunteered that he hated the smell of coffee, and the combination of burning coffee and decomposition had just about done him in. Only the blessing of an empty stomach had saved his county-wide reputation. Lamar Whitten must have sensed something was wrong with Brian that day because he would always look at Brian and smile when he volunteered to burn coffee grounds at subsequent decomposed scenes. Brian would always return Lamar's smile with a glance that would freeze a volcano.

Sometimes I got lucky. When I did it made all of the hours that I'd spent previously working over foul smelling decomposing bodies with nondramatic results almost seem worthwhile. One midmorning in the spring our lab received a call from Mr. Wayne Lathan, a funeral homeowner and coroner of Clark County. It seems that a group of state highway employees working on a state road in the southern portion of his county had found a skeletonized body off the shoulder some one hundred feet from the highway.

I wish I had a dollar for every time some highway worker found a decomposed body off the roadway. Interestingly, it's usually some distance from the highway itself, making me wonder what they're doing off in the woods. According to Mr. Lathan, there was no real need for us to go to the scene itself so he volunteered to help the scene personnel from the sheriff's office package and deliver the body to his funeral home where we could come and fetch it. I suggested that they make sure that they get a good portion of the dirt immediately below the body as they were scooping up the remains.

Later that afternoon the remains arrived at our lab. It wasn't an encouraging case. The body itself was almost totally skeletonized, with only a large fragment of adipocere-type material about the blue-jean-clad pelvis. Adipocere is a type of decomposition seen in relatively wet environments. It's a waxy decomposition of fatty tissue and has the consistency of tallow. The clothing was in an advanced stage of dry rot. As is routine, I took photographs of the body as it was presented to the lab, then had the autopsy assistants take full body X-rays to look for bullets or other foreign metal fragments. Upon viewing the X-rays, I could see no bullets or objects of interest.

On an almost totally skeletonized body there's obviously not much to examine. One point in the investigator's favor is that there is little or no smell, but even in a body that has decomposed to the point of skeletonization, we still attempt to accomplish the same tasks that we attempt in a freshly deceased body. These are our old buddies—determining the cause of death and the manner of death. In addition, identification of the remains takes on added importance as previously discussed.

In a body that's skeletonized, identification can get sticky. In this case, the fingerprints were obviously missing, but we were lucky in another way. Examining the skull, I could tell that the body was a black male by the architecture of the upper jaw, shape of the eye sockets, and the shape of the nasal opening. I thought it was a male because of the relatively thick bony prominences at the points of muscle attachment, due to the relative increased muscle bulk on males versus females and by the shape of the pelvis. The finding that was going to make identification simpler was the presence of multiple healed fractures along the left side of the skull. With healed injuries of this severity, the individual had to have spent a considerable period of time in a hospital.

After the examination of the skull I systematically began examining all of the individual bones of the body, basically reassembling them on a clean gurney. Initial inspection revealed nothing of particular interest. After all of the bones were removed from the body bag, I was left with a two foot by two foot pile of mud, sand, and adipocere, then for no reason I can explain in retrospect I had the technician take another X-ray of the pile of left-overs. I couldn't believe what I saw.

There, nestled in the pile, were four round radiodense objects that looked for the world like shotgun pellets. After going through the debris, I located four double 00 size shotgun pellets. I then began anxiously sorting through the fragments of clothing submitted with the body. On the front of the nylon shirt were defects that I felt were consistent with a shotgun entrance defect. Our firearms examiner, who examines these clothes for the record, agreed.

After finishing my dictation, I called the coroner who in this case was responsible for signing the death certificate. Having a fair amount of experience in these matters, he was amazed that we would be able to give a cause of death in such a decomposed body. Usually the best he would expect is a positive identification. When I related the fractures to the head he was equally surprised. The sheriff, while investigating this case, had mentioned a missing person from Mississippi who was allegedly taken at gunpoint from his home and brought to Clark County AL.

He'd been missing for about a year. Upon contacting the Mississippi authorities, we found that our missing person was a black male with the distinctive feature of multiple healed fractures on the side of his head sustained in a fight with an individual swinging a baseball bat. He'd been hospitalized for many months. Copies of the X-rays taken from the hospital were forwarded to our lab and a subsequent comparison with our autopsy X-rays resulted in a positive identification.

This case reaffirmed several points that I had been told by Dr. Riddick many times. First, no matter how decomposed a body, there's still information relating to the death that can be obtained. Second, one of the keys to a good forensic examination is a systematic approach where every step is carefully followed. Third, without access to good

X-ray facilities findings are bound to be missed. Fourth, sometimes if the investigator follows all of the above, he/she gets lucky.

People have asked me where I take the putrid bodies to do the thorough examination that the death investigation deserves. All of our examinations with few exceptions take place in a laboratory facility especially designed to handle all the cases from the freshly deceased to the markedly decomposed.

There are few words in medicine that conjure up more mental images than the word "morgue." It's slightly ironic that the term "morgue" itself actually refers only to the refrigerated facility located deep in the bowels of the hospital where dead bodies are stored awaiting pickup by the funeral home hired by the family to prepare the remains for burial.

In the mind of most of the lay public, however, the morgue is also the place where autopsies are conducted. This area is more correctly called the autopsy suite and although it's usually located adjacent to the morgue proper, it can actually be located some distance from the autopsy suite.

Most hospital personnel who have worked the night shift in a hospital have either experienced personally or have at least heard stories about the spooky feelings and experiences they've had when transporting a deceased body to the morgue in the middle of the night. It's almost a rite of passage to give this duty to the new guy or gal working the graveyard shifts.

Despite the fact that death isn't an unexpected outcome for many who enter a hospital for care, the hospital still goes to rather elaborate means to disguise deaths that have occurred in the hospital. The reasons for this are obvious. Death to a hospital is considered a failure. Hospitals are there to cure and heal. Besides, it's bad publicity for the hospital and staff to parade dead bodies along the halls passing patients and families of patients in the process.

Yet whenever there's a hospital death, the body must be removed from the patient care areas and transported to the morgue facility in a timely fashion. Whoever came up with the specialized cart used in the body transport deserves credit for making a difficult situation easier to accomplish.

Most hospital transport carts are built at a standard height that facilitates the transfer of the patient from their hospital bed to the rolling cart. The supine patient can then be rolled to radiology or surgery where they can again be easily transferred to the radiology or surgical table with a minimal amount of lifting. If these same carts were used to transport the deceased to the morgue, the sight of a body outline under sheets from head to toe would signal to everyone concerned that the orderly was transporting a dead body.

To get around the need to parade dead bodies around the hospital, a specialized cart is utilized. The body is initially transferred to a cart that's almost identical to all of the usual transport carts. This cart, however, has a crank mechanism that allows the body to be lowered to about three feet above the ground. A fake, draped cover supported by aluminum poles to appear like the usual cart surface is then placed above the body. This thick vinyl cover is at the same height and made to look like the normal surface of a transportation cart. In essence, the persons pushing the cart through the hospital hallways look as though they are pushing an empty cart when in fact there's a dead body located below that false top. Drapes that extend well below the level of the bodies on the carts on all four sides hide the true package being transported. Knowing this you will now never look at an empty transport cart rolling down the hall of your local hospital in quite the same way.

The morgue and autopsy suite in most community hospitals are usually small and not that frequently utilized. In many of the medical examiner's offices within the major metropolitan areas, however, the combined morgue and autopsy suite may occupy a large building just to be able to provide the floor space needed to handle the medical examiner's caseload. By the time that office space for the medical examiner and the necessary support personnel has been added, the facility can reach football field dimensions.

In most jurisdictions there's usually one hospital that handles all of the major trauma cases. It's the usual case that the medical examiner's office is located either on the hospital campus proper or at least nearby. The reason is that an intimate location keeps the need to transport bodies by vehicle to a minimum. It's much more cost effective to transport bodies down hallways than it is to motor them across town to be examined by the medical examiner. In many instances the main trauma hospital in a community is associated with a medical school training hospital. This allows the medical examiner's pathologist to participate in educational activities for the hospital residents.

I've had the experience during my career to be involved in the design and planning of two separate autopsy and morgue facilities. The first facility was built during my early years with Dr. Riddick in Mobile, AL. To be honest, I had little direct input into the process, but was able to learn and see what worked well and what worked not so well. I then used that information when I was more directly involved in the morgue and autopsy facility built in Pensacola, FL.

When most people think of an autopsy facility, they visualize stainless steel tables fixed in the center of the room designed such that the body must be wheeled in on a cart, then physically transferred to the autopsy table for the actual exam. This type of equipment requires that the body be lifted and transferred between the autopsy table and the transport cart at least two times. The term "dead weight" definitely comes into play with this sort of system, and by the end of a busy day, a morgue attendant can go home with back pains or more serious injuries.

To get around this issue, autopsy systems have been developed where the body is initially placed on a portable table which can be moved via wheels to a modified sink facility and the entire autopsy completed on the initial table/cart that the body was placed on when he or she first arrived in the office. This eliminates a lot of the lifting associated with the autopsy and makes it possible for the examination to be completely performed by one person without the aid of a denier. This is the type of facility that we had in Mobile, AL, and I made sure that we duplicated the same features when I was in charge of designing the new autopsy/morgue suite in Pensacola, FL.

One of the issues that occur in every medical examiner's office is the issue of space. How much room does the autopsy suite need to be to be able to function at that office's current volume of cases as well as the anticipated increase in caseload that's sure to come over the lifetime of the facility being built? It's always been my experience that hospital administrators allow the pathologist the liberty of designing the ideal facility in terms of equipment and size, then they systematically decrease the size over time as competing hospital needs interfere with the initial plans. To at least partially circumvent this possibility I intentionally indicated that I would need nearly twice the number of square feet for the morgue than what was reasonable. I thought that when the pencil pushers finished whittling down my allotted square footage I would at least be near the minimum size that would comfortably fill our needs.

In the case of the Pensacola autopsy suite, however, the hospital administration kept their word in terms of the space that they would give us. As a result, the autopsy/morgue complex located in Pensacola, FL, ended up being one of the most spacious in the state of Florida, if not the southeastern United States.

Another issue often overlooked when considering the autopsy/morgue facility for a medical examiner's office is the issue of decomposed and decomposing bodies. Because this is rarely an issue for the standard hospital morgue, it's sometimes overlooked until the first case of decomposed remains is brought into the building and the odor permeates everywhere. As stated elsewhere, the organic acids involved in the decomposition process can change a pleasant hospital stay on the third floor to disgust and wrenching when a bad body is brought into the hospital basement morgue.

Because of this issue, most morgue facilities have what is called a bad body room. This is usually a separate small autopsy work station which has its own ventilation system so that the smells generated by the case don't get sucked into the entire hospital. One of the lessons I learned from the construction of the Mobile autopsy suite is that the morgue designer cannot be too careful about odor control. In the Mobile laboratory, great pains were taken to isolate the odors coming from a decomposed case. A separate outflow ventilation system was installed to keep the smell to a minimum. Unfortunately, the ventilation outflow was placed so that when the bad body room's ventilation was switched on, the bad body room outflow blew directly into the hospital laboratory's ventilation intake. We made enemies every time a decomposed body arrived in our morgue.

The design of the bad body ventilation in the Pensacola morgue was a bit more hospital friendly. The outflow from the bad body suite was shunted to the roof of the hospital, then jetted straight up into the sky some three hundred feet before it begins to dissipate. It actually works pretty well for the most part.

On particularly humid days, not at all uncommon in Pensacola, the lay public sometimes talks about a strange odor that seems to linger around the hospital grounds. Some people find the smell mildly offensive while some people claim that it makes them hungry. Those of us who know that the source of the smell is a recently decomposed body just acknowledge the comments and try to keep a straight face and quickly change the subject.

The morgue coolers shown or discussed on all of the television shows always depict a refrigerated unit with large slide-out drawers that each contains a single body. This is a type of cooler seen most commonly in smaller hospitals that have relatively few bodies passing through their morgue at one time. The type of morgue cooler used in most of the larger medical examiner's offices is of the walk-in type. They're literally large insulated rooms with a souped-up refrigeration system that allows the carts that contain the dead bodies to be rolled into the cold environment.

The morgue cooler in Pensacola was about fifteen feet square and could easily hold fifteen to twenty bodies at a time. In case of an emergency situation, like an airplane crash, temporary shelving could be built inside the cooler to hold a larger volume of bodies. Fortunately, this has never happened. One advantage to the large open cooler type of morgue is that it can be put to additional uses. Early in my career, one of our investigator's family owned a watermelon farm. When the watermelons were ripe and ready for harvesting, the investigator would bring each employee a watermelon to take home. Before transporting the melons home, however, we discovered that an overnight in the morgue cooler brought the melon down to the ideal temperature for eating.

Some people are just not cut out for working with or around dead bodies. It usually doesn't take long to find out who they are. As part of their National Guard training in the mortuary division of the Guard, we commonly had three or four guardsmen assigned to our office during their one month active duty. The men and women assigned to us were being trained to handle the deceased from military as well as civilian events. In the Guard it was their job to aid in the identification and documentation of the deceased so that the remains could be returned to their loved ones for burial. Although the job was mostly clerical, it did require some contact with the bodies, so our morgue facility seemed a good place to gain that exposure. We, in turn, had access to free help.

In most instances, it only takes a day or two for the Guardsmen to get comfortable around the bodies. There's the rare individual, however, who can never adjust to handling dead bodies. One summer we had such an individual. This particular individual would go to any extreme to avoid having to touch or be with a dead body. How he ended up in the mortuary corps is beyond me, but there he was.

His peers used his discomfort to their personal advantage. They offered to handle the dead bodies if he would do all the jobs they didn't want to do. The whole deal fell apart one day when the fellow Guardsmen decided to play a practical joke on their skittish colleague.

On a morning when the cooler was empty of dead bodies, one of the guardsman took off his shoe and sock and tied an identification toe tag onto his big toe. He then went into the cooler, covered himself with a sheet, and waited for his colleague. Another guardsman assumed the part of ridiculing the corpse-shy guardsman, stating that it was his turn to do the morning check on the bodies and that because there was only one body in the cooler, he was going to have to go into the cooler by himself and check the toe tag.

With sheer terror in his eyes, the guardsman slowly opened the morgue door and stepped inside the cooler. He slowly walked over to the only stretcher in the cooler and reached for the toe tag to check the name. As soon as his hand touched the toe tag, the supine guardsman jerked his foot back and sat up quickly under the sheet. The guardsman who was the brunt of the joke jumped three feet straight up into the air, hit the ground, and ran out of the morgue, out of the building, and I suspect out of town.

We never saw that scared guardsman again. The rumor on the street was that he had transferred to some other service not associated with dead bodies. For his sake, I hope that was the case.

MY FRIENDS? THE LAWYERS AND COURTS

Although no one comes right out and states it, throughout medical school, there's a subtle distrust and, hence, dislike, ingrained into most physicians toward attorneys. The reasons for this are many. First, attorneys are the one group of individuals who, by their profession, can have a direct influence on a physician professionally. Second, the courtroom is the attorney's ballpark. Thus, if for any reason a physician is required to be in court, he's forced to play by the lawyers' rules. Physicians aren't used to being verbally abused or manipulated. Third, and probably most important, attorneys deal with each other and witnesses in a different way than physicians are used to experiencing. I'll apologize to all attorneys in advance and admit that this is my interpretation of a system that they call adversarial law. Basically both sides have a point of view that they try to get a jury to accept.

In criminal cases, the prosecution is usually a state-elected attorney who takes the evidence and tries to prove guilt. The defense attorney is hired by the defendant (person accused of a crime) and attempts to prove his client innocent. Basically this is done by each side calling witnesses who agree with their point of view. The other side then has an opportunity to question the other's witnesses, trying to disprove or discredit their testimony.

The interesting difference between attorneys and physicians is their relationship toward themselves and opposing witnesses during the trial. Within a legal framework all is fair and no holds are barred. It's reminiscent of two gladiators in an arena fighting to the death. In the process of trying to discredit a witness, they may ridicule, berate professional abilities, and twist words around to suit their cause, but, when the case is over, they may walk to a nearby bar and drink a friendly cocktail with the opposing attorney. They expect the opposing witness to join them.

Physicians, on the other hand, may say all sorts of degrading things about a colleague to fellow physicians but to someone outside the profession they tend to keep their opinions to themselves. One only has to look at the medical records of a patient whose case is being handled by multiple physicians to understand what I mean. Even if the therapy prescribed by one physician is, according to the next physician, "out in left field" the observer would have to know the medical case before he/she could pick out a true conflict.

Thus, when a physician is placed on the witness stand he may as well be in a foreign country. They're not used to having a nonphysician challenge their opinion, much less their professional integrity. As a result, their courtroom experiences are usually memorable, but less than positive.

In forensic pathology, we as physicians actually spend more time talking to attorneys than we do talking to fellow physicians. In fact, one major reason for forming the specialty was that pathologists felt that there was a need for a group of physicians trained to handle the legal aspects of death. As I readily admit to just about anyone, there are attorneys whom I personally like, but, as a profession, I'm not overly enamored with attorneys as a group. Part of the reason for this is as previously stated above, but more important I often find myself questioning the morality of the legal profession. As with most people, I've been raised with a fairly strong opinion as to what is morally right and what is morally wrong. I have problems with an individual who can accept a case and work hard to prove a guilty person innocent, especially if that person has confessed his guilt to the attorney in confidence. This said, however, the reader should rest assured that I would seek out the best attorney I know at manipulating the system if I should ever get into legal troubles.

The reader should also be advised that all attorneys are not created or elected equal. There are specializations among attorneys just as in the medical profession. It's perhaps worthwhile to briefly delineate the attorney types confronted by a forensic pathologist. Probably the most exposure any forensic pathologist has is with the prosecuting attorney or district attorney. This is an attorney elected by a population to represent their interests and argue their side in criminal cases. He's in effect the chief law enforcement officer in an area. Ideally, he should examine all cases and decide if there's enough evidence to prove and convict an individual of the crime. His goal is justice for both the innocent and the guilty. He, in turn, is answerable to his constituency each election for how well he has represented them. In my opinion a good district attorney shouldn't hesitate to end courtroom proceedings if it's proven to everyone's satisfaction that the defendant is innocent. This, however, is not always the case.

As an elected official, a district attorney's reelection hopes rise and fall with his batting average in court. As a result, the district attorney often feels pressure to prosecute a case even if the evidence against an individual is less than ideal. In addition, like most other government officials, they labor under too large a caseload for the amount of monies and personnel that they have to do the job.

The opponent of the prosecuting attorney in the criminal arena is the defense attorney. These attorneys are hired by the defendant to represent their side of a criminal case. They examine the available evidence, interview witnesses, and decide on the way to approach the case that will be most beneficial to their client. This may vary from a full out defense to prove innocence to arbitration with the district attorney's office to arrive at an admission of guilt to a lesser degree satisfactory to both the district attorney and the client. The defense attorney is usually paid for his services in advance as it's difficult to get payment from a client who's serving time in prison.

In my opinion, the defense attorney works at a considerable disadvantage in criminal proceedings. While the district attorney has the investigating powers of the police agencies, the scientific expertise of the crime lab, as well as the medical expertise of the coroner/medical examiner at his disposal, the defense attorney usually has financial limitations which prevent him from hiring his own expert witnesses.

A corollary to this is that in most areas a prosecuting attorney won't actively pursue a case without having the above advantages in his camp. In our area we strongly encourage defense attorneys to discuss the case with us before heading to court. This, however, doesn't happen as often as we'd like.

Although good criminal defense attorneys obviously do their clients a great service, most people agree that it would be suicide to represent yourself in court, sometimes I question their morality. Although I want them to defend their clients to the best of their abilities, it would be difficult for me personally to allow a person whom I knew was guilty of homicide to walk free based on a technicality that I, as his attorney, had found.

I suspect that attorneys reading this would volunteer, probably quite loudly, that I favor an inquisitorial type of judicial proceeding instead of the adversarial type of system. In an inquisitorial system both attorneys in the case work to reach a conclusion as to the guilt or innocence of a defendant. Proponents of the adversarial system maintain that the inquisitorial system makes it too easy for both attorneys to arrive at a conclusion beneficial to them, but detrimental to the defendant.

The next major area of contact between the forensic pathologist and lawyers is in the civil area of litigation. In this area someone feels that he/she has been wronged (called the plaintiff) by either a person, persons, or company/industry (called the defendant). Obviously in our instance the case involves some type of wrongful death.

If I thought that attorneys in the criminal area of the legal arena were aggressive, they don't hold a proverbial candle to civil case lawyers. One important reason for this is that instead of being paid a flat fee and expenses, the plaintiff attorneys in civil cases often get a percentage of the settlement (called a contingency fee). Obviously, the greater the settlement, the greater the lawyer stands to make from the case. The attorneys representing the defendant are usually kept on a retainer by a company or industry getting a fixed sum of money for handling trivial matters and additional funds for lengthy proceedings. They're under pressure to win cases because this type of client will quickly take his business elsewhere if the lawyer doesn't perform.

As you might imagine, this type of case can become big business. In fact, many firms specialize in one area of litigation, say, wrongful death. The firm may become so successful at this that it becomes more financially rewarding for the small firms to refer these cases to the specializing firm. There's the understanding that they will receive a referral percentage of the settlement and don't have to invest their time and efforts into the case personally.

It's also not unusual for these specialized firms to have expert witnesses on retainer to research and testify in their cases. One firm in Mobile especially known for their expertise have an MD-attorney who flies into Mobile from his home in Beverly Hills to take depositions and help handle medical malpractice cases.

The case that comes to mind in this regard is that involving the death of a young white female during the birth of her first child. The baby was born alive and healthy. During delivery of the placenta or after birth, the mother suddenly went into cardiac arrest and, despite aggressive resuscitative measures, was pronounced dead in the delivery room. How does an obstetrician walk into the waiting room and tell the expectant father that he has a beautiful baby girl, but that his wife has died? What happened and what if anything could have been done to prevent the mother's death? That's when a thorough autopsy examination can be of immeasurable help. That is where I came into the picture, no pressure there.

To add to the stress of the case, the obstetrician involved in the death was the same obstetrician who in some four weeks was due to deliver my own first born child, Sarah. Even before the autopsy examination was completed, our office was already receiving calls from the father's attorney wanting copies of all of our proceedings. This wasn't going to be easy. After finishing the autopsy examination proper, I had no definitive cause of death for the mother. All of the usual causes of sudden unexpected death to include pulmonary thromboemboli (blood clots breaking free within blood vessels and showering the lungs, resulting in shock and death), myocardial infarction (heart attack) and cerebral vascular accident (blood clot to the brain or rupture of a brain blood vessel) were all negative. The toxicology results were of no help in explaining the death.

When I examined pieces of lung tissue under the microscope, however, I had my answer. Impacted into the small arteries and capillaries of the lung tissue were masses of bizarre appearing cells mixed with skin cells and cheesy amorphous debris. This was a case of amniotic fluid embolism.

Throughout its entire development, the developing baby lives in or really floats in a compartment of fluid called the amniotic sac. The fluid in the sac is a combination of urine produced by the baby, fluid secreted by the placental tissues mixed with skin cells being sloughed by the baby during its forty week development. Normally during a routine delivery one of the first things to happen is for the amniotic sac to rupture and flow out of the mother's vagina (called breaking of the mother's water.)

When this happens all of the waste products excreted or sloughed from the baby are eliminated before the actual birth occurs.

In rare instances, some of the amniotic fluid gets trapped within the uterine cavity. Remember that the placenta functions to exchange oxygen and food between the circulation of the developing baby and the circulation of the mother. When the placenta separates from the lining of the mother's uterus, there's a brief period of open communication between the uterine cavity and the mother's circulation. If there's entrapped or lobulated amniotic fluid present, it can be sucked into the mother's circulation and travel up to her lungs where it occludes the pulmonary circulation, resulting in immediate shock and death. That's what happened in this case. Amniotic fluid embolism is unpredictable and unpreventable. If the amount and contents of the fluid is sufficient, the death of the mother is a certainty.

This case was my first exposure to a physician attorney who specialized in wrongful death cases. Some six months after the mother's death described above had occurred, I was scheduled to be deposed by the law firm in town who specialized in malpractice cases involving wrongful deaths on the death described above.

I was particularly nervous because I knew they had flown in their expert consultant who in addition to being an attorney, was also a board-certified anesthesiologist. As we sat before the court reporter and began the deposition, I was having bad vibes from the consultant. He was obnoxious and cocky with a strong component of condescension. I nervously delineated my findings, and after showing the consultant photos of my microscopic findings, he turned to the local attorney and stated that my findings were undeniable and that amniotic fluid embolization was one of the few entities left in medicine which were totally unpredictable and couldn't be prevented. He thanked me for my time, collected his papers, and caught the next plane back to Beverly Hills where I hope he stays until he dies.

Lest I come across as too critical of these attorneys, I need to add that physicians with acknowledged expertise in areas of medicine have also begun to help as expert witnesses and consultants on both sides of the civil litigation fence. These "hired guns" are brought in to both defend an accused physician and testify against him. The reason for this is that any physician accused of malpractice must be shown to fall short of accepted standards of medical practice in his field. In some instances it's not unusual for the testifying physician to earn more income from the expert witness fees than he does from his practice or medical school faculty position.

The role of the practicing forensic pathologist in all of these proceedings is basically the same as in criminal cases, to determine the cause and manner of death. In fact, unless the death occurs on the job, it's difficult to determine those cases which will go to court. As a result, it behooves us to be as thorough as possible on all noncriminal cases.

In fact, this is one area of death investigation where a medical examiner's investigators can shine. As previously stated, it's unusual for the police to take an active investigative interest in these cases; they have their hands full with criminal cases. Most of the actual investigative footwork is therefore done within a medical examiner's office. Having as many facts as possible is particularly important if the case goes before a civil court and multiple lawyers representing multiple clients are asking rather pointed questions to exonerate their clients. It's, therefore, the forensic pathologist's lot to deal continually with attorneys and testify in court. Obviously many physicians would be appalled to have to spend so much of their time in court. Forensic pathologists, however, tend to enjoy it.

Personally, I approach each court appearance as a personal challenge to explain the findings of the death as plainly as possible to the jury and at the same time match wits with the attorneys in the case. Despite my reservations about our judicial system, I freely acknowledge that it's the best in the world and the only avenue available to a people as well as an individual to see that justice is done.

This chapter wouldn't be complete without mentioning the actual courtroom setting and testimony. I'll never forget my first testimony in court. Fortunately, the trial took place in a small county in the northern part of our jurisdiction. Needless to say, I had read and reread my report and felt prepared to tell the truth. It would be a gross understatement if I said I was nervous; I was petrified to the point that I was visibly shaking. As I approached the witness stand to be "sworn in," I literally had to tell my legs to work. After the swearing in, the prosecuting attorney began by asking me questions about my professional background to reveal my qualifications as an expert witness in medical death investigation.

I knew that this was coming and was counting on using this time in talking about my background to get myself settled down and able to testify about the case at hand. Just as I began to talk about my educational background, however, the defense attorney stood and conceded to my expert status as a physician. The judge accepted me as an expert witness.

Although probably a compliment that the court would so readily accept me as expert witness, I had counted on that time to calm down and get my mouth working right. As a result, my testimony on the case, at least as it sounded to me, was awkward and babbling. After the prosecuting attorney had finished his questioning, the defense attorney waived his right to ask any cross-examination questions. I felt sure that, as awkward as my direct testimony had been, he felt that any further questions attempting to impeach my testimony could only backfire against him and his case. During the hour drive home after court, I did some real soul searching as to my abilities to adequately testify in court.

In retrospect, however, I realized that my real problem had been in translating medical terminology into everyday language. You see, for the past eight years I had been working in an environment that used a totally different vocabulary to communicate. I was quite fluent in using this vocabulary to communicate with other medical personnel and seldom needed to translate the terminology to lay people. Suddenly, however, I was thrown into the courtroom environment where I was expected to explain my autopsy results in a language that would be easily understood by the jury. The pregnant pauses that had occurred during my testimony were due to my search for everyday language that would explain what I was trying to say.

Prior to my next court appearance I not only reviewed my autopsy notes, but also practiced presenting my findings in layman's terms. I left the stand feeling much better about my testimony. Interestingly, physicians in other medical specialties have more than once complained that forensic pathologists come close to losing their medical standing because of this tendency to revert to everyday language to explain medical situations.

I've often heard physicians make the statement that they would much rather testify in a deposition than actually going to the courtroom to testify. This immediately tells me that the person speaking is a rookie in terms of his/her medical-legal experience.

For the uninitiated, a deposition is a legal proceeding where a witness answers questions posed by both lawyers from both sides of the case along with a court reporter, who transcribes the questions and answers verbatim. The reason most rookies prefer the deposition is that it's usually conducted in the more relaxed atmosphere of a hospital conference room or attorney's office. Unlike the formal courtroom scene where the witness sits in front of the jury, judge, attorneys, and defendant, the deposition is a much more relaxed atmosphere.

In point of fact, this is exactly what the deposing attorney wants. He or she hopes to put the witness in a relaxed, nonthreatening environment where he/she will drop their guard and say much more than he/she would say in a more formal court setting. So, as the witness quietly sits in a comfortable chair, drinking fresh coffee with access to fresh Danish, he/she is really being manipulated into a feeling of false security that increases the chances that the questioning attorney will gain information that he or she can use to discredit their subsequent testimony in the following formal court proceeding.

An additional point that the testifier needs to remember is that, unlike the actual courtroom testimony where the witness can at least be partially protected from questions that are inappropriate by objections of the opposing attorney and sustained by the judge, in the deposition, all and any questions can and are posed and must be answered under oath. This can lead to some embarrassing moments.

I personally experienced this at the hands of one particularly obnoxious defense attorney when I failed to give him the answers that he thought I should provide. Toward the end of the deposition he looked me in the eye and asked why I was lying about my findings in the particular case under discussion. I turned to the court reporter, who as usual was a particularly attractive female, and asked her if we were still on the record, that is, if she was continuing to record our conversations. When she replied in the affirmative, I turned toward the defense attorney and slammed my fist on the conference table, looked him directly in the eye, and stated the following: "Tell me that I'm short and I would have to admit that you're correct. Tell me that I'm ugly and I would admit that you may have a point. But don't you ever, ever again accuse me of lying under oath." After my outburst, that particular attorney always treated me with the utmost respect. If a medical examiner doesn't have the confidence of the court that he'll always tell the truth, he or she has nothing.

As alluded to earlier, the courtroom environment is totally unlike any other situation experienced by the physician. Part of the reason for this is that the witness, even if an expert witness, is considerably restricted in telling his story by the questions asked by the attorneys representing both sides. Although the prosecuting attorney usually gives his witness more open ended questions that allow the expert to better explain his findings, it's not uncommon to leave the stand feeling frustrated because pertinent information available from autopsy examination wasn't adequately brought out in the court proceedings. This, of course, can be at least partially avoided by pretrial conferences between the attorneys representing both sides and the physician testifying as an expert witness. Unfortunately, this isn't done as often as it should be done. On controversial cases, in fact, I have often called the prosecuting attorney and set up an appointment to review the autopsy findings. There is nothing worse than both the witness and the prosecutor being surprised by each other's questions and answers.

Another aspect of the courtroom that's unnerving to the testifying physician is the power of the circuit court judge. As an individual with a fair number of years of educational training and responsibility, I like to think of myself as a professional in terms of my medical abilities and in my devotion to my work. As such, I expect to be treated as a professional in my dealings with law enforcement agencies, attorneys, and the court. Although far and away we find this to be the case, there are episodes that have been humorous, but only in retrospect.

One such case occurred immediately after the delivery of my daughter, Sarah. The delivery had been complicated, requiring an emergency cesarean section to get Sarah out alive. Because of the trauma of a prolonged labor superimposed on the emergency surgery, Beth wasn't immediately able to care for herself, much less a newborn baby. To help out at home I took off two weeks from work with the instructions to my office that I would be unavailable except to testify in court.

Things went well for the first few days as I attempted to play Mr. Mom at home. As is usually the case, however, on the morning that Beth and Sarah were due for follow-up visits to their respective physicians, I received a call from the office stating that I was needed in court in a county to the north of Mobile. They wanted me there at 11:00 a.m. As it was 9:00 a.m. at the time of the call to my home, I would have to leave immediately to have any chance of arriving at court on time. I told the receptionist relaying the call that there was no way that I could make it to court by that time and that I would be there by 1:00 p.m. barring any unseen problems.

As I hung up the phone, I was trying to think of how I was going to get Beth and Sarah to their appointments and still make it to court. When I relayed the message to Beth, she immediately exploded in anger. She wanted me to call the court and tell them that I couldn't come. I was finally able to contact a friend to take care of my family and calm Beth down to a reasonable level of anger. I raced northward to my court appointment pleased with myself that I would be able to get everything accomplished that day with a minimum of inconvenience to all parties concerned.

Sometimes, however, you can't please everybody. When I arrived at court, the district attorney informed me that the Judge wanted to see me as soon as I arrived. I was in big trouble. I walked to the judge's chambers feeling like a schoolboy called to the principal's office.

As I sat across from the judge's desk he opened up with both barrels. I sat quietly for some ten minutes allowing the judge to ventilate. I'm sure that my face was a bright red as I fought back my feelings of embarrassment and outrage. When the judge had spoken his mind, I attempted to explain my side of the story with as much tact and composure as I could muster. I apologized to the judge and the court and, after explaining my circumstances, volunteered that I would try never to be tardy for his court again. He hesitantly accepted my apology and allowed me to subsequently testify in court.

I left the court that day humiliated and angry. Everyone in court knew that I had received a good "chewing out" from the judge, yet I was in no position to argue. I was playing in his ballpark, and although my professional credentials were comparable to his, he had all the power on his team. It would have easily been his option to throw me into jail for contempt of court. I was totally at his mercy and knew it. Although he could easily cancel court on any day for any reason, my job requires me to be completely available at a moment's notice.

Being a reasonable person, I readily acknowledge that without these strict requirements it would be impossible to get any case tried; however, I can't help but think that judges have too much unbridled power in our society. This said, let me confess that I made sure from that time forward that I was always a little early for court in this judge's cases.

MALPRACTICE:
THE SUIT THAT NEVER FITS COMFORTABLY

One area of litigation that strikes near and dear to every physician's heart and pocketbook is the matter of medical malpractice. The physicians in Mobile County at one point had lost over three million dollars to civil claims of medical malpractice within a three month period. There appears to be no relief in sight. Even those physicians who have avoided claims personally have been penalized through escalating malpractice insurance premiums. Some physicians are markedly restricting their sphere of medical practice to obtain lower premium rates. Some are even getting out of the practice of medicine altogether.

I wish I had the answer to this complicated problem, but I don't. Although I personally feel that physicians have brought some of this headache down upon themselves by obtaining and projecting the image of financial extravagance all the while encouraging and sometimes believing the infallible, somewhat obnoxious godlike image bestowed upon them by the lay public.

Obviously the attorneys have done their share by encouraging the public to seek satisfaction through the legal system for larger and larger sums of money over more and more trivial injustices. This is also fueled by the contingency type arrangement with their clients; the larger the cash settlements involved, the larger the amount of money the attorney of record stands to make.

Medicine as practiced today is a combination of art, science, and technology. It has in many respects become like our country's space program. When things go well, it's acknowledged as miraculous. It soon, however, becomes completely taken for granted. Miracles are routinely seen and therefore routinely expected, but when things go wrong, they can go wrong rapidly. These instances are then considered tragic; for example, a space shuttle explodes and we lose seven astronauts. Likewise with increasing medical technology, miraculous things are always happening, but always with the potential for tragedy just around the corner waiting to show its ugly head when least expected.

By the time I had my first real near tragic experience I had already had four years of medical school training and some five years of medical specialty training. Although all of these years were filled with episodes of tragedy or near tragedy, it wasn't until I had an episode striking close to home that I could understand the fear and helplessness that accompanies the experience. As Beth went into labor with Sarah, our first child, I was too busy thinking of the joy of the occasion to even contemplate that anything could go wrong. Beth was young, healthy, and more than physically able to deliver a child.

After some twenty hours of labor and two hours of pushing, however, it became obvious that Sarah had inherited the Cumberland big head and wouldn't fit through Beth's pelvis. In addition, as verified by the fetal monitor, Sarah was beginning to suffer from the prolonged labor. The decision was made to perform an emergency cesarean section to deliver Sarah. Still expecting the event to go smoothly, the obstetrician invited me into the operating room to witness Sarah's arrival.

The anesthesiologist arrived shortly thereafter and began to put Beth to sleep. He used both analgesics and epidural medications hoping to render Beth pain free and nearly unconscious. He then followed this with a medicine that interfered with her ability to contract her muscles (a curare type drug). This allowed the obstetrician to begin the surgery without having to fight Beth's abdominal muscles to get at the baby and at the same time kept her from fighting the anesthesiologist's attempts to manually breathe for her. Unfortunately, this medication also made it impossible for Beth to breathe on her own.

The key to the success of the induction was to get an endotracheal tube into Beth's airway so that air could be manually pushed into her lungs. At first the tube seemed to go in quite easily, but as the anesthesiologist continued to push air into the tube, Beth began to turn a progressively deep shade of blue. The endotracheal tube was in her esophagus and not her trachea. During this same time, the obstetrician was informing the anesthesia team that the blood at the surgical site was getting blue. I, meanwhile, realized what was going on and was biting my tongue to keep from screaming, something that in this situation would be counterproductive. The anesthesiologist pulled out the tube and reinserted it only to have the same result. I was now really worried. I began having visions that in one fell swoop I was going to lose both my wife and unborn child.

On the third attempt the tube was correctly placed and Beth's color began returning to normal. Sarah was subsequently delivered, and although initially neurologically depressed, she quickly came around. I, however, had had my first close brush with personal loss and have never forgotten it.

After I had caught my breath and regained my wits I finally got up the nerve to ask myself if I would have been tempted to sue for malpractice had Beth or Sarah or both been lost in the procedure. After some real soul searching I decided that I wouldn't have sued. All physicians and staff involved in the case had responded and performed as per accepted medical standards. It was only a relatively simple technical procedure that had caused our troubles; it wasn't mal or bad medical practice. Beth was just a difficult person to intubate. The experience did, however, drive home the point that despite all of the medical technology and expertise available, things can and do go wrong, sometimes very quickly. I can now better understand the anger and frustration that the survivor of a loved one who has been lost during a medical procedure must feel, particularly when he/she lacks a realistic understanding of the limitations of medical science.

Professionally, cases of potential malpractice are always difficult for the forensic pathologist. Since forensic pathologists are usually employed by a government agency separate from the hospital where the death has occurred, we're often requested to do potential malpractice death cases as a relatively unbiased investigator.

From our technical point of view these cases can be difficult because there's often not an anatomic cause of death that in and of itself is responsible for the patient's demise. Quite often, the patient is sick unto death before going into surgery; thus, it's difficult to separate presurgical problems from problems that either materialized during or became worse because of the surgery. Finally, some people undergo anesthesia and just never wake up for no good reason. The subsequent autopsy examination doesn't explain their death.

As previously stated, any issue suddenly becomes more real and important when you are intimately involved. Malpractice litigation is no exception. It's a standing joke with friends and people I know who are not involved in death investigation that malpractice is obviously not one of the hazards of my job; how can a pathologist be sued by a dead person? Actually, I carry malpractice insurance just like any other physician. I readily admit, however, that my premiums are not nearly as expensive as an anesthesiologist's, but on two separate occasions was certainly glad that I had it.

It's routine in our office to autopsy all persons who die from trauma. We attempt to hold fast to this rule unless there are serious protests from the family and the case is obviously not important to the court to take a stand against their wishes. As a result, it's policy to autopsy all fire victims, even if there has been a period of hospitalization between the incident and their death.

I arrived at work one Saturday morning to find a five-year-old black female who had been trapped in a house fire about a week previous. She had spent the previous week in the hospital's burn unit, but because of the severity and extent of her burns had died. I performed the autopsy and sent the body to the funeral home requested by the mother. About a week later I signed the death certificate and thought nothing more about it. Two days later, however, I received a call from the mother stating that there was an error on her copy of the death certificate. (Although we try to be careful with these important documents, occasionally errors do occur.) She went on to explain that on the certificate, I had indicated that I had performed an autopsy.

She, however, had denied permission for an autopsy immediately after her daughter's death in the burn unit. I knew I was in trouble. I tried to explain to the mother that indeed an autopsy had been performed, but not at the hospital. Instead, the autopsy had been conducted at the Mobile County Coroner's Office. This was standard procedure. I explained that it was potentially useful to her and her family should insurance problems arise later or if someone raised the issue of child abuse against her or some member of her family. It was obvious that I wasn't getting my point across. She simply couldn't understand how I could do an autopsy against her will. She felt that her daughter had already suffered enough and that the autopsy had added to that suffering. I don't think that she ever understood that the autopsy was done in the public interest and by law.

A few weeks passed and I was just beginning to feel that the issue had blown over when I opened a letter from a local law firm stating that I was going to be sued for performing an autopsy against the family's wishes. I envisioned my embryonic career going up in smoke. Although I had been involved in multiple cases of suspected malpractice before, this was the first time I had been a defendant. Although I had done the autopsy under state statute, I did not feel all that confident that it would hold up. I immediately called the Mobile County District Attorney, State Attorney General's Office, and our department headquarters to discuss the matter. They seemed just concerned enough about it to make me worry even more.

Finally, after many letters from state attorneys at various levels of government, the lawyer representing the mother conceded that he hadn't realized that the autopsy had been done under state law. He withdrew his suit. Thus, after some three weeks of worrying, I could breathe a sigh of relief. Although this case did not even come close to going to court, it did give me a better feel for those physicians who are pulled into the courtroom arena to defend themselves. It's not a pleasant experience.

Not three years after my initial brush with personal involvement in malpractice litigation, I was struck again. The case involved the deaths of two white males in a single vehicle automobile crash. Allegedly the state troopers and emergency personnel responded to the scene and determined that both occupants had died in the crash. The officers then removed the billfolds from the bodies and began their scene investigation.

Instead of calling the medical examiner's office to the scene, the troopers elected to have the bodies transported to the University of South Alabama Medical Center Emergency Room to be pronounced dead. The troopers contacted the respective families of the crash victims and informed them that their sons had been transported to the hospital.

In the emergency room the nursing staff noticed that neither of the bodies had identification cards attached. The ambulance crew had no idea who was who in terms of identify. The head nurse finally reached one of the troopers on the phone and was given a verbal description of the identities based on their respective injuries. In the meantime, both families had arrived in the emergency room and were informed that their respective sons had arrived "DOA" with severe injuries from the crash. Allegedly the intern discouraged the families from viewing the bodies because of the severe trauma. The nursing staff subsequently tagged the bodies with identification toe tags based on the trooper's verbal descriptions. The bodies were then transferred to the medical examiner's morgue.

Since it was my weekend on call, I arrived at the office at around 8:00 a.m. Roy Tex, the investigator on call, informed me that we had two bodies from a single-vehicle crash. He went on to state that we hadn't been called to the scene and that the bodies had been pronounced dead and identified in the hospital emergency room. Roy indicated he was attempting to locate the investigating troopers to obtain details on the crash.

I glanced at the emergency room medical records and noted that both families had been present in the emergency room after the bodies had been brought in. Since both bodies had appropriate identification tags signed by the emergency room nurse, I assumed the bodies had been appropriately identified. As part of my routine, I took Polaroid identification photographs of both victim's faces. The autopsy examinations that followed showed injuries of the severity commonly seen in automobile fatalities. After the autopsies were completed, the bodies were released to the funeral homes requested by the families and soon forgotten in the flood of new cases.

All seemed well until Wednesday of the next week. At about 8:00 p.m., I received a call from investigator Huey Mack Jr. stating that there had been a problem with the identification of the two fatalities from the previous Saturday. Although the funeral services for both victims were to be closed coffin, the family of one of the victims had requested that they have an opportunity to privately view their son. Allegedly, they walked into the viewing room to discover that it wasn't their son in the coffin. Needless to say, the family as well as the funeral home people were upset. A quick call to the funeral home handling the other victim's remains confirmed our worst fears. He had already been buried. Allegedly, the family had declined the opportunity to view the remains before the closed casket service. He'd been buried the previous day. My investigators quickly organized a meeting of both funeral homes and both families. Using the Polaroid photos taken at autopsy, the switch of identities was confirmed and steps initiated to correct the error. Early the next morning the buried victim was exhumed and the bodies returned to their respective (correct) funeral homes. Both bodies were buried that same day.

Immediately after the error had been corrected, our department began an intra-laboratory investigation to see what had gone wrong. We also contacted the department director, attorney general's office, and my malpractice insurance carrier to abreast them of the potential for litigation. For several days things were quiet, not unlike the calm before the storm, but everyone involved knew that it was just a matter of time.

Some two weeks later I was scheduled to be off from work and had made an appointment for a routine dental checkup. After my dental cleaning, the dentist, a personal friend, strolled into my exam room and asked me how much money I had. Thinking that he was trying to get a free lunch out of me, I stated that I had enough for two meals at a reasonably priced restaurant. He replied that he didn't think that would be enough and handed me the morning newspaper. The front page of the metropolitan section had a headline that immediately caught my eye, "Family files suit over body mix-up." My heart skipped several beats as I hurried to read the associated article. Not only had I been named in the suit with my name printed in the article, I also learned that I was being sued for a sum of two million dollars, an amount of money I have difficulty fathoming even to this day. The article went on to state that Dr. Riddick was being sued for a similar sum. I thought that interesting because I had performed both autopsies and therefore both cases were my responsibility. To be honest, it did relieve some of my anxieties to see Dr. Riddick's name with mine in the article.

The next few weeks weren't at all reassuring. Although our malpractice insurance carrier hired a top notch firm to defend us, it soon became difficult to maintain my workload with the malpractice cloud hanging over my head. After the first week I grew tired of trying to explain what had happened to my friends. Though I realized that they were only trying to be helpful, the jokes about burying my mistakes began to wear on my nerves. The fact that the attorneys chosen by the insurance company to represent me were actually hired to represent the insurance company's best interests was driven home when I received a letter from my carrier informing me that my coverage was limited to one million dollars per incident and that it might be in my best interest to retain an attorney to represent my uninsured liabilities.

To add insult to injury, the other family eventually filed suit against all those named in the suit by the first family. Again a letter from my insurance arrived to inform me that although their attorneys would handle the additional lawsuit, my total coverage per incident remained one million dollars. It therefore might be in my best interest to obtain legal counsel to protect my uninsured interests.

The lawsuit soon began to infiltrate all aspects of my life. My reaction was to avoid any form of social interaction because I didn't want to talk about it. The more my friends, especially, attorney friends, told me not to worry, the more I worried. Even though I knew that none of this misidentification was truly my fault, I began to feel like the child who feels guilty because he's been accused. Dr. Riddick's friendship during this time became priceless. Though not as deeply involved in the cases as I was, he was also being sued and thus could be a true ally. He did this and more as he voluntarily helped with the case preparation and buffered me from the state bureaucracy, which tends to meddle in details in an attempt to show concern.

Time does heal all wounds, and as the months passed I was eventually able to put some of my feelings into perspective. My attorneys filed for a summary judgment immediately. This basically asked the judge to exclude Dr. Riddick and myself from the suit, in this case, because we were performing our duties as government employees under statute law. The judge elected not to exclude us until after the discovery process, the depositions of witnesses in the cases. Almost a year after the suit was filed all of my anxieties began to surface again. As part of the discovery process I was scheduled to give my deposition in the case.

With deposition strategies learned through bitter experience and confirmed by my attorney during my predeposition conference, I began my deposition. It's probably an understatement to say that this deposition was important. Everyone in the room knew that what I said and how I said it would determine whether or not my involvement in the suit would continue or stop. As I sat in the chair waiting to begin, I thought it was much easier testifying on cases where I was only an objective witness. Defending myself was no fun and something to be avoided in the future.

After an hour of intense concentration and attention to the implication of all the questions posed by the plaintiff's attorney, I walked out of the deposition. My assessment was that, though I had stumbled on a few questions, I had essentially done alright. The smile on my defense attorney's face was reassuring. After an hour or two of mutual consolation with Dr. Riddick who had also been deposed, I made a concerted effort to forget all about the events surrounding the lawsuit. Six weeks later my attorney called to inform me that I had been dismissed from the suit by the judge.

I felt as though a weight had been lifted from my shoulders, and for about three hours I felt great. After my post-suit euphoria, however, I became angry and depressed. After all, hadn't I simply been doing my job as a public servant that Saturday morning? Wasn't that my name in the newspaper accusing me of switching the bodies? Wasn't it me who had to endure the jokes and well-meaning questions from friends and acquaintances? Yes, it was, in all the above. To be honest, I still find myself struggling with my feelings. Although I considered countersuing both families and their attorneys immediately after the summary judgment, I finally came to the conclusion that for my own peace of mind I'd be better off just walking away. After my dismissal from the case there was no newspaper article expounding my innocence, and I knew that there never would be. I would just have to learn to live with that.

Some months later it suddenly came to me that one of my biggest disappointments from the suit was that I had quickly found that I wasn't exempt from the judicial system that I had been hired to serve. Although I wouldn't have expected to be able to commit murder and walk away free, I did believe that because of my service to the court, the judges, district attorneys and countless defense attorneys I had assisted over the years someone would come to my aid. Maybe they did and I just didn't hear about it. More important, maybe I shouldn't have expected their help in the first place. Maybe I should have had enough faith in the judicial system to know that because I was innocent, I would be found innocent.

I'm sorry to say that I didn't and still don't have that much faith in the system. If anything, I've become more skeptical with the intervening years. I think too often it's not the right that triumphs but instead the side with the better, more eloquent attorney or attorneys.

The other lesson I've learned is that the real difference between empathy and sympathy is the rite of passage. Although I'm still called upon to testify in malpractice death cases and I still do my best to tell the truth regardless of whom it benefits, I find myself sympathizing and empathizing with the physician being sued. This is especially the case when I perceive that he was sincerely trying to do his job conscientiously and to the best of his abilities. I think most physicians still do.

THE WORST-CASE SCENARIO: MURDER AT RANDOM

Susan Morris

There is one type of killer whom every medical examiner hopes to avoid during his or her career. This is the sexual deviant who uses his charm to get his victims to drop their guard and then uses his size, strength, or physical restraints to incapacitate and control them. These individuals, usually males, get their sexual gratification by the control that they have over their victim and the fear that it generates. They usually start down their deviant path at an early age, beginning with acts of voyeurism and animal torture. Because of their need for higher and higher levels of stimulation to achieve sexual gratification, their crime eventually progress to rape and finally murder.

As with any addiction or compulsive behavior, the interval between acts of violence may at first be measured in months to years, but the perpetrator soon needs to not only increase the level of physical violence but also shorten the time between acts to stay satisfied. It's not unusual for this type of individual to initially lead a normal life actively involved in society, but maintaining this Mr. Hyde–like persona hidden from those with whom he comes in contact. Eventually, the urges become more and more difficult to control and occur with greater frequency until the individual goes off on a spree of attacks trying without success to satisfy his desires. The impulses can become so controlling that they often cause the perpetrator to make mistakes that ultimately lead to his/her arrest and incarceration.

All men have a prominent sexual overlay to their lives. I've often told my wife and daughter that they do not want to know the thoughts going through the heads of men they pass on the street or bump into at the supermarket. Humans are sexual animals, and the testosterone flowing through the veins of all post pubescent males causes them to look at and think about women in a crude sexual way. Men, by their nature, are basically looking at all the women they pass as though they were picking which food to order off a restaurant menu, essentially evaluating all women as potential sexual mates. Because I know what goes on in my mind, I've always been concerned about the clothes that my daughter and wife wear. By wearing what they think is stylish and currently in fashion, they may in fact be pushing the sexual buttons of men with whom they come in contact. This was particularly an issue with my daughter who, by imitating the dress of the latest pop stars, not only looked inappropriately dressed to me but also sent the message that she was more sexually sophisticated and interested than she actually was or cared to be. It remains one of those ironies that a daughter can dress in an outfit that looks like a hooker to someone my age all the while thinking that she's merely being stylish.

The sexual deviants I'm talking about fall far outside the normal range, even well beyond those males who look at each woman as a challenge to be conquered, a proverbial notch on their guns (no pun intended). These men are not looking for sexual excitement or satisfaction for the sake of sex but instead are feeding off the fear of their victim and the physical control over them to get their sexual release. Although actual sexual assault is often used to generate fear and helplessness, it can often be a minor component or even absent because this assailant gets his real sexual release through the torture and killing of his victim. These are sick men and extremely dangerous because they often have extremely high IQs and are extremely good at disguising their true motives and covering their tracks. Unlike the sociopath who's unable to know right from wrong, these individuals know what they're doing is wrong but are unable to control the urges. They're not the common murderer in that they often don't know their victim prior to a chance encounter. This makes them all the more frightening, especially when I have just dropped my daughter and her friends off at the local mall.

My closest encounter with an individual who met many of the traits described above occurred in January of 1993. Susan Morris was a young college student raised in Pensacola, FL. She graduated from a local high school and was taking college courses at the nearby University of West Florida (UWF). UWF was a relatively new state university located just north of Pensacola on a bluff overlooking a bay feeding into the Gulf of Mexico. The campus was in its adolescent phase with a rapid growth in student enrollment and its facilities scattered over the many acres of yet-to-be-developed woods and abundant parking lots. The abundance of parking lots played a role in campus logistics because UWF was predominantly a commuter school, having placed their emphasis on building classroom space while allowing dormitory facilities to lag behind. The end result was classroom and administrative facilities were scattered widely across a beautiful wooded campus with parking lots located at varying distances from the classrooms, often in isolated locations.

Susan Morris was a classic example of the type of student who attended UWF. Her long brown hair and her petite frame were topped off by a cute face that lit up a room when she smiled. Susan, like many of the students at UWF, lived at home, worked a part-time job, and commuted to her classes in a red Toyota. Unlike many of the young adults her age, Susan had a close relationship with both her mother and father, was active in a local Methodist church, and wasn't seriously dating anyone in particular. She was the ideal daughter who let her parents know where she was at all times and never failed to report in when she was going to be late arriving home.

One Monday evening, Susan left for a night class on the UWF campus and was never seen alive by her parents again. The parents' worry began when she was late coming home and failed to call. The local police and campus police were unhelpful, thinking the parents were overreacting to a young college girl who was probably with friends or a boyfriend. The parents knew better, so they went to the UWF campus to look for her themselves. They drove through the many parking lots on campus unable to find Susan or her car. The next day, the search by law enforcement actively began with no success. Finally, after a several-day search of the campus and surrounding areas, Susan's body was finally discovered in some woods on campus in a shallow grave.

Eric Scott Branch was a twenty-one-year-old white male on the run from authorities in Indiana. Because of an apparent clerical error, Eric had been inadvertently released from prison where he was serving time for aggravated sexual assault. He had come to the Florida Panhandle and was cruising the beaches of the so-called Redneck Riviera in an effort to avoid the Indiana authorities. While in Panama City, FL, Eric had hooked up with a local woman and had sexually traumatized her before fleeing the area ahead of an outstanding warrant for sexual battery issued by the Bay County Sheriff's Office. Branch had been driving a family-owned 1982 Pontiac Bonneville since leaving Indiana, and after visiting with his brother briefly in Pensacola, he decided to ditch his vehicle and steal a local car not being actively sought by police.

Branch had become a person of interest for several reasons after Susan's disappearance. He was identified as driving a small red vehicle on the UWF campus on the day after Ms. Morris's disappearance and was noted to have a recent hand injury, which he attributed to a bar fight. Branch had been described as wearing a pair of black-and-white checkered shorts.

Branch's Bonneville was subsequently found in the Pensacola regional airport parking lot. Forensic evaluation of its contents revealed boots and socks with blood splatters that matched Susan Morris's DNA profile. Two days later, Eric Branch was spotted in Bowling Green, KY, with Susan Morris's Toyota recovered in a parking lot in Bowling Green the next day. Forensic analysis of the vehicle showed a blood stain matching Susan's DNA on the back of the passenger's seat. When Branch was arrested later in Indiana, he had a pair of white-and-black checkered shorts in his possession stained with his own blood type.

In the early evening of January 13, I received a call from the Florida Department of Law Enforcement stating that I was needed out at the UWF campus. The whole community had been holding their breath, hoping that Susan would be found safe and sound. It was a Wednesday night when I received the call, and I remembered leaving my wife a note so she would know my whereabouts when she came home from church. My note stated, "Co-ed found, don't wait up."

When I arrived at the scene, the body was located in a shallow grave not far from one of the UWF parking lots. As the crime scene analysts and I systematically uncovered the body, I observed that the body changes were consistent with the amount of time that Susan had been missing. Although I went about my job in a professional manner, my heart stayed up in my throat. Lying before me was the nude body of a beautiful young woman who had been bruised and battered beyond recognition. The autopsy the next day confirmed that the body had been savagely beaten, stomped, and ultimately strangled. Her eyes were blackened, her lips were split in multiple areas, and there were deep bruises located in multiple areas of her body. Injuries suggested that she had been raped and sodomized, and a tree branch had been jammed up her vaginal vault. It was without a doubt one of the worst cases of blunt force trauma that I've ever seen inflicted without an obvious weapon of some sort being used. The other thing that this degree of injury indicated to me was that Susan had most probably put up a valiant fight in her attempt to escape her assailant. I can still remember talking to both parents and hoping that they didn't ask the question that parents always ask when one of their children has died. I had promised myself years ago that, when I went over autopsy findings with the family, I would answer all their questions truthfully but would only answer the specific questions asked. I never wanted to lay additional grief on a family who wasn't ready to receive it. I also made it a point to emphasize to the family that I would always make myself available to them to answer any questions that might arise in the future. In this case, I had to admit to the parents that Susan had suffered considerably before she finally passed.

It was over a year before the case was able to work its way through the circuit court system. Although the time that this process took allowed the prosecution the opportunity to fine tune their case for the trial, the prolonged interval was long enough that the trial reopened all the wounds that the family had suffered at the initial trauma, forcing them to relive it again in detail. I was thankful that Susan's father and mother both left the courtroom when I was called to testify. This allowed me to comfortably go into detail about Susan's injuries and the amount of pain and terror that she probably suffered before she died. I wanted the jury to have a realistic concept of what had occurred, the severity of the injuries, and how Susan had suffered.

The jury subsequently found the defendant guilty of first-degree murder and by a 10–2 vote recommended death. The judge followed the jury's recommendation and confirmed the death sentence, adding an additional life sentence for sexual battery and five years' incarceration for grand theft of Susan's car.

In the state of Florida, capital murder verdicts with the death penalty seem to go on forever. From the standpoint of justice, I can understand the need for conscientious oversight when someone's life is on the line, but from the perspective of a busy medical examiner's office, the appeals with the repeat court testimony take up a significant amount of time with all depositions, court proceedings, autopsy reports, and notes that must be reviewed before appearing again in court. The Branch case was no different. In late 2006, I received a call from the state attorney's office stating that I would be called to testify as part of the appeal process. Because the defense was looking for anything it could use to overturn the conviction, paid experts from many of the forensic fields were there testifying for the defense.

It was interesting for me in that it was one of the few times that another board-certified forensic pathologist from another state had been asked to testify against my findings and seek any areas where he disagreed with my conclusions. I was actually allowed to sit in the courtroom and listen to him pick apart my findings without him knowing that I was present. Although he could find several small issues to disagree with me when interpreting the findings, even he had to admit under oath that he couldn't dispute my major findings and that our differences were over minor, significant issues. When his testimony was over, I walked across the room and introduced myself. I thought he was going to choke on his tongue when he realized that I had heard what he had said about my work. That in itself was worth the price of admission. The appeal process turned out to be a backhanded compliment regarding my abilities as a forensic pathologist.

The end result of all of the above was that Eric Branch today sits on Florida's death row awaiting denials on his now-diminishing avenues of appeal. I know that there isn't a day that goes by when both of the Morris parents don't stop to think about their daughter and what might have been. I'm sure they would agree with me in that we'll never fully understand what makes a man like Eric Branch tick or why God places such distorted humans in our midst. I hope the execution of Eric Branch will help bring a modicum of closure to the Morris family. I also hope that they realize that there are some of us who will never forget Susan Morris or the pain that they have suffered because of their loss.

Jennifer Robinson

Some people are just plain wicked and need to be kept out of contact with society. While I'm willing to concede that humans for the most part can fit well into our society and contribute, I disagree with those sociologists who maintain that all people are basically good and that they only act badly because of some nurture issue experienced growing up. They believe that, with adequate help and support, everyone can become useful members of our society. My personal opinion is that all people are basically evil, and it's only a thin veneer of civilization applied by parents, peers, and mentors that makes the average person able to contribute to society. We're all basically selfish, self-centered animals who have learned manners because we've found that it's the best way to serve our own needs. There's also a small subset of humans who cannot or at least choose not to live within our social norms. They're basically predatory animals without a conscience and no concept of right or wrong. This type person is dangerous because he/she is usually bright, often handsome or charming, and has learned to use his/her gifts to achieve their evil purposes. They prey on the unsuspecting and care nothing for the other person's wants or needs. They have the uncanny ability to sense those individuals who are submissive or naive. Society needs to find them and either indefinitely confine or execute them.

The only thing scarier than this type of asocial person is when two of these individuals team up and work their evil together, a situation like that seen with Hickock and Smith in 1959 documented by Truman Capote in his book, *In Cold Blood*. Instead of doubling the amount of harm committed by the combination, it tends to increase geometrically. The two sick personalities feed off each other to make a bad situation even worse.

I've only had one case that would qualify for this dual subtype of serial killers. In my case the suspects eventually found guilty of murder were named Jeremiah Rodgers and Jonathan Lawrence. Jeremiah Rodgers was twenty-one years old, while Jonathan Lawrence was twenty-three years old. Both young men lived in the community of Pace, FL, a growing bedroom community of Pensacola, FL, located in Santa Rosa County. Both men were native to Florida, and both began to display criminal behaviors with mental problems in their early twenties, requiring prison sentences, which included court-ordered hospitalization in the infamous Chattahoochee Hospital for the criminally insane in Florida. It was there in 1993 that they met each other and developed a relationship based on their shared worldview. After serving their prison sentences in the mental hospital, they returned to Pace, FL, where they stayed jobless and lived with various relatives or girlfriends from the area.

Their first known dual excursion into the arena of major crimes was a murder that occurred on April 9, 1998. On that night, they coaxed Justin Livingston, a twenty-year-old schizophrenic cousin of Lawrence, out onto a Navy helicopter landing and training field. Once they knew that they had arrived without being seen, Rodgers stabbed Justin once in the back with a bowie knife, then attempted to strangle him with his rolled-up T-shirt. Just as Justin was almost certainly dead, Lawrence repeatedly stabbed Justin in the back in rapid succession, seeming to enjoy the new sensation of stabbing a human being. They then rolled the body into a blanket and transported it out into the adjacent countryside and buried him before returning home. Their alleged motive for the killing was that Lawrence hated Justin because he was always hanging around bumming cigarettes and smoking their pot.

A slow, steady search for the missing Justin Livingston was conducted by the Santa Rosa County Sheriff's Office, but no viable leads were uncovered. Since the Pace area is a small community composed of multiple generations, everyone knew everyone, but no one had seen Justin. During the investigation, both Rodgers and Lawrence had been interviewed by the police, but they were never considered to be serious suspects during the early stages of the investigation. It would appear that Rodgers and Lawrence had committed the perfect crime, at least initially. Rodgers was smart enough to keep his mouth shut regarding the disappearance of Justin. Lawrence, however, was more than willing to talk to the investigators freely, giving them possible leads that went nowhere. The lead detective used Lawrence's willingness to talk about Justin's disappearance to convince him to take a voice analysis stress test. The detective promised Lawrence that if he passed the test, he would be completely eliminated as a suspect in the case. Lawrence volunteered to take the test, showing no fear that he might not pass.

The voice stress analysis is actually a more accurate version of the lie detector or polygraph. The vocal cords in the test subject's larynx are controlled by muscles that under normal circumstances vibrate or twitch at a rate of 8–12 Hz. All our muscles function in the same range and can be measured by an appropriate analyzer. Under relaxed situations, the vibration is located in the 8–9 Hz range. When the subject tells the truth when asked a question, the vibration stays in the 8–9 Hz range. When the subject lies in response to a question that might have negative consequences, the body's autonomic nervous system releases stress hormones, especially adrenalin, which causes the vibrations of the vocal cords to increase into the 11–12 Hz range. Since this response is governed by the autonomic or automatic part of our nervous systems, the subject doesn't have the ability to control the vibration result. Although useful as an investigative tool to include or eliminate suspects in a case, it's still not accepted as evidence in a court of law.

As suspected, Lawrence failed the test dramatically, with every question he was asked regarding Justin's disappearance showing that he was lying. Although not enough to arrest Lawrence, it was enough to mark him as a prime suspect in the case. In the weeks after the death of Justin Livingston, Jeremiah Rodgers hadn't been idle. He was actively pursuing Jennifer Robinson, an eighteen-year-old senior at Pace High School who worked part-time after school at a convenience store located near her home. Jennifer was an attractive, strawberry blonde standing five foot three and slightly overweight at 140 pounds. Rodgers made it a habit to drop by the convenience store whenever Jennifer was working and was constantly asking her to go out with him on a date. After a month of constant pressure, Jennifer agreed to go out with Rodgers on May 7, 1998. Rodgers picked up Jennifer at her home, and after meeting Jennifer's mom, they went out "driving around and hanging out with friends." As Rodgers and Jennifer drove away from the house that evening, Jennifer's mother had no idea that that was the last time she would see her daughter alive.

As stated earlier, Rodgers and Lawrence had the type of symbiosis that the two together was much worse than any one of the two separately. They would sit for hours together planning all types of horrors that they wanted to inflict on those they disliked. Unfortunately, Jennifer was to be the star in their next production, and all the equipment necessary to complete their plan had been prepared. Rodgers convinced Jennifer that they should pick up his friend Lawrence and use his truck to drive out into the countryside. Lawrence didn't have the charm and good looks of Rodgers and was quiet during their drive. Once out in the woods far from any sign of civilization, Rodgers began mixing Jennifer and himself drinks of Mountain Dew and pure grain alcohol, an odorless, tasteless, extremely potent form of alcohol. With little or no experience drinking alcohol, the mixture soon began to do its work on Jennifer. Under the influence of the alcohol, Rodgers claimed that Jennifer performed oral sex on him, and once he was able to develop another erection, they had consensual intercourse. Lawrence, meanwhile, had wandered off so that Rodgers could have his fun with Jennifer. He rejoined the two, and they prepared to head out of the woods.

They had just started out of the woods in their vehicle when Rodgers told Lawrence to stop. He ran into the woods, coming back shortly to claim that there was a marijuana field nearby, and asked Jennifer to come see it. Once they had returned to the truck and were just about to get in, Rodgers pulled a revolver from his waistband and shot Jennifer in the back of her head. She died immediately.

This is the point at which the story becomes even more bizarre. Rodgers and Lawrence lifted Jennifer's body onto the tailgate of the truck. Lawrence then pulled out a scalpel-type knife that he had brought and cut off all of Jennifer's clothes. He then had sex with her dead body twice. Lawrence then took out a ziplock bag and, using his knife, carefully cut the calf muscles off Jennifer's right lower leg, dissected off the overlying skin and fat, and then placed the muscle into the ziplock bag. The bag containing the muscle was then placed into an ice cooler that he had brought along. Before he was finished, Lawrence took multiple Polaroid photos of Jennifer in various obscene poses, one showing the knife he had used sticking out of her vagina.

Finished with their work, they both climbed back into the truck to head back home, only to discover that the truck wouldn't start due to a dead battery. Rodgers and Lawrence both walked the five miles to a convenience store phone where Rodgers called his live-in girlfriend to pick them up and take them to Lawrence's house to get Rodger's car to return to the crime scene.

Once they had returned to the body and truck, Rodgers used the scalpel to make flaplike incisions on both sides of Jennifer's forehead. After a few more pictures, they cleaned up the area, burned Jennifer's clothes, and buried her body in a shallow grave a few yards off the road. They then went their respective ways, acting as though nothing untoward had occurred.

The beauty or curse of living in a small Southern town is that everyone knows everyone's business because gossip travels faster than the speed of light. It was soon common knowledge that Jennifer was missing and that Rodgers was the last person known to be with her. Rodgers had an older brother living in the area who had been adopted and raised by a Pace family. Rodgers was beginning to panic as he realized that he would be the prime suspect in the disappearance of Jennifer Robinson. Jeremiah Rodgers went to his brother for help. He told him that it was Lawrence who had killed Jennifer and in the process showed him the Polaroid photos of Jennifer's body. Before his brother could help, however, Rodgers was confronted by male friends of Jennifer and her mother who were looking for answers to her disappearance. Rodgers knew that he was in way over his head and decided to run. He managed to get to his car and headed to Lake County, FL, where he had grown up and where his sister still lived.

The world was also crashing in on Jonathan Lawrence. Rodgers's brother had called the sheriff's office and told them about his conversation with Jeremiah, the Polaroid photographs, and the confession that it had been Lawrence who killed Jennifer. When the sheriff detective arrived to interview Lawrence, he asked if Lawrence had a Polaroid camera or Polaroid photographs. Lawrence denied having either. During the interview, Lawrence also gave the detective permission to search his home. Pieces of torn Polaroid photographs of Jennifer were recovered. Lawrence was placed under arrest.

One of the advantages of being in law enforcement during the digital age is that information can be sent quickly and efficiently to various jurisdictions when a suspect is on the run. For whatever reason, Rogers had decided to go home, the first place anyone would look for him. I suspect that he needed a place where he felt comfortable and secure enough to plot his ultimate escape. It didn't work. Soon after he arrived in Lake County, he was arrested following a high-speed chase. He was transported back to Santa Rosa County where he immediately started confessing his innocence and implicating Lawrence as the real killer in Robinson's death.

While both Rodgers and Lawrence sat in the Santa Rose County Jail, they confessed to the murder of Jennifer Robinson as well as the murder of Justin Livingston. Although police had their suspects in both murders, they lacked the most important ingredient to a successful conviction in both cases, a dead body. Whenever two individuals commit a serious crime together and are both captured but jailed separately, it usually becomes a race to see which perpetrator can give the most information to the police while blaming the other guy for everything that happened. Lawrence was first to talk about the Robinson murder, but Rodgers was more than happy to cooperate on the Livingston death.

One aspect of an asocial personality is that the subject lacks the ability to feel the emotions that we all experience during certain situations. Because of this, they have to decide what emotions are appropriate for a situation, then attempt to mimic them. Some are better at this than others. During his interview with the Santa Rosa Sheriff's detectives, Lawrence didn't even try to mimic appropriate emotions. Rodgers was a bit more polished, probably because his pseudocharm had been his best survival tool in the past.

With a flat affect, Lawrence repeated the sequence of events that occurred on the night of Jennifer Robinson's death. After acknowledging that he knew where the body was buried, he agreed to take the detectives to the site of the burial. Later that same day, I was called out to the scene to help collect evidence and examine the body that proved to be Jennifer Robinson. Most medical examiners will claim that they're able to do their job and at the same time completely keep their emotions in check. I hope they're lying because in my opinion, it would take a real Mr. Spock to keep their feelings in check in certain cases. This was one of those cases for me. As I looked on the shallow burial site, I couldn't help but think that this could just as easily be my own fourteen-year-old daughter who had naively allowed herself to be charmed by a monster. Because the body had been placed in a shallow grave, flies had gained access to the body, depositing their eggs which had hatched into early maggot infestation around the mouth, nose, and eyes. The amount of decomposition was consistent with her death occurring some three days previously. The cause of death was confirmed as a gunshot to the back of her head with associated fractures of the base of the skull and trauma to the brain.

The sharp force injuries (cuttings) were all postmortem, that is, they had been inflicted after death. As the medical examiner involved in the case, I initially couldn't understand the purpose of the postmortem incisions. It wasn't a form of torture because they had been inflicted after Jennifer was already dead. The whole story wasn't fully explained until I was asked to come to the home of Jonathan Lawrence to help the sheriff's office execute a search warrant. Upon arriving at the scene, I was shown medical anatomy illustrations scattered around Jonathan's room. The real surprise, however, was when we opened the freezer and found Jennifer's calf muscle among the contents. Interestingly, sometime before, Iona Lawrence, Jonathan's mother, had developed a staph infection in her right leg, requiring hospitalization and prolonged home care. As a result, Mrs. Lawrence had atrophy and lost mobility in the leg, requiring her to use a cane and walk with an obvious limp. She claimed, to prove to investigators what a good boy Jonathan was, that he had taken a concern in her illness and nursed her consistently during the process of healing. It's ironic that the calf muscle harvested from Jennifer was the same muscle so atrophied on his mother. When asked the reason for cutting off the muscle and freezing it, Jonathan stated that he planned to cook and eat part of it and make the rest into jerky, depending on its taste.

The sheriff's department had now recovered one body, but the whereabouts of Justin Livingston was still unknown. When questioned about the whereabouts of Jennifer Robinson prior to his arrest, Jeremiah Rodgers had denied knowing anything. Now under arrest, he elected to be as cooperative as possible, hoping that his charm would again work in his favor. He told the sheriff's detectives everything from the Spencer Field location of the homicide to the burial location of Justin's body. Midmorning of the same day, I received a call from the Florida Department of Law Enforcement stating that they were being called to the suspected burial site of Justin Livingston and that the Santa Rosa Sheriff's Office had requested my presence at the scene.

The crime scene team from the Florida Department of Law Enforcement began a methodical excavation of the presumed burial site. Unlike the burial site of Jennifer Robinson, Rodgers and Lawrence had taken time to dig the hole several feet deep. The first body part uncovered was a snake-skin boot attached to a leg. We knew then that we were at Justin Livingston's burial site. The crime scene personnel were systematic in uncovering the body to avoid the loss of any associated trace evidence. Although by the time of recovery Justin's body had been buried for almost a month, the dry sandy soil in which the burial occurred pulled moisture from the body, resulting in a mummification rather than a waxy, putrefied saponification that can occur when the body is buried in a moist environment.

Once we had the body back at the morgue facility, the actual autopsy could begin. The external surfaces of the body were examined for any injuries or trace evidence as the clothing was systematically bagged and tagged for later examination by trace evidence personnel at the FDLE. Once fingernail clippings were obtained for trace evidence examination, the external body surfaces could be examined. The anterior or front of the body was unremarkable except for the decomposition changes due to the prolonged postmortem interval. The posterior thorax or back of the chest area was another story. There were twelve separate stab wounds to the back localized to two ragged horizontal lines. So far, the injuries noted fit the story given by Rodgers during his confession.

The internal portion of the autopsy examination involves opening the cranial cavity, chest cavity, and abdominal cavity to document any internal diseases or injuries. The internal examination of the chest cavity confirmed that all twelve stab wounds had entered the pleural or chest cavities. Both pleural cavities showed an accumulation of decomposing blood and tissue fluids confirming that the stab wounds that had entered both lungs had occurred at a time when Justin's heart was still beating and able to pump blood from the wounds that the stabbings had caused. Two of the wounds were of particular interest in that they both entered the right lung and penetrated deeper into the lung tissues than the other ten stab wounds. One of these wounds extended deeper into the right lung tissue than the other ten wounds, while the other completely perforated the lung and perforated the diaphragm to penetrate the underlying liver with a measured depth of penetration of six and a half inches from the skin surface of the back. If the story given by Rodgers is correct, the deeply penetrating wound on the right side may well have been the initial stab wound that sent Justin to the ground. The stab wound deep into the liver would be consistent with Rodgers's second lunge when Justin was on the ground and Rodgers summoned the nerve to plunge the knife deeper into the fallen Justin by holding on to the hilt and pushing down.

In some ways, this can become academic in that any or all stab wounds were potentially in and of themselves fatal if medical attention isn't rendered immediately. This means that both Rodgers and Lawrence are equally responsible for Justin's death. The remainder of the autopsy examination showed changes of decomposition and that Justin had previously had a kidney removed for unknown reasons.

It took more than a year for Rodgers and Lawrence's trial to come up in the judicial system. Since the death of Justin had occurred on federal property, the military-owned helicopter training field, the federal court had jurisdiction over that case. The real question for the federal prosecutor was whether or not to seek the death penalty under its federal jurisdiction. Knowing that this was a distinct possibility, the federal court had appointed each defendant two attorneys, one appointed solely because of their expertise in death cases in the federal court setting, the other to represent the defendant in the actual trial itself. Because the federal prosecutor at this point already knew that both Rodgers and Lawrence had already been charged with the murder of Jennifer and had decided to pursue a death penalty verdict under Florida state law, she agreed to not pursue a death verdict if both plead guilty to Justin's murder. Although saving them both from a possible death sentence in the federal court, it allowed their confession to be used against them in the state court where they could both be convicted and sentenced to death for Jennifer's murder.

Since both Rodgers and Lawrence had already admitted to killing Jennifer, the real question was whether the jury would recommend death for both defendants. In the Florida state court system, the jury votes on whether or not to render a death verdict, but it's really the judge who has the power to follow the jury's opinion or override the opinion and replace it with his own.

Since it had been Rodgers who had fired the gun that killed Jennifer, his jury had little difficulty arriving at a death sentence. Lawrence, because of his secondary role in the death, was a bit more difficult for the jury. Despite some resourceful defense work on the part of his attorney, Lawrence was also given a death sentence. They both will be put to death by either electrocution or lethal injection once their appeals are completed.

I suspect that there are many readers who feel that judicial execution is never warranted. As a physician who has spent a significant portion of his life learning how to lengthen and improve the quality of life of his patients, I understand that point of view. I'll also admit that historically, our judicial system has abused the death penalty, applying it to crimes that fell well short of what I would define as worthy of death. I also concede that the appeals process currently in place is exceedingly long and extremely expensive to the point that it would be less expensive to keep an individual in jail for his/her life than to pay for the costly appeals process. I would outrage the lobby against capital punishment if I failed to mention the cases where new evidence or some new technology such as DNA has proved the sentenced individual innocent of the crime for which he or she had been convicted.

Having said all of the preceding, I still firmly believe that there are certain murders that are so random and so motivated from the depths of a sick mind that displays no empathy or remorse for taking the life of another that a death sentence based on sound proof and rendered quickly is still a reasonable tool to be used discriminately by our society. I shudder to think what Rodgers and Livingston might have accomplished had they not been captured so quickly. Evil people like them just need to be eliminated by society.

TWO WRONGS NEVER MAKE A RIGHT: THE MURDER OF ABORTIONISTS

I'm rabidly pro-life. It's my considered opinion that once a human sperm hits a human egg, the resulting zygote is as much a human as I am sitting here typing at my computer. I also believe that the humanity that results from that miraculous collision has, by the very nature of its humanity, all the same rights and privileges that I claim as an American adult. The obvious corollary to this belief is that I think that the act of abortion is the killing of a human life and is morally wrong and should be legally wrong. Having said that, let me follow up by affirming that we are a nation of laws; and as citizens, we should to the best of our abilities comply with those laws and use the methods that we legally have available to us to change those laws if we feel that they're unjust or in error. Now I have a confession to make. In my job as medical examiner, I've autopsied more homicides where the abortionist is the victim than anyone else in the country. I've also testified against two murderers, thereby making me at least partially responsible for the ongoing imprisonment of one abortionist's killer and the judicial execution of another.

There are those individuals in the pro-life camp who would claim that my job as a medical examiner testifying against those involved in the killing of abortionists is a clear contradiction to my stance as a pro-life advocate. In response, I would refer them to my statements above where I defined my stand on this volatile social issue. In my opinion, murder is murder, whether it's inflicted upon a human still in the uterus or inflicted upon an individual who has unethically, but legally used his or her professional training to take another human's life. Although this "murder is murder" stance has allowed me to do my professional and legal duties with no loss of sleep or pangs of conscience, I'm not blind to the inconsistencies present in our current legal system as it pertains to abortion.

It was part of my usual duties to hold education sessions for the law enforcement agencies with whom I worked. Since it was a useful tool readily available to us, I often used cases currently under investigation or had been solved and were awaiting their turn in court. This had the advantage that everyone was usually familiar with the case and could relate to the facts that they were being given to an actual case. (Although I didn't make it a point to admit this openly, I've learned most of the homicide investigation techniques that I know by sharing with the police the forensic pathology that I applied to the individual cases while at the same time getting their investigative expertise in return.) One point of irony that I always bring up to both law enforcement and prosecuting attorneys in cases of infanticide is the amount of energy and treasure that the state of Florida commits to cases where a newborn is killed by a parent or caretaker while in many instances children are being killed at random at an abortion clinic down the street without anyone from the police or state prosecution even raising an eyebrow in acknowledgment. Unfortunately, that's how it will continue until the mind-set of the people and the laws are changed.

I also need to make another point to the reader which won't rest well with my fellow physicians. Physicians who dedicate their practice to performing abortions tend not to be the best physicians. To be honest, the abortion procedure isn't especially difficult from a technical viewpoint, and physicians who limit their practices to abortions tend to be physicians who were unable to succeed in a normal hospital-based practice. In addition, regardless of what abortionists tell you about their desire to help women through a difficult time in their lives, their true motivation is the easy money that the procedure generates. Any physician worth his salt will try to keep as much distance as possible between himself or herself and abortionists. Abortionists are considered to be the true bottom feeders in medicine by all their medical peers.

On March 11, 1993, I had my first brush with the violent side of the pro-life movement. I was going about my duties as a pathologist at Sacred Heart Hospital when I first heard about the abortionist shooting. Although this was the first abortionist-related shooting known to have occurred nationally, violence surrounding the abortion industry wasn't new to the Pensacola area. A group of activists had previously been convicted and had served prison time for the bombing of two doctors' offices and one abortion clinic in Pensacola on Christmas Day in 1984. At the time of this first shooting fatality, Pensacola had two functioning abortion clinics. The abortion clinic where the shooting had occurred was relatively new, having only been open for about a month. The victim, Dr. David Gunn, an ob-gyn aged forty-seven, wasn't a resident of Pensacola. He resided in Eufaula, AL, and commuted to the Pensacola office on his scheduled clinic days.

On the day of his death, Dr. Gunn had arrived at the clinic and parked his car behind his office. It wasn't uncommon for the clinic to be picketed by antiabortion activists on the days when elective abortions were scheduled. The protests usually consisted of the activists praying out loud, chanting, whistling, or even screaming at abortion providers as they came to work. The protesters on this particular day had allegedly stepped up their level of activity, with many of the protesters holding signs stating, "David Gunn Kills Babies." As Dr. Gunn was making his way from his car to the rear entrance to his clinic, Michael Fredrick Griffin, a thirty-one-year-old white male dressed in a gray suit, stepped forward and fired three shots from a .38-caliber snub-nosed revolver into Dr. Gunn's back. Witnesses stated that Griffin had yelled, "Don't kill any more babies," immediately prior to the shooting. An ambulance quickly arrived, and Dr. Gunn was taken to a local hospital where he died from his wounds. When the police arrived at the scene, Michael Griffin confessed to the shooting and surrendered his gun to the authorities.

I became involved in the case after Dr. Gunn had been pronounced dead at the hospital. In addition to interpreting and documenting the three lethal gunshot wounds, I also played a role in recovering one of the through-and-through fired bullets. Contrary to what is commonly assumed in a homicide gunshot case, it's extremely important to not only document each wound as to its entrance, exit, and path through the body but also recover all projectiles involved so that the prosecution can prove that all bullets were fired from the same gun and probably by the same person. Otherwise, the case falls into the "grassy knoll syndrome" named for the site where an alleged shooter aided Lee Harvey Oswald in the assassination of President John Kennedy. The absence of any of the fired bullets allows the defense to claim that another person was actively involved in the shooting, thereby raising the issue of reasonable doubt in the minds of the jurors.

One of the bullets produced a through-and-through-type wound, meaning that I could recover two of the bullets from my examination of the body while the third bullet was still located somewhere at the scene. Using the three wounds coupled with a reasonable approximation of Dr. Gunn's body position when the through-and-through wound was inflicted, I gave the scene investigators my best approximation of where the bullet might have landed. The next day, using a metal detector, the crime scene personnel were able to locate the bullet in the ground immediately below where I had projected it to have landed. It was one of the few times during my career when I actually felt like the television character Quincy.

What caused Michael Griffin to pull the trigger and kill David Gunn? Who or what caused him to violate the basic tenets of his morality so that a historically gentle man willingly stepped over a line that he would have never even considered crossing over previously? There are people in this world who are extremely impressionable. They tend to spend most of their lives in the background where they observe life more than live it. Unfortunately, there are also people in this world who are exceptionally charismatic. These people have the ability to convince and mold the impressionable individuals into subjects who not only catch the charismatic's vision but become enthralled and indoctrinated to the point that they lose all sense of proportion, often divorcing themselves from former friends and family in their quest to adopt and please the charismatic figurehead. This can be extremely dangerous, especially when the leader uses his abilities to separate the impressionable from their previous anchors of church, family, and friends. The end result can be a scenario like that seen with the Jim Jones Kool Aid mass suicide in South America. Even a lesser degree of attachment can be detrimental to some. I suspect that such was the case in Michael Griffin's association with a lay preacher at the Whitfield Assembly of God Church, John Burt.

No one knows for sure the strength of the connection between John Burt and Michael Griffin. We do know that Michael was a member of the same church as John Burt and had a membership in the pro-life group, Rescue America, where Burt served as the northwest Florida regional director for the national organization. Allegedly, at the church service the previous Sunday, Michael Griffin, in the presence of multiple protest organizers and participants, asked the congregation to pray for Dr. Gunn by name, hoping that Dr. Gunn would accept Christ and stop doing what the Bible states is wrong and start doing what is right. This was stated in the presence of a group of antiabortion supporters who claimed that killing an abortion provider was a justifiable murder. In addition, Griffin had inadvertently crossed paths with Dr. Gunn the morning of the shooting at a local filling station. Dr. Gunn was drinking a cup of coffee and reading a newspaper in his car when Michael Griffin was alleged to have approached Dr. Gunn and asked him if he would be killing any babies today. Dr. Gunn stated that he probably would, and after a brief attempt to get Dr. Gunn to change his mind, Michael Griffin walked back to his car and drove off.

As with most of these cases involving charismatic individuals, Michael Griffin did the wrongful deed and was sentenced to life in prison for murder, while John Burt, Mr. Charisma, got the publicity that he so desperately desired. Just to prove that there's some justice left in the world, in 2005, John Burt was sentenced to eighteen years in prison after being convicted of five counts of lewd and lascivious contact by improperly touching and propositioning a fifteen-year-old girl. I guess charisma doesn't necessarily work across the entire age spectrum.

It would have been nice to think that Pensacola was ready to pass the abortionists killing mantra to some other community, but such was not the case. With Michael Griffin in handcuffs and being led off to jail, Paul Hill, an excommunicated Presbyterian minister was more than willing to step into the limelight. Paul Hill was a forty-year-old white male who had been active in the anti-abortion movement for the previous ten years. Although born and raised in a Presbyterian family in South Florida, Paul had spent his teen years in the 1960s doing marijuana and LSD. In 1973, an alleged near drowning during a bad LSD trip convinced him to give up his drug abuse and commit himself to religion and the Presbyterian Church. After graduating from seminary in 1984, Paul was ordained into the Presbyterian Church in America (PCA). He soon found that the denomination was too liberal for his tastes and switched to the Orthodox Presbyterian Church (OPC), only to be unhappy with their "liberal" views. Hill relinquished his teaching elder status in the Presbyterian Church and ultimately joined an independent Calvinist church in Valparaiso, FL.

After the fatal shooting of Dr. Gunn in 1993, Hill appointed himself spokesman for all antiabortion terrorists claiming that the killing of abortionists was justifiable on the grounds of defending the lives of fetuses. He actively pursued opportunities to publicly defend his viewpoint, ultimately getting national exposure on television shows like *The Donahue Show*. While a guest on the show, Hill claimed that Dr. Gunn's murder was justified, actively debating the point with Dr. Gunn's son who was also an invited guest on the show. His radical viewpoint ultimately resulted in his excommunication from his home church. He started a car detail business in Pensacola which allowed him to support his wife and three children while still pursuing his antiabortion activities. As the self-appointed national spokesman for the radical antiabortion point of view, he was repeatedly asked the question, "If you believe it's justifiable to kill abortion doctors, why have you not killed one yourself?" To take his celebrity to the next level, that's exactly what Paul Hill decided to do.

On July 29, 1994, Paul Hill packed the shotgun that he had purchased and practiced shooting at a local range into a cardboard tube that he normally used to transport antiabortion posters to the Ladies Center abortion clinic. He arrived at the clinic at 6:45 a.m. and hid the shotgun in the grass near the front entrance of the Ninth Avenue clinic. At 7:27 a.m., a blue Nissan pickup truck transporting the abortionist, Dr. John Britton, from South Florida and driven by an escort, John Barrett, with his wife, June, riding in the jump seat behind the passenger's seat, pulled into the clinic driveway. As they entered the clinic property, the truck passed by Paul Hill as he stood just outside the property's fence on the clinic driveway. According to Hill, he then picked up the shotgun and moved to a position allowing him a direct shot at the truck. James Barrett was positioned between Hill and the abortionist, so he fired three shots into the driver's side of the truck, hitting James Barrett in the head and neck, causing his body to fall out of the way so he could get a clear shot at Dr. Britton. Next, Hill fired five more rounds from the shotgun, hitting Dr. Britton about the head and neck. Several of the pellets also wounded but did not kill June Barrett in the rear jump seat of the truck. Paul Hill then set down the shotgun and calmly walked away from the weapon with his hands down and visible. He was subsequently arrested and held without bond.

I was attending an early-morning educational meeting at the hospital that Friday morning, hoping for an easy day that would allow me to slip into my two weeks' vacation without any unnecessary trauma during my last prevacation day at work. I was sorely disappointed. During the educational presentation, my secretary came to get me out of the meeting, explaining that the police needed me at a homicide scene. I could see my dream of a quiet slide into my vacation slowly start to vanish. The scene was just down the street from the hospital, and although it was at most a ten-minute drive under normal conditions, the police, television crews, fire department, and state crime scene vehicles and personnel turned the trip into a forty-minute excursion. Once on site, the scene itself was easy enough to interpret, but I also knew that with two deaths due to multiple shotgun wounds, it was going to take a long time to fully document the injuries at autopsy. In addition, I couldn't start my examinations until the crime scene was completely processed. My time issue was further complicated by the fact that the combination of multiple pieces of evidence coupled with the high-profile status of the case ensured that I wouldn't get started with my examinations until much later in the afternoon. Knowing that I had tickets to fly to Chicago with my family the next morning, I dreaded the call home to explain to my wife why I wouldn't be able to fly off with them the next day. Fortunately, I was able to convince my autopsy help to work late into the night, and we finished both autopsies at three the next morning. I dictated my reports and was able to catch the flight out of Pensacola with my marriage and family intact.

The case in terms of my testimony was interesting from the perspective that the trial was conducted in both the federal and state court systems. The reason for the dual trial was that this case was to be the inaugural trial of a recently passed federal law that was at least in part initiated because of the Gunn homicide. The statute was called the Freedom of Access to Clinic Entrances (FACE) law. In addition to having to testify in the state judicial system, I was given my first opportunity to be qualified as an expert medical witness in the Pensacola federal court.

The tactic that Paul Hill's defense tried to use was the affirmative defense justification, the defense claiming that Paul Hill's actions should be viewed as defensive acts to prevent the murder of the unborn fetuses rather than an act of retribution. The court refused to accept that defense. Thus, Paul Hill in essence mounted no defense at all. He was found guilty of capital murder and was sentenced to die at the hands of the state of Florida.

This was thankfully my last case where an abortionist was murdered because of his or her willingness to perform that procedure. The whole "abortion as a woman's right" continues to be a volatile issue in our society. I continue to believe that life is precious and worth preserving whether the person lives inside or outside the womb. Hopefully someday, we as a culture will come to appreciate how precious a resource human life is; any human life continues to be. The endings of both cases were as tragic as the beginnings. On September 3, 2003, Paul Hill was executed by lethal injection at the Florida State Prison. He's survived by his wife and three daughters. Michael Griffin is currently serving a life sentence for murder at the Okaloosa Correctional Institution in Crestview, FL.

EPILOGUE

When I went to medical school, I had no idea that my career would revolve on crime scenes, autopsies, lawyers and the courtroom. I don't think I could have experienced nearly as much as I would have encountered had I stuck to my early family practice leanings. Although I readily acknowledge that this specialty is not for everyone, those who do serve in the role of medical examiner make a huge contribution to the judicial system and at the same time function as a type of quality control for both law enforcement and the courtroom itself.

As you have read this volume, you have noticed from time to time that I mentioned my wife, Beth, and her reactions to my career, especially when it intersected with our home life. It seemed that every vacation or family outing we planned was continually subjected to the whims of the ongoing caseload of the job or interrupted by a court system that made unreasonable demands on my time by requiring me to testify on their schedule and not mine. Of course, the ball games, performances, and other activities of my children that I missed are too numerous to mention. Although many times irritated and occasionally outright angry, Beth has been a real trooper throughout my career. It would have been impossible for me to maintain the emotional equilibrium and avoid the depression of the job without her continuous support. I readily admit that I married way above myself.

When there's no one able to give the deceased's side of the story, it becomes quite easy to miss important details. The medical examiner does just that. He or she uses information gleaned from past medical history, background information including the scene of death, and of course, the autopsy examination to tell the victim's story and help convict those who are guilty, but just as important, prove the innocence of the truly innocent.

There are hundreds of forensic pathologists like myself across America who continue to perform their duties in the face of governmental cutbacks in both equipment and personnel. Beth is fond of recalling the times that I stood beside my state-issued car, kicking the fenders and screaming out loud because it had once again broken down on the way to or from a crime scene. Only large amounts of time can convert those memories from initial screams of anger to current smiles of nostalgia. Please remember that the cutting-edge instrumentation seen on television crime scene programs is rarely available to the journeyman like myself. Only you the public can remedy those issues.

Finally, my purpose in writing this volume has been to describe my career in a style and vocabulary that a man or woman on the street can read and understand. If nothing else, I hope that this feeble attempt at explaining death investigation has shown the practical value of the medical examiner's office in death investigation and certification. I submit that it's an office that needs your political and financial support in your local community.

Manufactured by Amazon.ca
Bolton, ON